New Black Feminist Criticism, 1985–2000

New Black Feminist Criticism, 1985–2000

Barbara Christian

Edited by
Gloria Bowles, M. Giulia Fabi,
and Arlene R. Keizer

University of Illinois Press
Urbana and Chicago

Frontispiece photo by Jane Scherr

© 2007 by Najuma Henderson
Manufactured in the United States of America
1 2 3 4 5 C P 5 4 3 2 1
∞ This book is printed on acid-free paper.

Library of Congress Cataloging-in-Publication Data
Christian, Barbara, 1943-2000.
New Black feminist criticism, 1985–2000 / Barbara Christian ;
edited by Gloria Bowles, M. Giulia Fabi, and Arlene R. Keizer.
p.   cm.
Includes bibliographical references and index.
ISBN-10 0-252-03180-6 (cloth : alk. paper)
ISBN-13 978-0-252-03180-9 (cloth : alk. paper)
1. American literature—African American authors—History and criticism—Theory etc.
2. American literature—Women authors—History and criticism—Theory, etc.
3. Feminist literary criticism—United States.
4. Feminism and literature—United States.
5. African American women in literature.
I. Bowles, Gloria. II. Fabi, M. Giulia (Maria Giulia) III. Keizer, Arlene R. IV. Title.
PS153.N5C48   2007
810.9'928708996073—dc22   2007015805

Contents

Acknowledgments

The editors would like to thank Najuma Henderson, Barbara Christian's daughter, for her support of this project and for her afterword. We would also like to thank Najuma Henderson and Marvina White for their establishment of a Barbara T. Christian scholarship fund for students of African American studies at Berkeley. Royalties for this book will be donated to the fund.

We gratefully acknowledge the collaboration of Sarah Berkowitz and Osvaldo Gomez, both students at Berkeley, who were research assistants during the early stages of this project, as well as the work of Jeannette Lee and Mario Sifuentez, graduate students at Brown, who also served as research assistants. Ms. Lee's help in applying for permissions was especially important. The editors thank Brown University for grants that covered the cost of permissions.

Finally, we would like to thank Elaine H. Kim, Gabrielle P. Foreman, and Thalia Kitrilakis for supporting this project from the very beginning, and Willis G. Regier, director of the University of Illinois Press, for his patience, generosity, and expert advice, which proved crucial for the completion of this volume.

Introduction

GLORIA BOWLES, M. GIULIA FABI,
AND ARLENE R. KEIZER

Among the founding mothers of contemporary African American and black feminist criticism, Barbara Christian holds a central place. From the publication of her groundbreaking *Black Women Novelists* in 1980, to her untimely death in 2000 at the age of 56, Christian was a preeminent critic, whose writing, teaching, activism, and public lecturing around the world influenced generations of students and scholars and helped to inspire and shape the unprecedented interest in African American literature and culture that characterized the last decades of the twentieth century and is continuing in the twenty-first.

Her essays and reviews included in this posthumous collection, *New Black Feminist Criticism, 1985–2000,* span the last fifteen years of her career and offer a privileged point of entry into the rich world of Christian's thought and writings on African American literature, on black women's unique contributions to that tradition, on the everyday uses of beauty and literature, and on the personal and social impact of the imaginative worlds created by African American women and men in their writings.

Born in St. Thomas, Virgin Islands, in 1943, Christian attended college in the United States. The 1960s found her in New York, doing her graduate studies in contemporary British and American literature at Columbia, where she completed her Ph.D. with distinction in 1970, with a dissertation entitled "Spirit Bloom in Harlem. The Search for a Black Aesthetic during the Harlem Renaissance: The Poetry of Claude McKay, Countee Cullen, and Jean Toomer." During that time, she was also an activist and teacher at the City College of New York, where she was an English instructor in the SEEK program, a program, as she would recall in later years, "designed to uplift apparently uneducable black and Puerto Rican youth by giving them the skills to enter city colleges."[1] In some of her essays, including

"Being the Subject and the Object: Reading African-American Women's Novels," reprinted in this collection, Christian wrote eloquently about how this experience influenced her lifework as a critic, pedagogue, and public intellectual.

In 1971, she was hired as assistant professor at the University of California, Berkeley, where she would work for the following thirty years. Active in the struggle to establish the African American Studies Department on her campus, in 1978 she would become the first black woman to receive tenure at Berkeley, in 1986, the first to be promoted to full professor, and in 1991, the first to receive the campus Distinguished Teaching Award. Chair of the African American Studies Department for five years (1978–83) and of the Ph.D. program in ethnic studies from 1986 to 1989, Christian received prestigious awards for her work as teacher, activist, and scholar.

Christian's contributions as a critic are indeed outstanding. Her first volume, *Black Women Novelists: The Development of a Tradition, 1892–1976*, which won the Before Columbus American Book Award in 1983, was the first book-length study of the African American female literary tradition. It is now a much-quoted classic work of criticism, but when it was originally published, in 1980, *Black Women Novelists* was a pathbreaking scholarly work. The outcome of systematic and painstaking research at a time when the works of early black women writers were still largely unavailable and out of print, *Black Women Novelists* established authoritatively the idea of an African American women's novelistic tradition stretching from the nineteenth to the end of the twentieth century. Despite the publication of important early black feminist essays by Barbara Smith and Alice Walker, for instance, the academic standing of that critical approach was still a matter of contention. In later years Christian would remind her graduate students and her readers of how difficult it had been to find a publisher interested in a volume of criticism on black women writers and of the many rejection letters she had received before Greenwood Press decided to publish her manuscript. Against these odds, *Black Women Novelists* succeeded in reconstructing an African American female literary tradition and in opening the way for the scholarly interest in early African American women writers that would characterize the 1980s and 1990s. At the same time, the extensive close readings in the last chapters of the volume brought to the attention of scholars and readers three contemporary women writers who have since then become internationally famous and an integral part of the American literary canon: Paule Marshall, Alice Walker, and Toni Morrison.

Versatile, eloquent, open to literary experimentation, and engaged with changes in the academy and in society, Christian was a prolific writer of essays and book reviews. In 1985, she collected some of her pieces in *Black*

Feminist Criticism: Perspectives on Black Women Writers, a volume that defined distinctive new approaches to reading black women novelists and poets. Christian devoted attention to writers of the present and the past, and did not shrink from addressing feminist topics, including lesbianism, at a time when debates surrounding *The Color Purple* and the representation of black men in African American women's fiction made such subjects quite controversial. Christian's compelling introduction to *Black Feminist Criticism* and her retrospective headnotes, which provide illuminating information on the context in which each individual piece was originally thought and written, afford readers the privilege to follow the "thinking and feeling process" of a scholar's mind and her reflections on her own critical practice, as well as on the impact of gender (and especially motherhood) on her writings and the sense of responsibility connected with analyzing and promoting the artistic creativity of a socially oppressed group. Christian's reflections also communicate the contagious enthusiasm of the professional scholar who never forgets to enjoy the beauty and power of the works she reads and studies.

In the 1990s, Christian worked, as before, on several fronts. She coedited scholarly books such as *Female Subjects in Black and White: Race, Psychoanalysis, Feminism* (1997), published a casebook on Alice Walker's "Everyday Use" (1994), and contributed to encyclopedic volumes that increased the availability of African American literature among teachers and the general public, including the first *Norton Anthology of African American Literature* (for which she was the contemporary editor) and the *Harper Collins World Reader.* She also participated in important documentary films on African American culture and history; consolidated her reputation as a speaker who lectured locally, nationally, and around the world; and continued to work in the community and for social justice. As Professor Gabrielle Foreman, a former graduate student of Christian's, has said, "Fighting the backlash against affirmative action, which decreased the presence of students of color in higher education, remained one of her central passions," as emerges also from some of the essays included in *New Black Feminist Criticism.* At the time of her death, Christian was still actively thinking about a variety of different scholarly projects, including a book on Toni Morrison.

The groundbreaking quality of Christian's criticism, the breadth of her knowledge, her intellectual courage, and her scholarly determination to being both rigorous and readable, as well as her ethical commitment to literature and criticism as crucial for envisioning and bringing about social change, retain a compelling contemporary relevance. These characterizing features of her work emerge vividly and engagingly from the essays collected in *New Black Feminist Criticism.* Under the auspices of Christian's daughter and heir, Najuma Henderson, whose afterword closes this volume, *New Black Feminist Criticism* has been edited by a former colleague of Christian's at Berkeley, Gloria Bowles, and by two of her former graduate students, now professors, M. Giulia Fabi and Arlene R. Keizer. The driving forces of this collaborative project were admiration for Christian's brilliance and generosity, as well as the conviction of the continued importance of her lifework and vision. The aim of this collection is, therefore, to make her most recent writings more readily available not only to the many who already know and prize her work, but also to new generations of students, scholars, and general readers. Passing on knowledge was a key preoccupation of Christian's, and it is also the aim of the editors in publishing this collection of her essays.

Since it was necessary, for space reasons, to select from the many writings Christian published between 1985 and 2000, the editors have chosen those that were most significant and original, at the same time privileging the essays that are most difficult to find and that would provide a sense of the variety of Christian's critical output. As a result, some essays that have been published in well-known and readily available anthologies or reference volumes are missing from *New Black Feminist Criticism*. For this reason, and for the interested reader's convenience, a selected bibliography of Christian's work has been included at the end of the volume.

New Black Feminist Criticism is divided into three sections that foreground some of Christian's key critical concerns and are preceded by introductions: "Defining Black Feminist Criticism," "Reading Black Women Writers," and "Black Feminist Criticism in the Academy." In keeping with her emphasis on the inextricability of the practice and the theorizing of literary criticism, there is no explicit nor implied hierarchical value in the sequence of the sections. Section I, "Defining Black Feminist Criticism," is arranged to highlight Christian's articulation of major concepts and questions raised by the development of black feminist criticism and her demonstration of her own critical methodologies. The section closes with one of Christian's best-known essays, "The Race for Theory," and a talk she gave almost ten years later, "Does Theory Play Well in the Classroom?" in which she revisited and in some ways revised the earlier argument. In section II, "Reading Black Women Writers," the essays have been ordered chronologically, a choice Christian herself made in editing her 1985 collection that has inspired this one. Section II includes also some of Christian's book reviews, in recognition of the importance she attributed to them and as particularly effective examples of her intellectual openness and nuanced readings. Section III, "Black Feminist Criticism in the Academy," begins with a wide-ranging interview of Christian by graduate students and is then arranged thematically. The goal is to give a sense of her evolving critical concerns and of her sensitivity to and interventions in the expanding field of African American literary criticism. The material included in this anthology has been reprinted in its original form; only obvious orthographic and mechanical errors have been silently corrected. In keeping with the editors' goal to keep Christian's intellectual legacy alive, all royalties from this book will go to the Barbara T. Christian Memorial Fund.

The essays in *New Black Feminist Criticism* show Christian at her most eloquent. Hers is a wide-ranging, authoritative voice. In *New Black Feminist Criticism,* we hear the teacher and scholar who has been immersed for thirty years in the words of writers such as Toni Morrison, Alice Walker, Paule Marshall, and Gloria Naylor. We hear the intellectual and academic who has actively supported and encouraged students and scholars in other marginalized fields, including women's studies and Asian American studies, by tirelessly reading, critiquing, and promoting their work. We hear as well the citizen and university activist who laments the demise of affirmative action and thus the decreasing number of students who will carry on the broad cultural work connected with black feminist criticism.

Christian is scholarly, passionate, lyrical and sometimes polemical. She is always clear and forceful, as she felt strongly that if writing is not written about, it disappears. She saw herself as one who brings illumination to works of art. In fact, her essays explicate, as they illuminate the tradition in which her authors write. She guides the reader into new literary territory, on an intellectual journey replete with beauty, courage, and a commitment to social justice. The editors hope that many, now and in the future, will be the students, scholars, and general readers interested in embarking on this journey. To paraphrase what she wrote in commemorating Audre Lorde, though we no longer have the privilege of seeing Barbara Christian, we will always hear her. She left for us her work.

New Black Feminist Criticism,
1985–2000

PART 1

Defining Black Feminist Criticism

Introduction
ARLENE R. KEIZER

The essays in this section highlight the metacritical dimension of Barbara Christian's analytical writing. In spite of the range and abundance of Christian's writing on African American literature and culture, she has become known as the author of "The Race for Theory," an essay that sparked a polarizing controversy among African Americanist literary critics in the late 1980s and reverberated into the next decade.[1] In their haste to attack the essentialist aspects of "The Race for Theory," critics disregarded two crucial components of that essay: its argument for an expanded definition of theory and its articulation of Christian's own critical methodology. Far from being antitheoretical, Christian theorized through literature, using the knowledge represented by writers and their characters as a basis for thinking about African American literature as a whole. "The Race for Theory" articulates a practice as surely as it critiques another. Throughout her career, Christian was dedicated to analyzing and critiquing, when necessary, the practice and the general direction of literary criticism.

Two threads run through the essays in "Defining Black Feminist Criticism." One is the opposition between knowledge and theory. What Christian insists upon, over and over again, is the idea that what the subaltern knows may not easily fit into an available theoretical framework. Her concern was that such knowledge not be silenced simply because it is incompatible with prevailing systems of thought. In fact, that incompatibility, difference, or insubordination was, for her, one of the most important qualities of literary texts. Christian envisioned literary criticism as elegant backtalk that would support the contrary impulses of the literature itself. She recognized that some deemed her incapable of producing a comprehensive black feminist literary theory, but she made it clear that this was, in fact, a refusal of a demand from the reigning critical establishment. In "The Race for Theory," she writes, "I, for one, am tired of being asked to produce a black feminist literary theory as if I were a mechanical man. . . . Since I can count on one hand the number of people attempting to be black feminist literary critics in the world today, I consider it presumptuous of me to invent a theory of how we *ought* to read." And yet, she produced one of the most substantial and influential collections of black feminist literary theorizing that we have, in addition to nurturing dozens of new black feminist literary critics (too many of us now to be counted on one or even two hands).

Another significant thread tying these essays together is denoted by variations of the term "fixing." Versions of this word appear in every article, and in some it is repeated several times. In "But What Do We Think We're Doing Anyway," "What Celie Knows That You Should Know," "The Race for Theory," and "Does Theory Play Well in the Classroom?" Christian insists upon the danger of fixing the literary text with "theory" like a fly in amber. For her, black feminist literary practice demands that the dynamism of fiction, poetry, and drama be matched by an equally dynamic criticism. Frameworks that seek to subdue or oversimplify the idiosyncrasies and the fluidity of literary works are anathema to her. In "Fixing Methodologies: *Beloved*," however, Christian goes further, identifying and analyzing the reparative properties of Toni Morrison's use of West African spiritual traditions. By reading *Beloved* as a "fixing ceremony," a healing practice, Christian also points toward the possibility of criticism that might function in a similar way. She crafts the essay as a "fixing methodology" that can serve as a model for other critics who want to use knowledge that comes from "below" as part of their interpretive strategies.

Finally, one of the most important principles that Barbara

Christian imparted through her writing and her pedagogy was the significance of naming one's personal relationship to the literature about which one writes, even if one does not explicitly discuss that relationship in one's scholarly essays. She herself did this consistently and courageously, while knowing and counting the cost of her "lifesaving" critical practice.

1 But What Do We Think We're Doing Anyway: The State of Black Feminist Criticism(s) or My Version of a Little Bit of History (1989)

In August 1974, a rather unique event occurred. *Black World,* probably the most widely read publication of Afro-American literature, culture, and political thought at that time, used on its cover a picture of the then practically unknown writer Zora Neale Hurston.[1] Under Zora's then unfamiliar photograph was a caption in bold letters, "Black Women Image Makers," which was the title of the essay by Mary Helen Washington featured in the issue. Alongside the Washington essay were three other pieces: an essay now considered a classic, June Jordan's "On Richard Wright and Zora Neale Hurston: Notes Towards a Balancing of Love and Hate"; an essay on major works of Zora Neale Hurston, "The Novelist/Anthropologist/Life Work," by poet Ellease Southerland; and a short piece criticizing the television version of Ernest Gaines's *The Autobiography of Miss Jane Pittman,* by black psychologist Alvin Ramsey. It was not particularly striking that the image of a black woman writer graced the cover of *Black World;* Gwendolyn Brooks's picture, for example, had appeared on a previous *Black World* cover. Nor was it especially noteworthy that literary analyses of an Afro-American woman writer appeared in that journal. That certainly had occurred before. What was so striking about this issue of *Black World* was the tone of the individual pieces and the effect of their juxtaposition.

Mary Helen Washington's essay sounded a strong chord—that there was indeed a growing number of contemporary Afro-American women writers whose perspective underlined the centrality of women's lives to

First published in Cheryl A. Wall, ed., *Changing Our Own Words: Essays on Criticism, Theory, and Writing by Black Women* (New Brunswick, N.J.: Rutgers University Press, 1989), 58–74. The title of this essay is a riff on Gloria T. Hull's title, "What It Is I Think She's Doing Anyhow," in Barbara Smith, ed., *Home Girls: A Black Feminist Anthology* (New York: Kitchen Table Women of Color Press, 1983), 124–42.

their creative vision. June Jordan's essay placed Hurston, a relatively unknown Afro-American woman writer, alongside Richard Wright, who is probably the best known of Afro-American writers, and illuminated how their apparently antithetical worldviews were *both* necessary ways of viewing the complexity of Afro-American life, which Jordan made clear was not monolithic. Ellease Southerland reviewed many of Hurston's works, pointing out their significance to Afro-American literature and therefore indicating the existence of major Afro-American women writers in the past. And in criticizing the television version of *The Autobiography of Miss Jane Pittman,* Ramsey objected that that commercial white medium had omitted the message of struggle in Ernest Gaines's novel and turned it into an individual woman's story—a foreshadowing of criticism that would be repeated when, periodically, images of black women from literature were translated into visual media.

What the configuration of the August 1974 *Black World* suggested to me, as I am sure it did to others, was the growing visibility of Afro-American women and the significant impact they were having on contemporary black culture. The articulation of that impact had been the basis for Toni Cade's edition of *The Black Woman* in 1970.[2] But that collection had not dealt specifically with literature/creativity. Coupled with the publication of Alice Walker's "In Search of Our Mothers' Gardens" only a few months before in the May issue of *Ms.,*[3] the August 1974 *Black World* signaled a shift in position among those interested in Afro-American literature about women's creativity. Perhaps because I had experienced a decade of the intense literary activity of the 1960s, but also much anti-female black cultural nationalist rhetoric, these two publications had a lightning effect on me. Afro-American women were making public, were able to make public, their search for themselves in literary culture.

I begin my reflections on the state (history) of black feminist criticism(s) with this memory because it seems to me we so quickly forget the recent past. Perhaps some of us have never known it. Like many of us who lived through the literary activism of the sixties, we of the eighties may forget that which just recently preceded us and may therefore misconstrue the period in which we are acting.

Less than twenty years ago, without using the self-consciously academic word *theory,* Mary Helen Washington articulated a concept that was original, startling even, to many of us immersed in the study of Afro-American literature, among whom were few academics, who knew little or cared less about this literature. In "Black Women Image Makers" Washington stated what for me is still a basic tenet of black feminist criticism: "We should be about the business of *reading, absorbing,* and giving *critical* attention to those writers whose understanding of the black woman can take us *further*" (emphasis mine).[4] The names of the writers Washington listed, with the exception of Gwendolyn Brooks, were then all virtually unknown; interestingly, after a period when poetry and drama were the preeminent genre of Afro-American literature, practically all of these writers—Maya Angelou, Toni Cade Bambara, Paule Marshall, Toni Morrison, Alice Walker—were practicing fiction writers. While all of the writers were contemporary, Washington implied through her analysis that their vision and craft suggested that previous Afro-American women writers existed. Hence Zora Neale Hurston's picture on the cover of this issue connoted a specific meaning—that of a literary foremother who had been neglected by Afro-Americanists of the past but who was finally being recognized by her daughters and reinstated as a major figure in the Afro-American literary tradition.

It is important for us to remember that in 1974, even before the publication of Robert Hemenway's biography of Hurston in 1977 or the reissuing of *Their Eyes Were Watching God,* the articulation of the possibility of a tradition of Afro-American women writers occurred not in a fancy academic journal but in two magazines: *Ms.,* a new popular magazine that came out of the women's movement, and *Black World,* a long-standing black journal unknown to most academics and possibly scorned by some.

Walker's essay and *Black World's* August 1974 issue gave me a focus and are the recognizable points that I can recall as to when I consciously began to work on black women writers. I had, of course, unconsciously begun my own search before reading those pieces. I had spent some portion of the late sixties and early seventies asking my "elders" in the black arts movement whether there were black women who had written before Gwendolyn Brooks or Lorraine Hansberry. Younger poets such as Sonia Sanchez, Nikki Giovanni, Carolyn Rodgers, June Jordan, and Audre Lorde were, of course, quite visible by that time. And by 1974, Morrison and Walker had each published a novel. But only through accident or sheer stint of effort did I discover Paule Marshall's *Brown Girl, Brownstones* (1959) or Hurston's *Their Eyes Were Watching God* (1937)—an indication that the contemporary writers I was then reading might too fade into oblivion. Although in the sixties the works of neglected Afro-American male writers of the Harlem Renaissance were beginning to resurface, for example, Jean Toomer's *Cane,* I was told the women writers of that period were terrible—not worth my trouble. However, because of the conjuncture of the black arts movement and the women's movement, I asked questions I probably would not have otherwise thought of.

If movements have any effect, it is to give us a context within which to imagine questions we would not have imagined before, to ask questions we might not have asked before. The publication of the *Black World* August 1974 issue as well as Walker's essay was rooted in the conjuncture of those two movements, rather than in the theoretizing of any individual scholar, and most emphatically in the literature of contemporary Afro-American women who were able to be published as they had not been before, precisely because that conjuncture was occurring.

That the development of black feminist criticism(s) is firmly rooted in this conjecture is crystal clear from a pivotal essay of the 1970s: Barbara Smith's "Toward a Black Feminist Criticism," which was originally published in *Conditions II* in 1977. By that time Smith was not only calling on critics to read, absorb, and pay attention to black women writers, as Washington had, but also to write about that body of literature from a feminist perspective. What *feminist* meant for Smith went beyond Washington's emphasis on image making. Critics, she believed, needed to demonstrate how the literature exposed "the brutally complex systems of oppression"[5] — that of sexism, racism, and economic exploitation which affected so gravely the experience and culture of black women. As important, Smith was among the first to point out that black lesbian literature was thoroughly ignored in critical journals, an indication of the homophobia existent in the literary world.

Because the U.S. women's movement had begun to extend itself into academic arenas and because women's voices had been so thoroughly suppressed, by the middle seventies there was a visible increase of interest among academics in women's literature. Yet despite the existence of powerful contemporary Afro-American women writers who continued to be major explorers of Afro-American women's lives—writers such as Bambara, Jordan, Lorde, Morrison, Ntozake Shange, Walker, Sherley Anne Williams (the list could be much longer)—little commentary on their works could be found in feminist journals. In many ways, they continued to be characterized by such journals as black, not women, writers. Nor, generally speaking, were critics who studied these writers considered either in the Afro-American or feminist literary worlds—far less the mainstream literary establishment—to be working on an important body of literature central to American letters. By 1977, Smith knew that the sexism of Afro-American literary/intellectual circles and the racism of white feminist literary journals resulted in a kind of homelessness for critical works on black women or other third world women writers. She underlined this fact in her landmark essay: "I think of the thousands and thousands of books which have been devoted by this time to the subject of Women's Writing and I am filled with rage at the fraction of these pages that mention black and other Third World women. I finally do not know how to begin, because in 1977 I want to be writing this for a black feminist publication."[6]

At that time, most feminist journals were practically all-white publications; their content dealt almost exclusively with white women as if they were the only women in the United States. The extent to which the mid-twentieth-century women's movement was becoming, like its nineteenth-century predecessor, infected by racism seemed all too clear, and the split between a black and a white women's movement that occurred in the nineteenth century seemed to be repeating itself.

Smith seemed to believe that the lack of inclusion of women-of-color writers and critics in the burgeoning literature on women's voices was due, in part, to "the fact that a parallel black feminist movement had been slower in evolving," and that that fact "could not help but have impact upon the situation of black women writers and artists and explains in part why during that very same period we have been so ignored."[7] My experience, however, suggests that other factors were more prominently at work, factors Smith also mentioned. In calling for a "body of black feminist political theory," she pointed out that such a theory was necessary since those who had access to critical publications—white male and, increasingly, black male and white female critics—apparently did not *know how* to respond to the works of black women. More accurately, I think these critics might have been resistant to this body of writing which unavoidably demonstrated the intersections of sexism and racism so central to Afro-American women's lives and therefore threatened not only white men's view of themselves, but black men and white women's view of themselves as well. Smith concludes that "undoubtedly there are other [black] women working and writing whom I do not know, simply because there is no place to read them."[8]

I can personally attest to that fact. By 1977 I was well into the writing of the book that would become *Black Women Novelists: The Development of a Tradition* (1980) and had independently stumbled on two pivotal concepts that Smith articulated in her essay: "the need to demonstrate that black women's writing constituted an identifiable literary tradition" and the importance of looking "for precedents and insights in interpretation within the works of other black women."[9] I found, however, that it was virtually impossible to locate either the works of many nineteenth-century writers or those of contemporary writers, whose books went in and out of print like ping-pong balls. For example, I xeroxed *Brown Girl, Brownstones* (please forgive me, Paule) any number of times because it simply was not available and I wanted to use it in the classes I had begun to teach on Afro-American women's literature. At times I felt more like a detective than a literary critic as I chased clues to find a book I knew existed but which I had begun to think I had hallucinated.

Particularly difficult, I felt, was the dearth of historical material on Afro-American women—that is, on the contexts within which the literature had evolved—contexts I increasingly saw as a necessary foundation for the development of a contemporary black feminist perspective. Other than Gerda Lerner's *Black Women in White America* (1973), I could not find a single full-length analysis of Afro-American women's history. And despite the proliferation of Afro-American and women's history books in the 1970s, I found in most of them only a few paragraphs devoted to black women, the favorites being Harriet Tubman in the black studies ones and Sojourner Truth in the women's studies ones. As a result, in preparation for my book, I, untrained in history, had created a patchwork quilt of historical facts gathered here and there. I remember being positively elated when Sharon Harley and Rosalyn Terborg-Penn's collection of historical essays — *The Afro-American Woman* (1978)—was published. But by then, I had almost completed my manuscript. If Afro-American women critics were to turn to black women of the past for insights, their words and works needed to be accessible and had to be located in a cogent historical analysis.

As well, what was stunning to me as I worked on *Black Women Novelists* was the resistance I experienced among scholars to my subject matter. Colleagues of mine, some of whom had my best interest at heart, warned me that I was going to ruin my academic career by studying an insignificant, some said nonexistent, body of literature. Yet I knew it was fortunate for me that I was situated in an Afro-American studies rather than in an English department, where not even the intercession of the Virgin would have allowed me to do research on black women writers. I also found that lit crit journals were not interested in the essays I had begun to write on black women writers. The sustenance I received during those years of writing *Black Women Novelists* came not from the academic/literary world but from small groups of women in bookstores, Y's, in my classes and writers groups for whom this literature was not so much an object of study but was, as it is for me, life-saving.

Many contemporary Afro-American critics imply in their analyses that only those Afro-Americans in the academy—college faculty and students— read Afro-American literature. I have found quite the opposite to be true. For it was "ordinary" black women, women in the churches, private reading groups, women like my hairdresser and her clients, secondary school teachers, typists, my women friends, many of whom were single mothers, who discussed *The Bluest Eye* (1970) or *In Love and Trouble* (1973) with an intensity unheard of in the academic world. In fact most of my colleagues did not even know these books existed when women I knew were calling these writers by their first name—Alice, Paule, Toni, June—indicating their sense of an intimacy with them. They did not necessarily buy the books but often begged, "borrowed," or "liberated" them—so that book sales were not always indicative of their interest. I had had similar experiences during the 1960s. Postal clerks, winos, as well as the folk who hung out in Micheaux's, the black bookstore in Harlem, knew Baldwin's, Wright's, Ellison's works and talked vociferously about them when many of the folk at CCNY and Columbia had never read one of these writers. Ralph Ellison wrote an extremely provocative blurb for *Our Nig* when he pointed out that Harriet Wilson's novel demonstrated that there is more "free-floating" literacy among blacks than we acknowledge.

No doubt we are influenced by what publishers say people should read or do read. When I began sending out sections of *Black Women Novelists,* practically all academic presses as well as trade presses commented that my subject was not important—that people were not interested in black women writers. Couldn't I write a book on the social problems of black women? Affected by the rhetoric à la Moynihan, most of these presses could hardly believe black women were artists—a point we might remember as some of us today minimize the craft and artistry of these writers in favor of intellectual or social analysis. In response to these comments I could not point to any precedents, for in 1978 there had not been published a full-length study of black women writers. I believe if it were not for the incredible publicity that Toni Morrison's *Song of Solomon* received in 1978, and the fact that one of my chapters was devoted to her work, I would not have been able to publish *Black Women Novelists* when I did. Smith was right on target when she suggested that there might be other black women critics writing and working about whom she did not know because there was no place to read them.

That situation began to change by 1980, however. And I think it is important for us to recall some of the major signs of that change. One such sign was the black sexism issue of the *Black Scholar* published in May/June of 1979 which grew out of black sociologist Robert Staples's extremely critical response to Ntozake Shange's play *for colored girls who have considered suicide when the rainbow is enuf* and Michele Wallace's critique of the sexism in the civil rights movement—*Black Macho and the Myth of the Superwoman* (1979).[10] In his critique of Shange and Wallace, Staples insinuated that black feminists were being promoted by the white media—a stance that would be reiterated years later by some critics in the *Color Purple* debate. Although the debate among the Afro-American women and men on the issue was not a specifically "literary" debate, its very existence indicated the effect

Afro-American women's literature was having on Afro-American intellectual circles. What was also interesting about the debate was the intense involvement of Afro-American women writers themselves who unabashedly responded to Staples. Audre Lorde put it succinctly: "Black feminists speak as women and do not need others to speak for us."[11]

Such speaking had certainly ignited the literary world. In the 1970s black women published more novels than they had in any other decade. Some, like Morrison and Walker, were beginning to be acknowledged as great American novelists. Poets such as Lorde, Jordan, Sherley Williams, and Lucille Clifton, to mention a few, were clearly literary/political activists as well as writers in the Afro-American and women's communities. And many of these writers, most of whom were not academicians (e.g., Walker in "One Child of One's Own," Lorde in "The Uses of the Erotic"), were themselves doing black feminist criticism. Increasingly, even academicians could not deny the effect this body of literature was having on various communities in American life. Simultaneously, critical essays and analysis began to appear in literary academic as well as in more generalized intellectual journals.

That a black feminist criticism was beginning to receive attention from the academic world was one basis for Deborah McDowell's essay "New Directions for Black Feminist Criticism," which originally appeared in an academic journal, *Black American Literature Forum,* in 1980.[12] In responding to Smith's call for a black feminist criticism, McDowell emphasized the need for clear definitions and methodologies, a sign as well of the increasing emphasis on theory surfacing in the academic world. She asked whether black feminist criticism was relegated only to black women who wrote about black women writers. Did they have to write from a feminist/political perspective to be black feminist critics? Could white women/black men/white men do black feminist criticism? a question which indicated that this literature was beginning to attract a wider group of critics.

McDowell's questions continue to have much relevance as more and more critics of different persuasions, genders, and races write critical essays on Afro-American women writers. Just recently, in April 1988, Michele Wallace published a piece in the *Village Voice* which seemed almost a parody of the August 1974 *Black World* issue.[13] The piece was advertised in the content listing with the titillating title "Who Owns Zora Neale Hurston: Critics Carve Up the Legend," and featured on the first page of its text was a big photograph of Zora, who had become the darling of the literary world. Wallace counter-pointed the perspectives of black women, black men, white women, even one prominent white male critic who had written about Hurston. Everyone apparently was getting into the act, though with clearly different purposes, as Wallace insinuated that Hurston had become a commodity. Wallace's own title for her piece, "Who Dat Say Who Dat When I Say Who Dat?" spoken as if by Hurston herself, underlined the ironic implications of the proliferation of Hurston criticism, much of which, Wallace implied, was severed from Hurston's roots and most of which ignored Hurston's goddesslike mischievousness.

"Who Dat Say Who Dat When I Say Who Dat?" took me back to McDowell's essay and her suggestions of parameters for a black feminist criticism. In addition to the ones articulated by Washington in 1974 and Smith in 1977, McDowell emphasized the need for both contextual and textual analysis—contextual, in that the critic needed to have a knowledge of Afro-American history and culture, and women's situation within it, and textual, that is, paying careful attention to the individual text. If one were to combine Washington's, Smith's, and McDowell's suggestions, few of the critical works cited by Wallace would even come close to doing black feminist criticism. Wallace acceded that "Black literature needs a rainbow coalition," but she wondered if some critical approaches did not silence Hurston. While Hurston's and other Afro-American women's writing are deep enough, full enough to be approached from any number of perspectives, their work demands rigorous attention as does any other serious writing.

The question as to who the critic is and how that affects her/his interpretation was very much on my mind when I put together *Black Feminist Criticism* in 1983–1984.[14] In thinking about my own attempts to do such criticism, I increasingly felt that critics needed to let go of their distanced and false stance of objectivity and to expose their own point of view—the tangle of background, influences, political perspectives, training, situations that helped form and inform their interpretations. Inspired by feminist discussions about objectivity and subjectivity, I constructed an introduction to my volume that, rather than the usual formal introduction found in most lit crit books, was intended to introduce me in my specific context. It was a personalized way of indicating some of my biases, not the least of which was the fact that the literature I chose to study was central to an understanding of my own life, and not *only* an intellectual pursuit. Such exposure would, I thought, help the reader evaluate more effectively the choices I had made about the language I used, the specific issues I approached, the particular writers I emphasized. By then I realized I did not want to write about every contemporary Afro-American woman writer—some did not speak to me—and that the extent of my own personal involvement with the writer's work was one aspect of my doing black feminist criticism.

But even more to the point, I thought that black feminist criticism needed to break some of the restricted forms, personalize the staid language associated with the critic—forms that seemed opposed to the works of the writers as well as the culture from which they came—and forms that many readers found intimidating and boring. In the introduction dialogue I used call and response, jazz riffs, techniques found in writers like Hughes and Hurston, as well as the anecdote, a device I had found so effective in the essays of Jordan and Walker, as ways of reflecting on my own process.

In fact the form of the book was based on the idea of process as a critical aspect of an evolving feminist approach—that is, a resistance to art as artifact, to ideas as fixed, and a commitment to open-endedness, possibility, fluidity—to change. These qualities were significant characteristics of the writers I studied. Inspired by Jordan's adroit use of headnotes in *Civil Wars,* I compiled a collection not of every essay I had written between 1975 and 1985 but examples of writing events I considered necessary to doing black feminist criticism—most of which were not essays written originally for academic outlets. For me, doing black feminist criticism involved a literary activism that went beyond the halls of academe, not because I had so legislated but because in practice that is what it often, happily, had to be.

I also intended the book to be a tracing of that journey some of us had been making since 1974, a journey guided by what I considered to be another important element of doing this type of criticism, that is, on being a participant in an ongoing dialogue between the writer and those who were reading the writer, most of whom were not academics and for whom that writing was life-sustaining, life-saving. As the race for theory began to accelerate in 1984, I became concerned that that dialogue was drying up as critics rushed to construct theories in languages that many writers abhorred and which few readers understood or enjoyed or could use. In particular I was struck by a talk I had had with one major writer who told me she had gone to a lit crit panel on her work but could not comprehend one word, nor could she recognize her work in anything that was said. To whom, she asked, were we critics speaking?

Finally, I used the phrase *Black Feminist Criticism* as the title of my book because it seemed to me, in 1984, as it still does that few black women critics were willing to claim the term *feminist* in their titles. *Women* was an acceptable term, but the political implications of the term *feminist* meant that it was fast giving way to the more neutral term *gender.* I believed it was important to place the term on the black literary map, so to speak, even if it were only a reminder of an orientation no longer in vogue.

My introduction was an appeal to practice as one decisive factor in defining a black feminist criticism. In 1985 Hortense Spillers contributed another point of view. Along with Marjorie Pryse, she edited a volume entitled *Conjuring: Black Women, Fiction, and Literary Tradition,*[15] which included essays by black and white women as well as black men. The subtitle was particularly striking to me since the volume privileged fiction, as had the majority of such collections, including my own. And I began to wonder why, in this rich period of Afro-American women's poetry, that genre was being so summarily ignored.

Spillers's afterword, entitled "Cross-Currents, Discontinuities: Black Women's Fiction," made it clear that "the community of black women writing in the U.S. can be regarded as a vivid new fact of national life." She defines this community as "those composed of fiction writers, as well as writers of criticism who are also teachers of literature."[16] In emphasizing the overlapping of these categories, she saw that the academy was fast becoming the site of this community and pointed to one reason why perhaps criticism had taken the direction it had. She might have added as well that new development might be one reason criticism had become so focused on fiction. Perhaps intellectual analysis is more suited to fiction and the essay than it is to poetry and drama—genres that insist on the emotions, the passions, the senses as well as the intellect as equally effective ways of knowing.

In characterizing Afro-American women's fiction as a series of discontinuities and relating these discontinuities to other American writing—to Faulkner, Dreiser, Wright—Spillers constructed a picture of American literature unthinkable in the academic world of 1974. And by using language associated with "new" critical approaches, she demonstrated how an overview of Afro-American women's fiction converged with the more conventional American literary tradition. Her essay extended the perimeters of black feminist criticism(s) in that they could now be situated in the study of American letters as an entirety. Spillers was clearly responding to the impetus for revised canons by showing how Afro-American women's fiction intersected with the currents of other literatures in the United States.

Canon formation has become one of the thorny dilemmas for the black feminist critic. Even as white women, blacks, people of color attempt to reconstruct that body of American literature considered to be *the* literature, we find ourselves confronted with the realization that we may be imitating the very structure that shut our literatures out in the first place. And that judgments we make about, for example, the BBBs (Big Black Books) are determined not only by "quality," that elusive term, but by what we academicians value, what points of view, what genre and forms we privilege.

We finally must wonder about whether this activity, which cannot be value free, will stifle the literatures we have been promoting. For while few white male American critics feel compelled to insinuate "white" literary works into *our* characterizations of American history and culture, we are almost always in a position of having to insinuate our works into their schema.[17] Spillers concludes her afterword with a provocative statement:

"The day will come, I would dare to predict, when the black American women's writing community will reflect the currents of both the New new critical procedures and the various literatures concurrent with them."[18] One might also turn that statement around. We might wonder, given that Afro-American women's writing is so clearly at the vortex of sex, race, and class factors that mitigate the notion of democracy at the core of "traditional" American literatures, whether one might want to predict the day when other literatures will reflect the currents of the black American women's writing community.

While Spillers was still concerned with Afro-American women's literature as a recognizable literary tradition, Hazel Carby, in the introduction to her *Reconstructing Womanhood* (1987), was positively negative about the use of the term *tradition*. In "Rethinking Black Feminist Theory," Carby insisted that black feminist criticism has "too frequently been reduced to an experiential relationship that is assumed to exist between black women as readers and black women as writers who represent black women's reality" and that "this reliance on a common or shared experience is essentialist and ahistorical." Her book, she stated, "does not assume the existence of a tradition or traditions of Afro-American intellectual thought that have been constructed as paradigmatic of Afro-American history."[19]

In what frame is her book situated? Carby tells us that her inquiry "works within the theoretical premises of societies — 'structured in dominance' by class, by race, and by gender and is a materialist account of the cultural production of black women intellectuals within the social relations that inscribed them."[20] As Valerie Smith pointed out in her review of Carby's book in *Women's Review of Books*, *Reconstructing Womanhood* signals a new direction in black feminist criticism in that Carby is not as much interested in Afro-American women writers as she is in constructing a black female intellectual history.[21]

Ironically, in reconstructing that history, Carby turns to creative writers/novelists. Perhaps that is because Afro-American writers, female and male, are central, pivotal, predominant figures in Afro-American intellectual history. Why that is so would take volumes to investigate, but one explanation might be that the usual modes of European/American intellectual production were not accessible to or particularly effective for Afro-Americans. That is, the thoroughly rationalist approach of European intellectual discourse might have seemed to them to be too one-dimensional, too narrow, more easily co-opted than narratives, poetry, nonlinear forms where the ambiguities and contradictions of their reality could be more freely expressed and that in these forms they could address themselves to various audiences — their own folk as well as those readers of the dominant culture. In any case, a large number if not the majority of those considered intellectuals in the Afro-American world, female or male, were or attempted to be creative writers—which might account for some of the focus Afro-American intellectual critics have had on creative literature.

No doubt Carby's emphasis on the reconstruction of a black female intellectual history is needed. And that history can now be imagined and speculated about by her and others, as it could not have been even a decade ago, because the words and works of Afro-American women of the past are more accessible. Yet Carby's approach, as she articulates it, does not seem to allow for other emphases within the arena of black feminist criticism, and the work she can now do is possible because others pursued different orientations from her own. Twenty years ago, scholars who used the language and approach she uses (and it is indeed a primarily academic language) were completely opposed to the inclusion of gender as central to their analyses and in fact called that term "essentialist." Nor could Carby be doing the work she is doing unless a space for it was created by a powerful contemporary Afro-American women's literature which in part comes out of the very paradigm she denies. What, I wonder, would Frances Harper or Pauline Hopkins think of her denial of the possibility of Afro-American literary history?

In addition, as my and other overviews of the development of Afro-American literature suggest, there is more of an inclination in the academic and publishing worlds (and we might ask why) to accept sociological/political analyses of black writers—female, male—whether they be from a materialist or bourgeois point of view, than to conceive of them as artists with their own ideas, imagination, forms. This seems to be a privilege reserved for only a few selected white men. Finally one must ask whether the study of an intellectual tradition necessitates the denial of an imaginative, creative one? Who is to say that the European emphasis on rational intellectual discourse as the measure of a people's history is superior to those traditions that value creativity, expression, paradox in the constructing of their historical process?

Carby's introduction brings the debate as to what black feminist criticism is full circle, back to Mary Helen Washington's essay in the August 1974 *Black World,* in that Washington's assumptions about the relationship between black women's writings and the reality of a shared experience among black women are held suspect—a question worth pursuing. What is so riveting to me is that the term *black feminist criticism* continues to be undefinable—not fixed. For many that might seem catastrophic; for me it is an indication that so much still needs to be done—for example, reading the works of the writers, in order to understand their ramifications. Even as I cannot believe all that has been accomplished in the last fifteen years—a complete revision of, conceptualization of nineteenth-century Afro-American literature, and a redirecting of definitions in contemporary life about women's sexuality, motherhood, relationships, history, race/class, gender intersections, political structures, spirituality as perceived through the lens of contemporary Afro-American women—there is so much yet to do.

So—what do we think we're doing anyway? More precisely, what might we have to do at this juncture, in 1990?

For one—we might have to confront the positives and negatives of what it means to become institutionalized in universities.

Does this mean we will no longer respond to the communal/erotic art that poetry and drama can be because it is so difficult to reduce these forms to ideological wrangling? As Audre Lorde has so profoundly expressed, it is often in poetry that we imagine that which we have been afraid to imagine— that poetry is an important source of imagining new ideas for change.

Does our emphasis on definitions and theories mean that we will close ourselves to those, the many, who know or care little about the intense debates that take so much of our time in universities? Can we conceive of our literary critical activities as related to the activism necessary to substantively change black women's lives?

Does our scholarly advancement mean that more and more of us will turn to the study of past writers as a safer pursuit in the university which apparently has difficulty engaging in the study of present-day literatures? As necessary as the study of the past is, it is just as important to be engaged in the history that we are now making—one that has been so powerfully ignited by the contemporary writers.

In spite of the critical clamor, how many of us have actually produced sustained readings, critiques?

Can we ignore the fact that fewer and fewer blacks are receiving Ph.D.'s? In fact, only 820 in 1986. Although black women are not the only ones who can do feminist criticism, it would be a significant loss if they were absent from this enterprise.

Do we assume that this orientation will be here even at the turn of the century?

To whom are *we* accountable? And what social relations are in/scribing us?

Does history teach us anything about the relationship between ideas, language, and practice? By 2000 will our voices sound like women's voices, black women's voices to anyone?

What do we want to do anyway and for whom do we think we're doing it?

2   What Celie Knows That You Should Know (1990)

At a climactic moment in The Color Purple, *Mister taunts Celie:*
  Look at you. You black, you pore, you ugly, you a woman.
  Goddam . . . You nothing at all.
Celie retorts:
  I'm pore, I'm black, I may be ugly and can't cook . . .
  But I'm here.

I begin my discussion about ways in which the study of Afro-American women's literature might enrich and extend knowledge with that excerpt from *The Color Purple* because it so succinctly articulates two worldviews. Mister's assessment of Celie's worth emphasizes her nothingness because she exists in realms of powerlessness and therefore of nonexistence in the world as he sees it. Because Celie is nothing, how can she know anything? Celie's affirmation of her own existence does not deny his categories of powerlessness; rather she insists that nonetheless she exists, that she knows something as a result of being at that intersection of categories that attempt to camouflage her existence.

It is precisely that intersection of categories that Mister lists, those of race, class, and gender, which Afro-American women writers have had to explore in order to articulate their subjects' existence. It is the knowledge that comes from living at such a sharp intersection, a point of contending categories of nothingness, which is so central to the literature, from Harriet Wilson's *Our Nig,* the first novel by an Afro-American woman to be published in this country, to Toni Morrison's recent *Beloved.* If there is any persistent motif in this literature, it is the illuminating of that which is perceived by others as not existing at all. To be black, poor, and a woman in American society has historically appeared and continues to appear to be "nothing at all," as Mister so grandly proclaims. Yet in knowing what it is to be a black woman, one knows not only that one exists, but also some essential truths about those "intellectual" categories—gender, race, class—of which all human beings partake.

First published in David Theo Goldberg, ed., *Anatomy of Racism* (Minneapolis: University of Minnesota Press, 1990), 135–45.

Of course, the most obvious contribution that Afro-American women's literature can bring to knowledge is what it feels like, what it sounds like, what it means to be any number of black women in America. The exploration of this literature for those of us who are Afro-American women is to experience ourselves as subjects in contexts that help us to understand who we were as well as who we now are. In exploring ourselves as subjects, not only do we reflect on what *we* know, but we also know a great deal about those who are perceived as being "something" rather than "nothing at all." Let me demonstrate the interrelationship of these two aspects of knowledge by commenting on the first novel by an Afro-American woman to be published in this country, lest we conclude that such an orientation is due to prevailing black feminist ideology.

Harriet Wilson's *Our Nig* is both an expression of what it meant to be an indentured black girl enslaved in a white Northern household of the 1830s as well as an exploration of the ways in which race affects the relations among women. In writing her autobiographical novel, Mrs. Wilson presents Frado, her girl-protagonist, as brutally abused by her white Northern mistress, Mrs. Bellmont. Although they are both women, Mrs. Bellmont perceives Frado not as a girl but as a thing from which she intends to get as much work as possible. In this context, gender bonds are meaningless and race is the primary determinant of the power relations between these two women.

Still *Our Nig* underscores the effects of gender on Frado's life. Mag, her mother, is a working-class white orphan who is seduced at an early age by a prosperous white man and becomes pregnant. Although the child dies, it is that momentous event in Mag's life that plunges her into a life of abject poverty and social ostracism from which she is barely saved by Jim, a black man who marries her and is the father of her two children. Mrs. Wilson documents not only the results of Mag's fall from grace because she is a woman but also Jim's hard life as a black man who can barely support his family and who eventually dies from overwork. The author emphasizes how Mag's ostracism from society is due both to gender and race and how it affects her as a mother. Near starvation, this mother does what no mother is supposed to do. She abandons her child, Frado, precipitating the terrible existence the girl experiences at the Bellmonts'. Like Celie, Frado is poor, black, and a woman. Like Celie, Mrs. Wilson, the author of *Our Nig*, insists on telling her own story, insists on her own apparently unique experience even as she outlines the intersection of race, gender, and class factors that determined her childhood.

But not only does this intersection affect the actual story she tells, it is the very reason for Mrs. Wilson's authorship. She tells us in her preface that it was her need to support her ailing child that was the initial impulse for *publishing* her story. Because she is a wife abandoned by her husband and thus a poor mother, she tried, as did so many nineteenth-century American women, to make some money through writing. Nina Baym's study of white women writers of the nineteenth century indicates that economics was one major reason why so many of them became professional romance writers. Harriet Wilson's *Our Nig* suggests that like white women, black woman, also in need of income, sought to make a living through their pen.

But if that was her only intention, Harriet Wilson underscores it by constructing a story that she tells us in her preface may well offend her brethren. In the construction of her novel, she opposed the abolitionist conventions of black William Wells Brown's *Clotel* as well as white Harriet Beecher Stowe's *Uncle Tom's Cabin*. For through the character of Mrs. Bellmont she dramatically challenges their claim that Northern white women were the likeliest allies of suffering, oppressed blacks. In addition, Mrs. Wilson emphasizes that it is a fugitive slave turned abolitionist-lecturer who marries Frado and abandons her and her child, thus questioning the idea that all black abolitionists were committed to the women of their race. It is likely that it is precisely those challenges to prevailing ideas that plunged Mrs. Wilson's novel into oblivion. Not only was her venture unsuccessful, not only did her son die, but it was not until this decade that her novel was rediscovered.

Alice Walker's *The Color Purple* was published in 1983, the same year that Henry Louis Gates's edition of the newly discovered *Our Nig* was released, so it is unlikely that she was able to read that nineteenth-century novel while she was writing her own. Yet, although Mrs. Wilson and Walker wrote some hundred years apart, they exhibit similar attitudes about black women as subjects.

The Color Purple also focuses on intersections of race, class, and gender so evident in much of Afro-American women's literature. It is about a young black woman's freeing of herself from incest, rape, and wife-beating within a black patriarchal family as well as her growing understanding of her worth. She does this not only through the support and love given to her from her sister-in-law, Sofia, her lover-friend, Shug, and her blood sister, Nettie, but also through her writing. Her letters to God and then to Nettie are her meditations on her life, her attempt to understand her reality, even as they are a record of her society's structure. Like *Our Nig*, *The Color Purple* explores the relations within a family from the perspective of a black girl-woman even as it demonstrates how racism, sexism, and class values are modes of oppression that intersect.

Imagine Mister as another version of the hard-working Jim. In this context he is a Southern black of the Reconstruction period whose family is descended from slaves and slave owners and who has observed the means by which white men maintain power. Rather than marrying a white woman, as Jim did, an act that in the South would precipitate his death, he imitates the men who have oppressed him. For he inherits from his hard-working father not only property and middle-class status but the modes of behavior that white men, who are above him, exhibit. Those who are subject to his will, those with less power than he, are his female kin, his wife, and his children. Just as he must at all times call white men Mister, a symbol of his power relationship to them, he insists that those below him call him Mister.

Like Frado, it is the loss of her parents that leads to Celie's rape by her stepfather and her abusive marriage to Mister. Just as Frado is beaten and kept in her place, Celie is beaten and kept in *her* place. Just as Frado is a thing to be used, Celie is a thing to be used. But whereas Frado's only means of salvation during her childhood are the apparently compassionate but ineffectual white men who promise her heavenly rather than earthly release, Celie has access to other black women who help her to build trust in herself and to oppose Mister and all that might restrict her. Like Frado, it is Celie's knowledge that she *can* fight that is the beginning of her release from bondage. Unlike Frado, whose opponent is a white woman, Celie must fight a black man, her husband who does not love her and who desires another woman. Like Frado, Celie lives in a middle-class household. Yet neither of them, as black women, shares in whatever power that status is supposed to signify. Whereas Frado is "nig" in the Bellmont house, Celie is "wife" and therefore nonexistent in her husband's house. When Harpo, her stepson, asks his father why he beats Celie, Mister simply and emphatically states, "She my wife."

Both Mrs. Bellmont and Mister are clearly frustrated beings. We can surmise from Frado's description of her employer that rather than being "an angel of house," a concept that became the norm for women in the late nineteenth century, she is its "devil." Clearly the household she runs is not sufficiently engrossing for her; she lacks avenues, outlets, although Frado, her victim, has little awareness of the lacks her employer feels. Because Mrs. Bellmont is more powerful than Frado, she vents her frustration on the girl, as so many whites have on blacks. In contrast, Celie does learn why Mister is so frustrated. In his weakness and in his desire to hold onto the land his father bequeathed to him, he has given up Shug, the woman he loves but cannot own. Like Mrs. Bellmont, he assaults those weaker than he—his wife and his children. Both *their* stories suggest to us that dissatisfied people who too are restricted by society exercise power over others because they *can*.

Like Mrs. Wilson, Celie writes, against all odds, to affirm her existence. It is because Celie needs to understand what is happening to her that she writes her letters to God. Like Mrs. Wilson, Alice Walker published her novel to assert that Celies do exist, as they had in her own family. For Celie's character is based on Rachel, Walker's step-grandmother, just as Frado's experience is based on the life experience of Mrs. Wilson. Through her imaginative retelling of Rachel's story, Walker claims for her maternal ancestor that knowledge that is an intersection of sexism and racism, a racism peculiar to America, an intense sexism that was common through much of the world at the beginning of the twentieth century. That Alice Walker's novel has not been repressed, as Mrs. Wilson's was, is an indication of a literary activism among black women like Mrs. Wilson, rather than primarily a measure of these two writers' respective literary talents.

For there is no question that Mrs. Wilson had a fine sense of the demands of writing a narrative, despite her claims of ineptitude in her preface. *Our Nig* is written in a strong, fluent prose. There is in Mrs. Wilson's rendering of her voice a sense of conviction in her storytelling skills. And she buttresses that voice with quotations from innumerable poets so that the reader could not ignore her knowledge of literature. Like her protagonist, Frado, literacy is for her a source of consolation, a means by which she gives order and meaning to her experience. As important, the author writes her work in a form that combines the major elements of two major genres of the day: the sentimental romance and the slave narrative, interestingly two forms that her literary descendant, Alice Walker, would put to great use in writing *The Color Purple*. Despite her low status in the society, despite her claims that she was "nothing at all," Mrs. Wilson drew from the two literary traditions of which, it could be said, she was naturally a part—that of "women's" literature and that of "Afro-American" literature. She therefore undercut the idea that "free" black people of the day were not reading, were not scrutinizing those forms in which the dominant popular literature was being written. Ralph Ellison's blurb for the republication of *Our Nig* in 1983 put it succinctly: "Professor Gates' discovery confirms my suspicion that there was more 'free floating literacy' available to Negroes than has been assumed." To that comment I would add that black women, as well as men, strove for literacy and saw reading and writing as a means of articulating their existence as well as a potential for advancement in the society.

Yet, despite Mrs. Wilson's remarkable achievement, her work went unmentioned for over a hundred years by black as well as white scholars. It is not surprising that white scholars would not notice her novel since blacks and women were typically disregarded in the literary arena. Moreover, generally speaking, Afro-American scholars focused until recently on the men who wrote; yet they did include, if only in footnotes, the works of women like Frances Harper. What Wilson's omission from even their footnotes indicates is that she did not fit into the Afro-American political ideology of the day. Her truth raised questions about the complex intersection of issues. At a time when the emphasis was on abolition and uplift her story would have been an embarrassment to her brethren. Further, Harriet Wilson was clearly not a part of the visible Afro-American social and political groups of the time. That she managed to get her story published is itself a miracle.

During the 1970s, the influence of the black movement and the women's movement opened a space in which literary scholars began to question the established body of American literature. The result has been a revision of the literary canon and an investigation of what works of literature have been omitted from our national literary tradition as well as reasons for their omission. Clearly groups perceived as "other" were not supposed to have written literature worth considering. The space created by such questioning is surely one of the reasons why Henry Louis Gates could recognize *Our Nig* for the fascinating work it is. Still, that autobiographical novel's importance as an example of an Afro-American woman's attempt to forge a form out of the two literary traditions to which she was heir is just beginning to be examined.

For *Our Nig* is a part of both the Afro-American and the women's literary tradition. Such a fusion of traditions should be quite fascinating to literary scholars. Instead we are often restricted by our own categories of gender and race. If we look at the literary work that most focused on nineteenth-century American women's fiction, Nina Baym's *Woman's Fiction: A Guide to Novels about Women in America, 1820–1870* (published in 1978), we could not expect to find reference to *Our Nig*, since Gates's edition of that work was not released until 1983. Still it is surprising that in her study, published during a period of intense interest in Afro-American women's literature, Baym uses the word "woman" so uncategorically. She appears not to have investigated the possibility that Afro-American women attempted to write fiction. Nor does she qualify her title or her text with the accurate adjective, *white* women, since her study is devoted exclusively to that group of women. An investigation into whether Afro-American women wrote sentimental fiction may have resulted in conclusions somewhat different from the ones she reaches. For example, writers of sentimental fiction might not, if they were also black, have been primarily middle class (Harriet Wilson was not). Issues of class that Baym discusses in this might also have been affected by her inclusion of black women's fiction.

On the other hand, contemporary male Afro-American literary commentators sometimes ignore the existence of *Our Nig* as an indication that black women as well as white women wrote sentimental romances. In his review of Alice Walker's *The Color Purple* in the January 29, 1987, edition of the *New York Review of Books,* Darryl Pinckney asserted that the book is closer to Harriet Beecher Stowe's works than it is to those of Zora Neale Hurston, for, he continues, *The Color Purple* is a form of the sentimental inspirational fiction of the nineteenth century. In referring to Harriet Beecher Stowe, Pinckney attempted to disqualify Alice Walker as belonging to the tradition of Afro-American literature; rather he implies that she belongs to the tradition of white women writers.

Whether *The Color Purple* is inspirational sentimental fiction is a point we could debate. What I would like to stress is Pinckney's omission of the fact that Afro-American women writers, like Wilson and Frances Harper, were participating in the development of sentimental romances and that their participation in that genre ought to qualify it as part of the tradition of Afro-American literature. Despite his allusion to Zora Neale Hurston (who too could be said to have qualities of the sentimental romance in *Their Eyes Were Watching God*), Pinckney's assertion gives the impression that there are *not* important literary intersections among black and white writers, male as well as female, in this country. After all, one could, as he has, label Ishmael Reed's fiction "detective" fiction, a genre used by white men and women. More important is Pinckney's slightly hidden assumption that since black men did not often use the genre of the sentimental romance, that genre is not a part of the Afro-American literary tradition.

Harriet Wilson's use not only of the slave narrative so identified with black nineteenth-century writers but also of the sentimental romance in 1859, as well as its use in the works of other nineteenth-century Afro-American women, suggests that free black women were relating to literary forms that would best express their experience as both black and woman. This quest continues among our writers, for contemporary Afro-American women writers utilize forms that could be identified as belonging to different traditions. Their participation in such traditions is enriching rather than restrictive.

Despite her adroit use of different genres, Mrs. Wilson could well have predicted, given the constraints of her time, that she would be unsuccessful in her publishing venture. Yet she insisted on telling *her* story from her particular point of view. Her use of italics throughout her text, a device that emphasizes that she is relating a truth contrary to what readers have come to believe, is a sure sign that she sees her experience as knowledge that must be recognized by others. She is insistent that what she knows needs to be known by others. Her attitude is important in her narrative; for if only *she* knows what she knows, she is left alone, not only in physical desolation but in a void that devises her existence. Her writing and publishing her subversive story underlines her insistence on her own existence, her insistence that it be acknowledged, respected, recognized by others. Listen to the final sentence of *Our Nig*. In concluding her tale about those who have determined so much of what her life has been and has become, Frado tells us that "[she] has passed from their memories, as Joseph from the butler's, but she will never cease to track them beyond mortal vision."

It is her truth, despite the prevailing traditional or alternative modes of representing reality, that Frado knows, that Celie knows. It is that contrariness that is at the core of so much of Afro-American women's literature, a contrariness that has often resulted in being silenced as Harriet Wilson was or in being rebuked as Alice Walker has been. That contrariness is a measure of health, of the insistence that counter to the societal perception of black women as being "nothing at all," their existence is knowledge that relates to us all.

For not only do *Our Nig* and *The Color Purple* explore poor black women as subjects, they also give us a finely tuned sense of their protagonists' society. Because Frado and Celie are at the bottom of society's ladder, they are likelier to experience more of the various strata of society. Those who are in positions of power do not have to pay attention to all those beneath them. They can be ignorant of those facts they do not want to know. Contrary to Mister's statement then, that because Celie is black, poor, and a woman, she knows nothing, contrary to the assertion that powerlessness means ignorance, Celie must know a great deal in order to survive. The powerless are particularly attuned to those who possess more power than they do. For the powerless, knowledge is essential to survival.

In beginning her story with Frado's mother's two falls, first into the quagmire of gender restraints, then into the bottomless pit of racism, Harriet Wilson tells a different story from those versions that envisioned the North as the Promised Land. The author presents us with a hierarchical view of society. Mag is near the bottom because she is a poor orphan girl. But she falls even lower when she commits the sin of getting pregnant without the sanctions of marriage. In so doing she becomes even more economically destitute. In other words, her class status is related to her gender and to the fact that she does not obey society's conventions. Of course the man who seduces her is not demeaned by his act, for he is the conqueror rather than the conquered. But beyond that, Mag has neither family nor resources to force him to submit to her wishes. Mrs. Wilson's description of Mag's fate is a clear indication that the author understands power relations between the sexes in society and how gender is affected by class status: she tells us that Mag "knew the voice of her charmer, so ravishing, sounded *far above* her," and that she thought "she could ascend to him and become an *equal.*" Instead, he "proudly garnered [her virtue] as a trophy, with those of other victims and left her to her fate."[1]

As well, Mrs. Wilson describes Mag's fall into blackness in similar societal terms, for she knew marriages between Northern white women and black men were not acknowledged. Mulattoes exist, most of us have been told, because of relationships, most of them forced or illicit, between black women and white men. Thus, when Mag marries Jim, Mrs. Wilson emphasizes the differences in their reasons for their union. Jim sees Mag as a "treasure." He muses that "she'd be as much of a prize to me as she'd fall short of coming up to the mark with white folks." Mag accepts Jim because of her poverty and desolation. Mrs. Wilson comments, "You can philosophize, gentle reader, upon the impropriety of such unions, and preach dozens of sermons on the evils of amalgamation. *Want* is a more powerful philosopher and preacher. Poor Mag. She has sundered another bond which held her to her fellows. She has descended another step down the ladder of infamy."[2]

Issues of class, race, and gender, then, are interactive in Mrs. Wilson's story. And her rendition focuses on how fixed societal status is in her time, and how status affects personality. Mag is already low on the scale when the novel opens because she is poor and an orphan. But she *is* virginal, her one prize—what Wilson calls a "priceless gem." That gem, she thinks, is a means to rising above her place in society. But in "giving up" her virginity, she sinks even lower. She is now a poor *soiled* orphan girl.

Yet black people were even lower on the social scale than Mag, who is poor, who is a woman, who knows sex. Wilson's description of Jim's attempt to support himself and his family suggests that he is only slightly above the status of a slave. His blackness gravely affects his economic status, and his attempt, if only a psychological one, to move closer to the status of whites by marrying a white woman suggests how restricted he has been. Still, although Jim is lower in status than Mag, because he is black and she is white, he is still a man and can alleviate, if only for a time, her destitute condition. Neither Mag's nor Jim's attempt to improve their status by relating to someone above them is successful, however. Instead, they "descend another step down."

Frado inherits from her parents their low standing. Not only is she black like her father, she is a woman like her mother. And she is a child, a being of especially low standing in nineteenth-century society. Because her mother is white, she is shut out from black as well as white society. Since her mother is rejected by her community and mothers are usually the link to a community, Frado is left without any resources beyond her parents.

By situating Frado's story in American culture, Wilson tells us not only that race, class, and gender intersect but that they are never pure, exclusive categories. None of these categories exist on their own. Rather, there are men or women of one class or another, of one race or another. Because of the ways in which we have tended to study these categories, we mention them only when we speak of the "non's—nonwhite, nonmale, non-middle-class," that is, of what we assume to be the norm. But in today's world all human beings belong to at least one of these categories.

When we study Afro-American women's literature, we are compelled to see that when we say "woman," we often unconsciously mean *white women;* when we omit a racial designation, we tend not to differentiate gender *and* to mean nonwhite; when we say people, we mean those who are economically comfortable. Our adjectives—for example, black, poor, female—qualify what we have designated as universal. But suppose we begin to think in another way, that is, from Celie or Frado's perspective. Then the others are white; the others are men; the others are comfortable or powerful. From their perspectives, those are the ones who do not know what needs to be known. And if we did adopt their perspective, we could not so easily define "women," or "blackness." Is Frado's experience the experience of woman, as we have come to think of that category, in the nineteenth century? Is her experience *black,* as we tend to identify blackness? Is Celie's experience the experience of a middle-class person, as we usually describe it?

Theoretical frames become more difficult to assert and construct, for Frado's experience, as is Celie's, is a clear indication that not only Afro-American women but very few of us can possibly be described as the norm. Interestingly, theory, at least in literary study, appears to be central—absolutely necessary—today when referring to those who are perceived as the other. I wonder, if any one were to construct a "theory" about white male upper-class literature, what it would be called.

Nor does Afro-American women's literature establish any such construct as "the black woman's experience." What the literature emphasizes is both the variousness and the sameness of being a black woman in America. Contrary to many social science studies, in which black women are often *objects* of study, Afro-American women writers give voice to experiences that converge at certain points and are different at others. Our tendency to want to reduce any one group to a monolith is one reason why scholars as well as readers could not *imagine,* despite the text, that *The Color Purple* was about a black *middle-class* family. We have been so conditioned by images of poor Southern blacks that we find it difficult to conceive of any others, despite our knowledge that blacks in Georgia made great economic strides during Reconstruction.

The study of Afro-American women's literature also suggests that we should be cautious about labeling genres or particular forms as belonging primarily to one group or another. Wilson fuses the slave narrative and sentimental romance. *The Color Purple* is written in letters, the form used in the first English novels, a form associated with women's history, and uses both the slave narrative and the sentimental romance in its structure. These writers drew from existing forms and constructed new ones more suited to their needs—forms that compel us to read differently, to enter into their unique experience. And like jazz musicians, Mrs. Wilson's voice is distinctly her own, as Alice Walker's and Toni Morrison's are distinctly theirs.

In using the word "tradition," as I so consciously did in my first book, *Black Women Novelists,* I sought to delineate a specifically Afro-American female body of literature that has existed since the eighteenth century. That word was useful for me, and I hope for others, in that it brought into view writers who had been completely ignored by both Anglo-American and Afro-American literary scholars. By emphasizing that these writers, as a result of their social definition in America, could not help but reflect the intersections of race, class, and gender, I hoped to suggest the central importance of their work to American history, to American culture.

Such emphasis, however, ought not to suggest, as it sometimes does (particularly to scholars), that these writers are all the same, or that they are limited to or by that construct. In fact, the opposite is true. For what Celie knows, what Frado knows, is that denied the apparent advantages of being the norm, whether it is in the category of gender, race, or class, they *exist.* Their very existence expands those categories beyond their meaning. Frado's knowledge and Celie's knowledge stretch those categories and challenge our assumptions as to what they can mean.

The literature that Afro-American women write refutes the perception not only that their subjects are "nothing at all" but that their subjects can be reduced to categories so often imposed on those who are devalued. Perhaps that is one lesson it teaches those of us who are scholars. For we are often so tempted to want to *fix* our subjects of study in stone.

Toni Morrison's *Beloved* has, since its publication in 1987, received much acclaim from academic critics as well as more commercially included commentators. Reviewers almost unanimously proclaimed it a masterpiece. In just six years the number of critical essays published on this novel rivals those written on only a few other contemporary African American novels: Ralph Ellison's *Invisible Man* (1952), a favorite of American English departments, and Alice Walker's *The Color Purple* (1982), a favorite of women's studies departments. Like these two novels, *Beloved* has passed into the mainstream curriculum of our universities, at least for the time being. That passing could be seen as a measure of an increasing awareness of "multiculturalism" and "feminism" in the academy, an awareness for which many people of color and women writers and scholars have struggled.

Yet I am perturbed by the attention, by the *kind* of critical attention *Beloved* has tended to receive, or to put it in our current literary critical language, by the critical discourses that I fear are beginning to appropriate this complex novel. I am not worried that *Beloved* will be destroyed by these discourses, for given the novel's text, it is often illuminated by them. Rather, I am concerned that another critical approach, which I assumed would have resulted in some significant analyses, has not often been applied to *Beloved*. As a result, I believe, precisely at this contemporary moment, a desperate moment for African Americans as a group, the power of this novel as a specifically African American text is being blunted.

Unfortunately, what the critical reception of *Beloved* points to is that very little has changed in the academic/intellectual community as to who writes and who publishes. True, one would think that, given the supposed craze about African Americans and peoples of color in the widely publi-

First published in *Cultural Critique* 24 (Spring 1993): 5–15.

cized "Political Correctness Takeover," it would be impossible to claim that little has changed in the academy. Yes, increasingly, nuanced sophisticated criticism is being written on *Beloved*. I note, for example, the many sessions at recent MLAs that have included presentations on the novel. Feminists are exploring the paradoxical mother-daughter relationship at the center of the novel, especially from a psychoanalytic perspective. Some African Americanists are examining *Beloved* from the perspective of its revisioning of the history of American slavery, the way Morrison is able to probe those terrible spaces that nineteenth-century slave narrators could not write about. I myself have written about this aspect of the novel in an essay, "'Somebody Forgot to Tell Somebody Something'" [included in this volume].[1] Marxist critics are explaining Morrison's conscious linking of the relationship between production and reproduction as central to the American slavery system. Formalist critics are examining the theme of memory and the role of myth in the novel, and are celebrating its innovative techniques.

Even as I have drawn on these various perspectives in my thinking, teaching, and writing about *Beloved,* I am still struck by what I believe to be Morrison's virtually unique accomplishment in this, her fifth novel—that is, her use of the African traditional religious belief that Westerners call ancestor worship. When I peruse the critical commentary that, to date, has been written on the novel, I find few analyses that emphasize the point that this is a novel about that unspeakable event, the only event in the brutal history of African Americans about which Morrison has stated there is barely a whisper—that is, the Middle Passage.[2] That event is the dividing line between being African and being African American. It is the four-hundred-year holocaust that wrenched tens of millions of Africans from their Mother, their biological mothers as well as their Motherland, in a disorganized and unimaginably monstrous fashion. Yet for reasons having as much to do with the inability on the part of America to acknowledge that it is capable of having generated such a holocaust, as well as with the horror that such a memory calls up for African Americans themselves, the Middle Passage has practically disappeared from American cultural memory. What did, what does that wrenching mean, not only then, but now? That is the question quivering throughout this novel. Have African Americans, How could African Americans, How are African Americans recovering from this monumental collective psychic rupture?

Let me be clear, lest I be misunderstood. I have no argument with psychoanalytic, Marxist, or formalist interpretations of *Beloved*. Although at times I can be testy about any one of these approaches to particular texts, because of its richness of texture, *Beloved* does and should generate many and various, even contending, interpretations. Let me also be clear about another point. The perspective on this novel that I believe has been sadly lacking in critical discourse is not what some are currently calling Afrocentrism. In effect the use of the term *centrism* betrays the fact that Afrocentrism is generated from narrow nationalist Western thinking, that it is akin to Eurocentrism, which it apparently opposes but also mimics. Thus many contemporary forms of Afrocentrism undercut the very concept they intended to propose—that there are different interpretations of history and different narratives, depending on where one is positioned, in terms of power relations as well as distinctive cultures and that there are, given the various cultures of our world, multiple philosophical approaches to understanding life. The perspective I am proposing is one that acknowledges the existence of an African cosmology, examines how that cosmology has been consistently denigrated in the West, and explores its appropriateness for texts that are clearly derived from it. Since *Beloved,* as a sign of a continually developing African cosmology,[3] is as much about the period when Africans were forcibly displaced from their Motherland as it is about slavery in North America, it would seem logical for critics to consider how African belief systems might illuminate this text.

As is evident from the many critical pieces written on this subject, memory is a central theme in *Beloved.* Yet memory, as such, is not unique to ex-slaves. One question that came to mind as I first read *Beloved* was the particular form of this novel's process of remembering, and what memory specifically means for its characters. Certainly, one could discuss the meaning of memory in the novel in terms of the pre-Oedipal relationship between mother and daughter that Freud theorized about, or even in general terms about how any group of human beings (for example, the Jews) who had suffered a holocaust might have repressed that horrible memory, and the consequences of the refusal to remember. Morrison, however, not only points to this general phenomenon of collective amnesia but also, specifically, to why the Middle Passage was, for Africans, a most extreme violation of one of the basic tenets of West African cosmology.

For the past three years, I have been giving a talk called "*Beloved* as Ancestral Worship" to point to that extreme violation and to the process which Morrison in this text uses to expose and dramatize that psychic rupture perhaps for the first time in American literature in such a complex and haunting way. And I have been startled, when I have given that talk, that few teachers or students even know what the Middle Passage is, or that African philosophical traditions exist. As a result, the idea of an African cosmological approach to this literary masterpiece could not occur to them. In contrast to this response, I experienced a distinctly different and dramatic reaction to my talk at a workshop I did with "emotionally disturbed" black patients at a hospital near my university. Unlike so many others who found the novel difficult to follow, these patients felt it to be a healing experience, one that mirrored their sense of their own personal and communal history and returned them to a point, sometimes only short-lived, where they were willing to remember what they had decided they did not want to remember. For many of them, that remembrance had to do with their parents, grandparents, glimpses of ancestors that they had pushed away. Why had *Beloved* had such an effect on them? Somehow the novel recalled for these patients African American communal beliefs that they thought they had abandoned but had still retained.

I suppose, since my awareness of an African ancestral system did not emanate from my training as a graduate student, nor from my study of literary/ critical theory, I should not be surprised that teachers and students do not generally know about it. That this concept reverberates for me throughout *Beloved* has much to do with the fact that practices derived from African religions, specifically in relation to ancestor worship, still persist in the culture from which I come. Why these practices are not often known about by those outside the culture, or even used as a basis of analysis by those from within the culture, might have to do with a pervasive belief within American cultural institutions that Africa does not have a philosophical tradition. It might also have to do with the denigration of African ancestor worship by Western academics as superstition. Reading this novel and the studies generated by it has led me to wonder about the types of methodologies that we are exposed to in the American university and how they might be related to culturally dominant patterns in our society.

I certainly did not understand very much about what African ancestral worship was, or what it could mean, when I first read *Beloved*. But I did recognize something from my own Caribbean culture. I was struck by Morrison's representation of the character Beloved as an embodied spirit, a spirit that presents itself as a body. In the Caribbean, spirits are everywhere, are naturally in the world, and are not ghosts in the horror-genre sense of that term. The spirits, the ancestors, to quote a song by the black women's singing group Sweet Honey in the Rock, "are in the wind, in the trees, in the waters, in the rocks."[4] In an interview, Morrison herself reiterated that point: for African Americans, at least until the recent past, the experience of spirits communicating with the living was a natural one rather than some kind of weird, unnatural event. Hence her representation of the spirit character as a body.

Moreover, in my tradition, ancestral spirits must be nurtured and fed, or they will be angry or, at the least, sad. Even today, as they did when I was growing up, many of my folk, before an important event, pour what we call "libations." If one does not, the ancestors are not being given the respect they deserve. If ancestors are consistently not fed, or have not resolved some major conflict, especially the manner of their death, they are tormented and may come back to the realm we characterize as that of the living, sometimes in the form of an apparently newborn baby. So often I have heard someone in the Caribbean say, "This one is an old one and has come back because she needs to clear up something big." Although Beloved is not a newborn baby in terms of her apparent age, she acts as she would have if she were the age when she was killed by her mother. And there are many references in the text of the novel to her skin and eyes, which appear to be those of a newborn baby. What, I wondered, was Morrison doing? As if fixed at the age of her death, Beloved comes back looking for the face of the mother which is still her face, just as babies when they are around two, the age of the already-crawling baby, cannot yet see themselves as separate from their mother, and see her face as their face. Morrison seemed to be fusing age-old beliefs from African-derived cultures in the New World with the observations of mothers throughout the world, observations that have been validated by Western scientific psychological perspectives.

I was also struck by the way the character Beloved needs constantly to be fed, especially sweet things, the food that ancestors, even voduns like Erzulie, the Haitian vodun of love, relish. Like bodies, the ancestral spirits in my Caribbean context who come back to visit us eat and drink and are carnal. Yet they differ from the living in that while they do appear as bodies, their eyes and skin, like Beloved's, are those of newborn babes.

Stimulated by these memories from my African-Caribbean culture as well as by Morrison's own remarks in her interviews about the novel, I began to try to articulate whether and how African belief systems might be crucial to an understanding of the novel. In contemplating Morrison's epigraph to Beloved, "Sixty Million and more," I was reminded of a recurrent childhood event. I used to wonder aloud who my ancestors were, not only the elders we knew about in my family, but also those who had come from Africa. How had they gotten to the Caribbean? How had they managed to survive? I was also curious about why no one in my family, as "chauvinistic" a clan as you could find, ever talked about that transition from Africa to the New World. Some elders even tried to deny that we came from Africa and had been slaves, despite the presence of the Market Square where the inscription read that slaves had been auctioned there. Why, I wondered, did we pour libations? To whom were we pouring libations? What were their names? West Africans I knew also poured libations. Reading Beloved revived these questions. And listening to Morrison speak about her novel as a prayer, a memorial, a fixing ceremony for those who did not survive the Middle Passage and whose names we did not know, reinforced my desire to approach *Beloved* from an African perspective.

That desire led me to several studies and especially to John Mbiti's *African Religions and Philosophy,* which I had read years before as I was working on my first book. My exploration in this essay based on Mbiti's book is not meant as a definitive statement as to how *Beloved* might be approached from an African cosmological perspective, but rather as an indication that such an approach might be appropriate for this novel and might yield interpretations in keeping with contemporary African American concerns.

Even now I hesitate to use the term "African ancestor worship" without worrying about legitimate concerns that I might be denigrating African religions, for the practice I am about to describe has been so maligned in the West that even African scholars apologize when they use the term. The *Christian* African theologian John Mbiti warns us that in traditional West African societies, Africans do not worship their ancestors. Rather, they believe that when a person passes (and this phrase is important, as it is still consistently used by African Americans), that is, "dies," in the Western sense, they do not disappear as long as someone remembers them, their name, their character. Mbiti states: "So long as the living-dead is thus remembered, he is in the state of *personal immortality.*"[5] The acts of feeding the dead and pouring libations are meant as symbols, active symbols of communion, fellowship, and renewal. Thus continuity, not only of genes but also of active remembering, is critical to a West African's sense of her or his own personal being and, beyond that, of the beingness of the group.

Mbiti also points out that the ancestors are associated with their land, the piece of Nature that they inhabit. The people are the land, the land is the people. He tells us, "The land provides them with the roots of existence as well as binding them mystically to their departed. People walk on the graves of their forefathers, and it is feared that anything separating them from these ties will bring disaster to family and community life. To remove Africans by force from their land is an act of such great injustice that no foreigner can fathom it."[6] For West Africans, a particular tree, rock, or grove embodies that relationship between themselves as human beings in Nature, and other aspects of Nature that are often seen as separate from human beings. Thus, Nature is seen as a part of the human and the divine and is considered sacred in much the same way that churches in the Christian religion are considered sacred. In *Beloved,* Morrison uses this aspect of traditional African religions in her representation of the Clearing, that space from which Baby Suggs preached and the place to which Sethe, her daughter-in-law, comes to communicate with her elder when she has passed on.

In fact, Morrison's entire opus has explored that connection between the folk and the land. I will not dwell here too much on her theme of place and displacement in African American life, the sense of homelessness and the intense emphasis on home, since so much as been written on this subject. I will only note that she has, from her first novel, *The Bluest Eye,* moved increasingly further back in time to the point in her third novel, *Song of Solomon,* where Milkman, her protagonist, discovers his oldest ancestor, Solomon, in the land of Shalimar; in this novel, the land is as much a character as its human protagonists. However, although Morrison focused on Solomon's flying back to Africa in *Song of Solomon,* she was literally stopped in her tracks. For in order to get back to Africa, she had to confront the Middle Passage. Not until *Beloved,* her fifth novel, does she try to imagine that terrible space, and what it must mean for the Solomons of her third novel.

What does it mean when not only Morrison's protagonists in her first four novels but millions of African Americans in the New World are cut off from their "living dead," and cannot know their names and thus cannot remember them? In not being able to remember, name, and feed those who passed on in the Middle Passage, those who survived *had* to abandon their living dead to the worst possible fate that could befall a West African: complete annihilation. Mbiti tells us that to "'die' immediately" is "a great tragedy that must be avoided at all costs."[7] What a tragedy, then, when millions "die" immediately. In a sense, Morrison anticipates that psychic horror by using the wit and irony of the African American tradition in *Song of Solomon,* when she names the descendants of Solomon the Deads, their name being the result of an error in a white man's records. In *Beloved,* however, wit gives way to a facing of the tragic wrenching of that disnaming, not only for those who did not survive but also for those who did. She evokes that terrible space of being/nonbeing in one of the last passages of *Beloved.*

> Everybody knew what she was called, but nobody anywhere knew her name. Disremembered and unaccounted for, she cannot be lost because no one is looking for her, and even if they were, how can they call her if they don't know her name? Although she has claim, she is not claimed. In the place where long grass opens, the girl who waits to be loved and cry shame erupts into her separate parts, to make it easy for the chewing laughter to swallow her all away.
> It was not a story to pass on.[8]

Mbiti tells us that African time is not linear. Rather, the future, in the Western sense, is absent, because the present is always an unfolding of the past.[9] Thus every "future" is already contained in what Westerners call the "past." When one views the novel from this African cosmological perspective it is especially significant that the embodied past is represented by a girl-child/woman, the character Beloved. It is not surprising, then, that the spirit who is the most wrathful and most in pain is that of a child who dies in a violent, unnatural way, for the child represents the sustenance of both the past and the present as it becomes the future, not only for an individual family but also for the group as a whole. Moreover, in many traditional African societies women, as potential mothers, are the bulwark against immediate "death." For in giving birth to children, mothers produce those who are more likely to know and remember their ancestors. If one has no children, who will pour libations to you?[10] That valuable status that West African women have as mothers is, of course, a double-edged sword, not only for those who are "barren" but also for those who have children whom they cannot mother, which includes passing on the memory of their ancestors.

In *Beloved,* Morrison not only explores the psychic horror of those who can no longer call their ancestors' names, but also the dilemma of the mother who knows her children will be born into and live in the realm of those who *cannot* call their ancestors' names. Sethe's killing of her already-crawling baby is not only the killing of that individual baby, but the collective anguish African women must have experienced when they realized their children were cut off forever from their "living-dead" who would never be called upon, remembered, or fed.

In reenacting that plane of in-betweenness; in evoking the desire to forget the pain of wrenching from those whom one can no longer name; in dramatizing the dilemma of not remembering those who have betrayed you and sent you into the arms of the abusers; in insisting on recalling those who have loved you in spite of pain and the need to forget, whether in Africa, the slave ships, or American slave farms; in not being able to forget those who are the ground of one's being, the source of one's origins — Morrison has, in *Beloved,* not just written a powerful novel, she has designed a fixing ceremony. Like African art, her novel works in the world. In a process that is central to African spirituality, her fixing ceremony is not merely that of remembrance for the sake of remembrance, but remembrance as the only way to begin the process of healing that psychic wound, which continues to have grave effects on the present. Those whose names we can no longer specifically call know that we have not forgotten them, that they are our "Beloveds," and that unless they release us from the wrath of the past, the future will be tormented and fractured.

By exploring the novel from the point of view of African cosmology, one sees it for what it could be in the world: a prayer, a ritual grounded in active remembering which might result, first of all, in our understanding why it is that so many of us are wounded, fragmented, and in a state of longing. Then, perhaps, we might move beyond that fracturing to those actions that might result in communal healing and in a redesigning of the contemporary world called the "New World." In acknowledging and naming our holocaust we feed, remember, and respect those forgotten, raging spirits whom we call the past, whose bodies and blood fed, and continue to feed, the ground on which we walk.

4　The Race for Theory (1987)

I have seized this occasion to break the silence among those of us, critics, as we are now called, who have been intimidated, devalued by what I call the race for theory. I have become convinced that there has been a takeover in the literary world by Western philosophers from the old literary élite, the neutral humanists. Philosophers have been able to effect such a takeover because so much of the literature of the West has become pallid, laden with despair, self-indulgent, and disconnected. The New Philosophers, eager to understand a world that is today fast escaping their political control, have redefined literature so that the distinctions implied by that term, that is, the distinctions between everything written and those things written to evoke feeling as well as to express thought, have been blurred. They have changed literary critical language to suit their own purposes as philosophers, and they have reinvented the meaning of theory.

My first response to this realization was to ignore it. Perhaps, in spite of the egocentrism of this trend, some good might come of it. I had, I felt, more pressing and interesting things to do, such as reading and studying the history and literature of black women, a history that had been totally ignored, a contemporary literature bursting with originality, passion, insight, and beauty. But unfortunately it is difficult to ignore this new takeover, since theory has become a commodity which helps determine whether we are hired or promoted in academic institutions—worse, whether we are heard at all. Due to this new orientation, works (a word which evokes labor) have become texts. Critics are no longer concerned with literature, but with other critics' texts, for the critic yearning for attention has displaced the writer and has conceived of himself as the center. Interestingly in the first part of this century, at least in England and America, the critic was usually

First published in *Cultural Critique* 6 (Spring 1987): 51–63.

also a writer of poetry, plays, or novels. But today, as a new generation of professionals develops, he or she is increasingly an academic. Activities such as teaching or writing one's response to specific works of literature have, among this group, become subordinated to one primary thrust, that moment when one creates a theory, thus fixing a constellation of ideas for a time at least, a fixing which no doubt will be replaced in another month or so by somebody else's competing theory as the race accelerates. Perhaps because those who have effected the takeover have the power (although they deny it) first of all to be published, and thereby to determine the ideas which are deemed valuable, some of our most daring and potentially radical critics (and by *our* I mean black, women, third world) have been influenced, even co-opted, into speaking a language and defining their discussion in terms alien to and opposed to our needs and orientation. At least so far, the creative writers I study have resisted this language.

For people of color have always theorized—but in forms quite different from the Western form of abstract logic. And I am inclined to say that our theorizing (and I intentionally use the verb rather than the noun) is often in narrative forms, in the stories we create, in riddles and proverbs, in the play with language, since dynamic rather than fixed ideas seem more to our liking. How else have we managed to survive with such spiritedness the assault on our bodies, social institutions, countries, our very humanity? And women, at least the women I grew up around, continuously speculated about the nature of life through pithy language that unmasked the power relations of their world. It is this language, and the grace and pleasure with which they played with it, that I find celebrated, refined, critiqued in the works of writers like [Toni] Morrison and [Alice] Walker. My folk, in other words, have always been a race for theory—though more in the form of the hieroglyph, a written figure which is both sensual and abstract, both beautiful and communicative. In my own work I try to illuminate and explain these hieroglyphs, which is, I think, an activity quite different from the creating of the hieroglyphs themselves. As the Buddhists would say, the finger pointing at the moon is not the moon.

In this discussion, however, I am more concerned with the issue raised by my first use of the term, *the race for theory,* in relation to its academic hegemony, and possibly of its inappropriateness to the energetic emerging literatures in the world today. The pervasiveness of this academic hegemony is an issue continually spoken about—but usually in hidden groups, lest we, who are disturbed by it, appear ignorant to the reigning academic elite. Among the folk who speak in muted tones are people of color, feminists, radical critics, creative writers, who have struggled for much longer than a decade to make their voices, their various voices, heard, and for whom literature is not an occasion for discourse among critics but is necessary nourishment for their people and one way by which they come to understand their lives better. Clichéd though this may be, it bears, I think, repeating here.

The race for theory, with its linguistic jargon, its emphasis on quoting its prophets, its tendency towards "Biblical" exegesis, its refusal even to mention specific works of creative writers, far less contemporary ones, its preoccupations with mechanical analyses of language, graphs, algebraic equations, its gross generalizations about culture, has silenced many of us to the extent that some of us feel we can no longer discuss our own literature, while others have developed intense writing blocks and are puzzled by the incomprehensibility of the language set adrift in literary circles. There have been, in the last year, any number of occasions on which I had to convince literary critics who have pioneered entire new areas of critical inquiry that they did have something to say. Some of us are continually harassed to invent wholesale theories regardless of the complexity of the literature we study. I, for one, am tired of being asked to produce a black feminist literary theory as if I were a mechanical man. For I believe such theory is prescriptive — it ought to have some relationship to practice. Since I can count on one hand the number of people attempting to be black feminist literary critics in the world today, I consider it presumptuous of me to invent a theory of how we *ought* to read. Instead, I think we need to read the works of our writers in our various ways and remain open to the intricacies of the intersection of language, class, race, and gender in the literature. And it would help if we share our process, that is, our practice, as much as possible, since, finally, our work *is* a collective endeavor.

The insidious quality of this race for theory is symbolized for me by the very name of this special issue — Minority Discourse — a label which is borrowed from the reigning theory of the day but which is untrue to the literatures being produced by our writers, for many of our literatures (certainly Afro-American literature) are central, not minor, and by the titles of many of the articles, which illuminate language as an assault on the other, rather than as possible communication, and play with, or even affirmation of another. I have used the passive voice in my last sentence construction, contrary to the rules of Black English, which like all languages has a particular value system, since I have not placed responsibility on any particular person or group. But that is precisely because this new ideology has become so prevalent among us that it behaves like so many of the other ideologies with which we have had to contend. It appears to have neither head nor center. At the least, though, we can say that the terms "minority" and "discourse" are located firmly in a Western dualistic or "binary" frame which sees the rest of the world as minor, and tries to convince the rest of the world that it *is* major, usually through force and then through language, even as it claims many of the ideas that we, its "historical" other, have known and spoken about for so long. For many of us have never conceived of ourselves only as somebody's *other.*

Let me not give the impression that by objecting to the race for theory I ally myself with or agree with the neutral humanists who see literature as pure expression and will not admit to the obvious control of its production, value, and distribution by those who have power, who deny, in other words, that literature is, of necessity, political. I am studying an entire body of literature that has been denigrated for centuries by such terms as *political.* For an entire century Afro-American writers, from Charles Chesnutt in the nineteenth century through Richard Wright in the 1930s, Imamu Baraka in the 1960s, Alice Walker in the 1970s, have protested the literary hierarchy of dominance which declares when literature is literature, when literature is great, depending on what it thinks is to its advantage. The Black Arts Movement of the 1960s, out of which Black Studies, the Feminist Literary Movement of the 1970s, and Women's Studies grew, articulated precisely those issues, which came *not* from the declarations of the New Western Philosophers but from these groups' reflections on their own lives. That Western scholars have long believed their ideas to be universal has been strongly opposed by many such groups. Some of my colleagues do not see black critical writers of previous decades as eloquent enough. Clearly they have not read Wright's "Blueprint for Negro Writing," Ralph Ellison's *Shadow and Act,* Chesnutt's resignation from being a writer, or Alice Walker's "Looking for Zora." There are two reasons for this general ignorance of what our writer-critics have said. One is that black writing has been generally ignored in this country [the United States]. Since we, as Toni Morrison has put it, are seen as a discredited people, it is no surprise, then, that our creations are also discredited, but this is also due to the fact that until recently dominant critics in the Western World have also been creative writers who have had access to the upper-middle-class institutions of education and, until recently, our writers have decidedly been excluded from these institutions and in fact have often been opposed to them. Because of the academic world's general ignorance about the literature of black people and of women, whose work too has been discredited, it is not surprising that so many of our critics think that the position arguing that literature is political begins with these New Philosophers. Unfortunately, many of our young critics do not investigate the reason *why* that statement—literature is political—is now acceptable when before it was not; nor do we look to our own antecedents for the sophisticated arguments upon which we can build in order to change the tendency of any established Western idea to become hegemonic.

For I feel that the new emphasis on literary critical theory is as hegemonic as the world which it attacks. I see the language it creates as one which mystifies rather than clarifies our condition, making it possible for a few people who know that particular language to control the critical scene — that language surfaced, interestingly enough, just when the literature of peoples of color, of black women, of Latin Americans, or Africans, began to move to "the center." Such words as *center* and *periphery* are themselves instructive. *Discourse, canon, texts,* words as Latinate as the tradition from which they come, are quite familiar to me. Because I went to a Catholic Mission school in the West Indies I must confess that I cannot hear the word "canon" without smelling incense, that the word "text" immediately brings back agonizing memories of Biblical exegesis, that "discourse" reeks for me of metaphysics forced down my throat in those courses that traced *world* philosophy from Aristotle through Thomas Aquinas to [Martin] Heidegger. "Periphery" too is a word I heard throughout my childhood, for if anything was seen as being at the periphery, it was those small Caribbean islands which had neither land mass nor military power. Still I noted how intensely important this periphery was, for U.S. troops were continually invading one island or another if any change in political control even seemed to be occurring. As I lived among folk for whom language was an absolutely necessary way of validating our existence, I was told that the minds of the world lived only in the small continent of Europe. The metaphysical language of the New Philosophy, then, I must admit, is repulsive to me and is one reason why I raced from philosophy to literature, since the latter seemed to me to have the possibilities of rendering the world as large and as complicated as I experienced it, as sensual as I knew it was. In literature I sensed the possibility of the integration of feeling/knowledge, rather than the split between the abstract and the emotional in which Western philosophy inevitably indulged.

Now I am being told that philosophers are the ones who write literature, that authors are dead, irrelevant, mere vessels through which their narratives ooze, that they do not work nor have they the faintest idea what they are doing; rather, they produce texts as disembodied as the angels. I am frankly astonished that scholars who call themselves Marxists or post-Marxists could seriously use such metaphysical language even as they attempt to deconstruct the philosophical tradition from which their language comes. And as a student of literature, I am appalled by the sheer ugliness of the language, its lack of clarity, its unnecessarily complicated sentence constructions, its lack of pleasurableness, its alienating quality. It is the kind of writing for which composition teachers would give a freshman a resounding F.

Because I am a curious person, however, I postponed readings of black women writers I was working on and read some of the prophets of this new literary orientation. These writers did announce their dissatisfaction with some of the cornerstone ideas of their own tradition, a dissatisfaction with which I was born. But in their attempt to change the orientation of Western scholarship, they, as usual, concentrated on themselves and were not in the slightest interested in the worlds they had ignored or controlled. Again I was supposed to know *them,* while they were not at all interested in knowing *me.* Instead they sought to "deconstruct" the tradition to which they belonged even as they used the same forms, style, language of that tradition, forms which necessarily embody its values. And increasingly as I read them and saw their substitution of their philosophical writings for literary ones, I began to have the uneasy feeling that their folk were not producing any literature worth mentioning. For they always harkened back to the masterpieces of the past, again reifying the very texts they said they were deconstructing. Increasingly, as *their* way, *their* terms, *their* approaches remained central and became the means by which one defined literary critics, many of my own peers who had previously been concentrating on dealing with the other side of the equation, the reclamation and discussion of past and *present* third world literatures, were diverted into continually discussing the new literary theory.

From my point of view as a critic of contemporary Afro-American women's writing, this orientation is extremely problematic. In attempting to find the deep structures in the literary tradition, a major preoccupation of the new New Criticism, many of us have become obsessed with the nature of reading itself to the extent that we have stopped writing about literature being written today. Since I am slightly paranoid, it has begun to occur to me that the literature being produced *is* precisely one of the reasons why this new philosophical-literary-critical theory of relativity is so prominent. In other words, the literature of blacks, women of South America and Africa, etc., as overtly "political" literature, was being preempted by a new Western concept which proclaimed that reality does not exist, that everything is relative, and that every text is silent about something—which indeed it must necessarily be.

There is, of course, much to be learned from exploring how we know what we know, how we read what we read, an exploration which, of necessity, can have no end. But there also has to be a "what," and that "what," when it is even mentioned by the New Philosophers, are texts of the past, primarily Western male texts, whose norms are again being transferred onto third world, female texts as theories of reading proliferate. Inevitably a hierarchy has now developed between what is called theoretical criticism and practical criticism, as mind is deemed superior to matter. I have no quarrel with those who wish to philosophize about how we know what we know. But I do resent the fact that this particular orientation is so privileged and has diverted so many of us from doing the first readings of the literature being written today as well as of past works about which nothing has been written. I note, for example, that there is little work done on Gloria Naylor, that most of Alice Walker's works have not been commented on—despite the rage around *The Color Purple*—that there has yet to be an in-depth study of Frances Harper, the nineteenth-century abolitionist poet and novelist. If our emphasis on theoretical criticism continues, critics of the future may have to reclaim the writers we are now ignoring, that is, if they are even aware these artists exist.

I am particularly perturbed by the movement to exalt theory, as well, because of my own adult history. I was an active member of the Black Arts Movement of the sixties and know how dangerous theory can become. Many today may not be aware of this, but the Black Arts Movement tried to create Black Literary Theory and in doing so became prescriptive. My fear is that when Theory is not rooted in practice, it becomes prescriptive, exclusive, élitist.

An example of this prescriptiveness is the approach the Black Arts Movement took towards language. For it, blackness resided in the use of black talk which they defined as hip urban language. So that when Nikki Giovanni reviewed Paule Marshall's *The Chosen Place, the Timeless People,* she criticized the novel on the grounds that it was not black, for the language was too elegant, too white. Blacks, she said, did not speak that way. Having come from the West Indies where we do, some of the time, speak that way, I was amazed by the narrowness of her vision. The emphasis on *one way* to be black resulted in the works of Southern writers being seen as non-black since the black talk of Georgia does not sound like the black talk of Philadelphia. Because the ideologues, like Baraka, come from the urban centers, they tended to privilege their way of speaking, thinking, writing, and to condemn other kinds of writing as not being black enough. Whole areas of the canon were assessed according to the dictum of the Black Arts Nationalist point of view, as in Addison Gayle's *The Way of the New World,* while other works were ignored because they did not fit the scheme of cultural nationalism. Older writers like Ellison and [James] Baldwin were condemned because they saw that the intersection of Western and African influences resulted in a new Afro-American culture, a position with which many of the Black Nationalist ideologues disagreed. Writers were told that writing love poems was not being black. Further examples abound.

It is true that the Black Arts Movement resulted in a necessary and important critique both of previous Afro-American literature and of the white-established literary world. But in attempting to take over power, it, as Ishmael Reed satirizes so well in *Mumbo Jumbo,* became much like its opponent, monolithic and downright repressive.

It is this tendency towards the monolithic, monotheistic, etc., which worries me about the race for theory. Constructs like the *center* and the *periphery* reveal that tendency to want to make the world less complex by organizing it according to one principle, to fix it through an idea which is really an ideal. Many of us are particularly sensitive to monolithism since one major element of ideologies of dominance, such as sexism and racism, is to dehumanize people by stereotyping them, by denying them their variousness and complexity. Inevitably, monolithism becomes a metasystem, in which there is a controlling ideal, especially in relation to pleasure. Language as one form of pleasure is immediately restricted, and becomes heavy, abstract, prescriptive, monotonous.

Variety, multiplicity, eroticism are difficult to control. And it may very well be that these are the reasons why writers are often seen as *persona non grata* by political states, whatever form they take, since writers/artists have a tendency to refuse to give up their way of seeing the world and of playing with possibilities; in fact, their very expression relies on that insistence. Perhaps that is why creative literature, even when written by politically reactionary people, can be so freeing, for in having to embody ideas and recreate the world, writers cannot merely produce "one way."

The characteristics of the Black Arts Movement are, I am afraid, being repeated again today, certainly in the other area to which I am especially tuned. In the race for theory, feminists, eager to enter the halls of power, have attempted their own prescriptions. So often I have read books on feminist literary theory that restrict the definition of what *feminist* means and overgeneralize about so much of the world that most women as well as men are excluded. Seldom do feminist theorists take into account the complexity of life — that women are of many races and ethnic backgrounds with different histories and cultures and that as a rule women belong to different classes that have different concerns. Seldom do they note these distinctions, because if they did they could not articulate a theory. Often as a way of clearing themselves they do acknowledge that women of color, for example, do exist, then go on to do what they were going to do anyway, which is to invent a theory that has little relevance for us.

That tendency towards monolithism is precisely how I see the French feminist theorists. They concentrate on the female body as the means to creating a female language, since language, they say, is male and necessarily conceives of woman as other. Clearly many of them have been irritated by the theories of Lacan for whom language is phallic. But suppose there are peoples in the world whose language was invented primarily in relation to women, who after all are the ones who relate to children and teach language. Some Native American languages, for example, use female pronouns when speaking about non-gender-specific activity. Who knows who, according to gender, created languages? Further, by positing the body as the source of everything, French feminists return to the old myth that biology determines everything and ignore the fact that gender is a social rather than a biological construct.

I could go on critiquing the positions of French feminists who are themselves more various in their points of view than the label which is used to describe them, but that is not my point. What I am concerned about is the authority this school now has in feminist scholarship—the way it has become *authoritative discourse,* monologic, which occurs precisely because it does have access to the means of promulgating its ideas. The Black Arts Movement was able to do this for a time because of the political movements of the 1960s—so too with the French feminists who could not be inventing "theory" if a space had not been created by the Women's Movement. In both cases, both groups posited a theory that excluded many of the people who made that space possible. Hence one of the reasons for the surge of Afro-American women's writing during the 1970s and its emphasis on sexism in the black community is precisely that when the ideologues of the 1960s said *black,* they meant *black male.*

I and many of my sisters do not see the world as being so simple. And perhaps that is why we have not rushed to create abstract theories. For we know there are countless women of color, both in America and in the rest of the world, to whom our singular ideas would be applied. There is, therefore, a caution we feel about pronouncing black feminist theory that might be seen as a decisive statement about third world women. This is not to say we are not theorizing. Certainly our literature is an indication of the ways in which our theorizing, of necessity, is based on our multiplicity of experiences.

There is at least one other lesson I learned from the Black Arts Movement. One reason for its monolithic approach had to do with its desire to destroy the power which controlled black people, but it was a power which many of its ideologues wished to achieve. The nature of our context today is such that an approach which desires power single-mindedly must of necessity become like that which it wishes to destroy. Rather than wanting to change the whole model, many of us want to be at the center. It is this point of view that writers like June Jordan and Audre Lorde continually critique even as they call for empowerment, as they emphasize the fear of difference among us and our need for leaders rather than a reliance on ourselves.

For one must distinguish the desire for power from the need to become empowered—that is, seeing oneself as capable of and having the right to determine one's life. Such empowerment is partially derived from a knowledge of history. The Black Arts Movement did result in the creation of Afro-American Studies as a concept, thus giving it a place in the university where one might engage in the reclamation of Afro-American history and culture and pass it on to others. I am particularly concerned that institutions such as Black Studies and Women's Studies, fought for with such vigor and at some sacrifice, are not often seen as important by many of our black or women scholars precisely because the old hierarchy of traditional departments is seen as superior to these "marginal" groups. Yet it is in this context that many others of us are discovering the extent of our complexity, the interrelationships of different areas of knowledge in relation to a distinctly Afro-American or female experience. Rather than having to view our world as subordinate to others, or rather than having to work as if we were hybrids, we can pursue ourselves as subjects.

My major objection to the race for theory, as some readers have probably guessed by now, really hinges on the question, "for whom are we doing what we are doing when we do literary criticism?" It is, I think, the central question today especially for the few of us who have infiltrated academia enough to be wooed by it. The answer to that question determines what orientation we take in our work, the language we use, the purposes for which it is intended.

I can only speak for myself. But what I write and how I write is done in order to save my own life. And I mean that literally. For me literature is a way of knowing that I am not hallucinating, that whatever I feel/know *is*. It is an affirmation that sensuality is intelligence, that sensual language is language that makes sense. My response, then, is directed to those who write what I read and to those who read what I read—put concretely—to Toni Morrison and to people who read Toni Morrison (among whom I would count few academics). That number is increasing, as is the readership of Walker and Marshall. But in no way is the literature Morrison, Marshall, or Walker create supported by the academic world. Nor, given the political context of our society, do I expect that to change soon. For there is no reason, given who controls these institutions, for them to be anything other than threatened by these writers.

My readings do presuppose a need, a desire among folk who like me also want to save their own lives. My concern, then, is a passionate one, for the literature of people who are not in power has always been in danger of extinction or of cooptation, not because we do not theorize, but because what we can even imagine, far less who we can reach, is constantly limited by societal structures. For me, literary criticism is promotion as well as understanding, a response to the writer to whom there is often ṇo response, to folk who need the writing as much as they need anything. I know, from literary history, that writing disappears unless there is a response to it. Because I write about writers who are now writing, I hope to help ensure that their tradition has continuity and survives.

So my "method," to use a new "lit. crit." word, is not fixed but relates to what I read and to the historical context of the writers I read *and* to the many critical activities in which I am engaged, which may or may not involve writing. It is a learning from the language of creative writers, which is one of surprise, so that I might discover what language I might use. For my language is very much based on what I read and how it affects me, that is, on the surprise that comes from reading something that compels you to read differently, as I believe literature does. I, therefore, have no set method, another prerequisite of the new theory, since for me every work suggests a new approach. As risky as that might seem, it is, I believe, what intelligence means—a tuned sensitivity to that which is alive and therefore cannot be known until it is known. Audre Lorde puts it in a far more succinct and sensual way in her essay "Poetry Is Not a Luxury":

> As they become known to and accepted by us, our feelings and the honest exploration of them become sanctuaries and spawning grounds for the most radical and daring of ideas. They become a safe-house for that difference so necessary to change and the conceptualization of any meaningful action. Right now, I could name at least ten ideas I would have found intolerable or incomprehensible and frightening, except as they came after dreams and poems. This is not idle fantasy, but a disciplined attention to the true meaning of "it feels right to me." We can train ourselves to respect our feelings and to transpose them into a language so they can be shared. And where that language does not yet exist, it is our poetry which helps to fashion it. Poetry is not only dream and vision; it is the skeleton architecture of our lives. It lays the foundations for a future of change, a bridge across our fears of what has never been before.[1]

5   Does Theory Play Well
   in the Classroom? (1996)

I

The title of my presentation that I gave to the organizers of this conference is "Does Theory Play Well in the Classroom?" I'm going to deconstruct that title for a minute so that I can go on and talk about what I really want to talk about. And actually, it does move me into that because, as I looked at the title later on, I realized that by theory, we now mean a particular theory; of course, there have always been theories; we just didn't call them theories before. That is, we are always theorizing, and the reason why we are now using that word, rather than some other word, is something that we might reflect upon perhaps twenty-five years from now. Someone will ask the question, "Why is it that, in literary studies, the word theory, which was so often associated with science, is now being used?" It may have something to do with our sense of inferiority in this technological age. But in any case, if I were to rewrite that title, theory would have an "s" after it, or I probably would use the verb "theorizing," which I prefer to the concept of an artifact, such as a theory. And, of course, "the Classroom" does not exist. There are classrooms. Many different kinds of classrooms, different kinds of institutions; even in Berkeley, in my own department, I have many kinds of classrooms from year to year. So, as I looked at the title again, the only word that I really still agree with is "play." I hope we're going to do a little bit of that today.[1]

There are two different kinds of things I want to do, although they're related. The first is to conceptualize for you, a bit, the essay that you read, "The Race for Theory" [reprinted in this volume], for which I have become

First published in James F. Slevin and Art Young, eds., *Critical Theory and the Teaching of Literature: Politics, Curriculum, Pedagogy* (Urbana, Ill.: National Council of Teachers of English, 1996), 241–57.

notorious. And the second part, which is what I generally like to do, is to contextualize, or at least talk a little bit about, the way I teach Toni Morrison's *Beloved*. I think both are actually related, as I recall what it is I wanted to say in "The Race for Theory." And in the tradition of feminists (I consider myself to be one), I want to begin by giving a kind of a personal context as to why it is that this essay might have, in fact, been written.

Well, it takes me all the say back to where I come from, which is the Caribbean. I grew up in a culture, a society, in which there is a split of cultures which I often call "the highs" and "the lows" (I have written a piece with that title, in fact), where language and the way one approached knowledge differed from the school and the church to the street and what we called "the yard." And I think it was growing up in that society, where there was such a contrast between the languages that were acceptable in these two places, and which were really different, that made me so aware of how values are vested in the kind of language that one uses. So, for example, if you were in the yard in the street, what you do is, you "long talk" in the Caribbean, or you "lie." That's the kind of word you use. Or as some African Americans might say, you do a lot of "signifying." Of course, in the church and in the school, we spoke a kind of British English that was the only way in which you could be heard at the time. We see some of that occurring now in literary criticism where "signifying" has become "signification," and "long talk" has become the "vernacular."

The kind of literature that I read when I was going to school was primarily that which was imposed by the colonials, not necessarily a bad thing. But there was no recognition of the fact that there was a very strong oral, vital tradition of storytelling which focused a great deal on the sound of language—not only on what was said, but how it sounded. I gave you an excerpt from *Beloved* precisely because the neglect of sound is one of the major problems I have with the theoretical language that so many of us are being forced to use if we are to be promoted. Now, one of the reasons why that concerned me when I was growing up had to do with the contradictions involved in what was valued. That is, we all knew we wanted to get by and that the way in which we were weeded out of the system had very much to do with whether or not we sounded British or whether or not we sounded Caribbean.

So, or course, we learned to sound two ways. But even those who expected us to sound British would not allow us to sound that way if we were in the marketplace. Somebody who didn't know how to long talk was not going to make it in the society—even if they became the finest speaker of British English and knew all of the literature. Now this brings me to another point that I want to stress—that was important in my upbringing.

It's interesting that "Dover Beach" is a poem that you all received to read because, in fact, it was one of the poems that we not only read but had to memorize. And I must say that even though there were many, many critiques that we did of "Dover Beach" without our knowing at the time that we were deconstructing it, the fact that it sounded the way it sounded was also important because it meant that we remembered it, and we related to it in some way. One of the things that I do regularly in my classroom is to look at literature from the point of view of its muscularity—that is, to read it aloud so you hear it.

I think that is one of the problems that I find with theoretical frameworks dealing with literature today. Even as we talk about the vernacular, we do not see literature as the *embodiment* of principles, but rather a *statement* of principles. That literature is, in fact, sensual-erotic as well as intellectual; from my point of view, that is what intelligence means. So that's one of the first conceptualizations for the essay that I was to write many, many years later.

A second would be that when I finally did move into the academic world, it was not into literature but into literacy. I taught in a program called SEEK in City College, and the idea of that program was to teach apparently "uneducable" blacks and Puerto Ricans so that they could enter the city colleges. It was thought that they could not, in fact, do that, but one of the things we found, which of course makes perfect sense when you think about it, was that if we chose literature to which they could relate, to use a '60s term, they began to learn to read. They wanted to read. And again, this had not only to do with the content of the literature but the way it sounded; it was through that process that I got into African American literature. The excavating of texts that were no longer available was not only about the meaning but about the fact that the students became involved in the sound that was being made, and many of them, in fact, went on to learn to read and write and to become scholars and many other things. This experience, of course, would turn me around in terms of what I felt literature was about.

I realize that a third very important influence on "The Race for Theory"—and this I reflected on just in the last couple of weeks—was an essay that was written by Alice Walker called "In Search of Our Mothers' Gardens," in which I think that Walker really proposes a critical theory. I think that writers, very often traditionally, are the ones who are good theorizers. Walker asks the question, "From whence does my tradition come?" since, in fact, African American women, until recently, have not had the privilege of writing. "What is my legacy of creativity?"

At first she looks at "the written tradition" in which writers like Nella

Larsen participated; she found them, of course, in a state of what she calls "contrary instincts" (wonderful phrase, sounds good too), and what she means by that is that they are caught between the dominant society's definition of what literature is and the folk tradition from which they're coming. That was not satisfactory, really, in terms of a legacy, the ground that she needed to stand on, or what she felt she needed as a contemporary writer. Walker said she "finally . . . realized that instead of looking high, she ought to look low," and on that low ground she found the many black women who had expressed their creativity in forms such as quilting, storytelling—in all of the various forms that they had access to. For me, this is a completely different definition of art as well as literature. It is on the low ground, where the folk express their creativity, that Walker later on would be able to tap as a basis for her own literary creativity.[2] Therefore, the whole question of whether one has "a room of one's own" shifts, doesn't it? That is a third consideration in terms of the essay that I wrote.

And then the fourth, and perhaps the most important recently, is that I am situated in an African American Studies department at Berkeley that is twenty years old, and we have been trying to put together a coherent curriculum that deals with conflict as well as points of sameness in terms of relating to our students. I have classes in which students come from a variety of disciplines, large classes of people who come from all over the campus to study African American literature because they feel that it means something to their existence now and that these classes can help to explain where they are right now. I'm not just talking about African American students. In most of my classes, the majority of the students are not African American. Many, many of them are Euramerican, Chicano/a, Native American, all kinds of folk. The fact is that they come into the classroom because literature means something to them. That's partially because I am teaching a subject that has been fortunate enough to be graced by writers like Walker and Morrison and [Paule] Marshall and [John Edgar] Wideman and writers of that sort during the last twenty years, so students are interested in reading that literature.

What I am primarily interested in, in relation to my students, is how we get into a dialogue about the way that literature opens them up. The writer is really very much involved in a dialogue with the reader, and I see myself in relation to that dialogue between the writer and the reader, who is not likely going to become a literary critic. I also work extensively, though, with graduate students who are interested in African American literature, women of color literature, or whatever we want to call it. In fact, right now, I have marvelous graduate students. I do find, however, and I want to emphasize this point, that although many of them are acquainted with critical texts, the majority of them have not read the literature. I'm stunned sometimes, as I speak with students who are studying African American literature, that they have never read Frederick Douglass nor approached Ralph Ellison. It seems to me that there is something wrong there in terms of that kind of imbalance. It has partially something to do with the kind of undergraduate training that many of them are receiving right now, where critical texts have become so much of what they read that they are no longer reading the actual literature itself.

That's extremely important to me, the literature, not because I'm a naive romantic, but because, at least in the African American tradition, the creative writers are often the ones who have had the opportunity to theorize about the worldview of African Americans. African Americans, until recently, have not had access to what we call the academic institutions of the West. So their primary domain, in terms of writing for African Americans and their explanation of the world, has been in their literature. I think that the literature not only allows writers to express or, as many of the women writers feel, heal themselves, but it also allows them to relate to different audiences, what we sometimes call "double voice." This has been problematic for the African American writer in the sense that one has to write to "the dominant group" and also one's own group. Writing, therefore, that is very sensual and erotic, that is double-voiced and quoted, that includes chants and proverbs, that uses sound, is extremely important in order to relate to different audiences. It is much, much more difficult to appropriate that kind of literature than the abstract intellectual logic that one might get in some of the Western forms that we think of as theory.

Now I believe that theorizing takes many forms, that it can be, in fact, culturally specific. The idea that theory only takes the form of the analytical, abstract, logical essay is precisely the reason why I ran from philosophy to literature when I was in high school. I felt that when we studied heavy philosophy, something was missing there: there was a split between the head and the body. What I needed, for myself anyway, was a coming together, an interrelatedness of the fact that the body and the soul are one, to put it in the phrase of one of our writers, and I felt that this was what literature actually did, what philosophy could not do. So, that is one of the reasons I was profoundly disturbed at the conference at which "The Race for Theory" was written and given. For two days, most of us "minority scholars," as we were then called (a term I hate), got together and talked to each other, but not about the literature. I'm not sure exactly what we were talking about, but it was clearly very boring, alienating, and had very little to do with what I thought we were there for; it had something to do with mimicking what was thought to be the way in which one ought to talk about literature if one were to be validated or respected today.

The essay then became for me a riff. "The Race for Theory" not only says that we *are* a race for theory, but also that there *is* a race for theory. There are many such riffs in it, so sensual, playing with words to break up the kind of absolute deadening of atmosphere I felt we had fallen into at that conference.

I have to tell you the truth; I'm absolutely amazed at how "significant" this essay has become, since I wrote it in three hours, pretty much as a way of alleviating the boredom that I happened to be situated in. But, of course, it is serious play. I am willing to discuss, contest, and argue about this essay, partially because many black women critics who have agreed with me are now being characterized as "reactionary abolitionists" by some of our brothers, precisely because we are not into "theoretical criticism."

The language of theory is part of the process of making you feel uncomfortable enough to have to think another way. I can see some of what that language is about, except that I think it lacks the surprise and sensuality that I find in literary writers who also sometimes make you struggle. I mean, Toni Morrison makes you struggle, but you're loving it; there's a kind of a pleasure involved which I think is missing in theory, and I find this to be absolutely unacceptable. I think there are a lot of new and important insights that have come from "the new contemporary theory." But the way in which it is written, I think, indicates something about it that is problematic, and it has a great deal to do with a kind of puritanism, which may be because so much of it is French, but that may be my own bias! But, in other words, it doesn't have a kind of sensuality, and so I think it is very hard to play with it in the classroom.

I want to tell a story about that in relation to writers. There was another conference of African American writings, critics, and writers, and one of the writers, a very important writer, called me up in tears from the conference. She had been at a couple of sessions on her work, and she said, "I didn't understand one word . . . what's happening to my work?" And she was absolutely serious. She had taken all this time to craft it, and she went to sessions where she felt that her work was completely miscommunicated, not only in terms of the content, but in the way it was spoken about. I thought about that, and I came to feel very strongly about writers and about readers; perhaps I don't feel strongly enough about critics.

Many people interpret "The Race for Theory" as antitheory, which it is not. What it is, is against theory that is not related to literature. But, of course, it is a theoretical essay. My problem with high theory today is not with it in itself but with what I see happening in the way people are hired, appreciated, and seen in the academic community. In other words, if you are not doing theory, high theory, at least where I am at (at Berkeley), people do not think of you as doing very much, and you're not getting hired. People are promoted on the basis of high theory and so on, and so what I would like to see is something more democratic. That is partially what this piece is about.

I wonder if, in fact, there are different functions. Let me put it this way: some of us are interested in literature, and some of us are interested in theory, and some of us are interested in the relationship between these two and in whether or not it is possible to do all those things. I mean, I think these functions are all valuable. For a very long time in the African American tradition as well as in the West, the literary critics were often the artists. I think that there are certain kinds of tasks that we perform—one of which is that we study; we continue to focus on the contextualization of the literature. That is, we are looking at it continuously from another perspective. We are also looking at the way in which language is used in particular traditions and bodies of literature that writers themselves are not necessarily looking at because they are much more focused on what they are trying to express. We're very much involved, I think, in a dialogue between the reader and the writer, but, most important, I think that our writing is one of the ways in which their writing lasts. If writing is not written about, it disappears. So I see that as being one of the major roles of the critic. My daughter is always saying to me, "Well, you're a critic, that means you judge." That is one of the reasons the word "critic" is also problematic for me. Because when you say you're a critic, most people in the world think, "Oh, you're a critic. You say this book is good, and this book is bad, and this book is in between, and this book is. . . ." I don't think this is what critics do most of the time. I think they ought to be illuminating the works. That is a word I tend to use, "illumination." A very old-fashioned word, I know.

My problem concerns what is going on in terms of academic currency. Another way of putting it is that theory is a new and trendy thing. This has become what every university rushes out to get right now. Theory is on the cutting edge, and the question as to whether or not these theorists can teach literature in the classroom doesn't come up during the hiring process. I have been involved in feminist theory classes, and I'm very interested in that, and I'm very interested in what African American theory should be. But I actually think that African American theory comes out of the literature and the folk tradition, which is what I want to stress. I think that there are various ways to go about it. The problem is that, even though theorists are saying that they are the ones on the top, the hierarchy is developed, and so part of theory ought to be a deconstructing of the theorists themselves. That's also what I wanted to do in "The Race for Theory." It's a deconstructionist piece, contributing my perspective to the academic community.

I'm wondering what we mean by an academic community? The best conversations I have had about literature, I will tell you, have been in my kitchen, with women who had to read the works they were reading. In fact, they don't even call these readers by their last names; they call them Toni and June and so on, because they need it for their lives. They are part of an intellectual community we don't acknowledge. When I go get my hair cut, the women talk about Audre Lorde. I'm serious; this is actually happening. I think we have an erroneous idea, at least in the community I come from, that the only people who read these books are critics and students who are forced to read them in classrooms. Now I find that I'm not just talking about contemporary literature. We can talk about Toni Morrison's *Beloved,* and a lot of my friends who are not in the "academic world" have then gone back and read [Harriet Jacobs's] *Incidents in the Life of a Slave Girl* because they now know it.[3] So I don't know what we mean by an intellectual community, and I wonder about this split between the real world and the academic world.

The academic world is *in* the world. I mean, that's the problem. One of the things I'm concerned about my students knowing is what I call the "literary geography": the way literature gets produced, what writers really do, the power of reviews, what goes on in the background. In other words, I want my students to know that there is not only the text, but that there is also a context out of which this text is arising. This discussion going on among writers is about what I call the "literary geography," and it is related to the social and political geography of what is going on now. In this way, the text that they're reading from the nineteenth century is looked at in a completely different way because of what we're dealing with right now. In other words, one of my roles is to show them that the division between "the real world" and the world of the academy is not really there. The university exists precisely in the world; it is in it.

II

There are a few things I wanted to mention about Toni Morrison's *Beloved,* and it does relate to what we are talking about now. I've been doing an essay on the way in which Morrison's *Beloved* is being written about at present ["Fixing Methodologies: *Beloved,*" reprinted in this volume]. I find out that it is being written about very well — in fact, from a psychoanalytic point of view, a Marxist point of view, a poststructuralist point of view, and so on. But one of the ways it is *not* being written about, which is very much at the core of the novel, is from what I would call an African point of view. The novel itself, it seems to me as I read it, and teach it, and talk with people who have read it, is generated by the phrase "ancestral worship." The reason it is called *Beloved*—the beloved that it is dedicated to, the "Sixty Million and more" that it is dedicated to—has to do with a philosophical concept about ancestral worship that comes from Africa, which many African Americans, at least until lately, have believed. Now, many of us don't know what that (nor what the "middle passage") is, so we miss that completely in the novel. Even though Morrison has said this many times in her interviews, it's what I do not see coming up in the criticism.

What concerns me is why the African American perspective, which is central to the novel, is not being dealt with. Probably because most of us are not trained in this, are we? I want to spend the rest of my time this morning talking about how we might bring that perspective to bear on the novel so that we might better grasp this literature in its own cultural terms.

The novel is, without question, from an African American perspective, a revisioning of the narratives of the nineteenth century. Morrison was able to use an entire tradition that precedes her, revisioning slave narratives (particularly female slave narratives) as well as nineteenth-century African American novels. If you read enough of the tradition, you can see that this novel is the other side of *Clotel,* which was the first novel to be published by an African American man, William Wells Brown.[4] In *Clotel,* the mother kills herself for her child. She does escape slavery, the escape is successful, but she does not have her child. She goes back to get her child, and, in the process of going back to get her child, she is recaptured, and so she drowns herself. Morrison reverses that process and retells that story from a different perspective. In one of her essays, Morrison talks about how the novels of the nineteenth century and the historical novels that precede her all the way up to the 1970s focused primarily on the institutions of slavery rather than on the psyches of the slaves themselves. Now one of the reasons for that, of course, had to do with the goal of the novels of the nineteenth century, which was the abolition of slavery. Therefore, there was a strong indictment of the institution. Another reason for this focus on the institution of slavery stemmed from the fact that, as we moved into the twentieth century, most Americans, black and white, did not know enough about or want to remember the institution of slavery so that you could focus on the slaves as "individuals in communities."

So we can see Morrison, in her revisioning of the literary tradition preceding her, is filling in the silences, the spaces of the narrators who were not able to say or could not speak in that way, for multiple reasons. First, the narrators of the nineteenth century very often fell silent out of modesty (that is the word Morrison uses); because they were trying to persuade whites to abolish slavery, there were certain things they should not speak of because it would not help their case. Also, the scholarship on African American slavery from an African American historical perspective didn't come out until the 1960s; writers attempting to write historical novels before that period were confronted by the problem of ignorance. Many people didn't know, were not aware of, how the slave community existed; for a very long time, there was an assumption that there was not a slave community. Only through historical scholarship were writers like Morrison able to free themselves into imagining the psyches of their characters, rather than having to lay out a historical base. Finally, so many of the nineteenth-century African American writers did not write about these things because they did not want to remember them, because, if they did, they could not go on. So Morrison, upon hearing that and going back to where it is that they did not want to go, asks, "Why didn't they pass it on? What didn't they pass on?"

African Americans have sung many songs about slavery, but the one area (and Morrison looked and looked and looked) that they are virtually silent on is the "middle passage." The middle passage is the horrifying journey of the slave ships from the West Coast of Africa to the Caribbean and to the U.S.; in that passage across the Atlantic, there are different estimates about the millions and millions of Africans who died from disease or killed themselves or whatever. It was a tremendous and horrendous passage; people were packed in ships like cargo. Much of the historical data comes from slave traders, the captains of ships who repented because of how terrifying a situation it was. They wrote what we might call "exposés" of the process. So that section in the novel, where you have Beloved, Sethe, Denver, and the voices intermingling, is, among other things, about the middle passage. Beloved, when she talks about the man with the pointed teeth and his hot thing and so on, could be talking about being in the hull of the ship and coming out of the water; it's both a death and a birth and a horrendous memory.

In writing *Beloved*, Morrison was asking a simple question: "Why? Why are they silent about that?" Her sense was that the process of healing involves remembering; healing can only begin when you remember that which you don't want to remember. I was talking about this to a group in Hawaii a year or so ago; they were all Japanese Americans whose families had never told them that they had been in internment camps, and, therefore, they did not understand why, in fact, they were doing what they were doing.

For Jews, with their history of the concentration camps, the situation is just the same. In other words, the process of remembering is part of the process of healing. That's one of the reasons why I think Morrison wrote this novel, and why there are so many historical novels being written right now by African Americans.

The historical event that forms the basis for this novel is the true story of Margaret Garner, a slave woman in Ohio who attempted to escape across the Ohio River; as she was being recaptured, she killed two of her children. Morrison discovered this story, which, by the way, was a very well-known event that the abolitionists made much of. Morrison, one of the most influential black editors of the last twenty years, came upon this story in the process of researching *The Black Book*, a scrapbook of African American history.[5] What really happened to the factual Margaret Garner is that she was recaptured and tried, not for the crime of killing her children, but for stealing herself, a crime of property that resulted in her return to slavery.

Now, for many reasons, it's important to note the difference between the event, the historical, factual event, and what Morrison does with it. African American literature is often turned primarily into a history lesson and is not looked at as literature. Morrison looks at this event from a writer's point of view which is specifically her own and, as she does in all her work, she deals with the paradox of the event. What Morrison does is to try and move into the issue of how you claim your own freedom. That is, how does one claim one's own freedom? It is one thing to be legally free; it's another thing to *claim* that freedom. For Morrison, in *Beloved*, part of the process must be reconciliation and healing. That is, remembering that which you don't want to remember in order to be healed is part of the process to freedom. So the novel focuses on characters who were born slaves and who are attempting to free themselves.

The question Morrison asks is, while one can understand why Sethe kills her child, does she have a right to do it? Beloved, who actually embodies the past, gives flesh to that experience. The senses, the sounds, the words do that. By bringing Beloved into the picture, the child coming back, Morrison explores one way of reconciling oneself in a physical way with the past, so that one can move forward into the future. So Morrison actually changes the Garner story; the event signals to the writer the possibility of the story.

Teaching the differences between the story of Margaret Garner and this novel is one of the ways I often move into the teaching of the novel itself. The core of the novel is about the claiming of freedom, a central question for African Americans from the time of slavery to the present. For Morrison, a great deal of that claiming of freedom has to do with remembering, collective remembering, and the process of going through that remembering to the point of healing. In changing the Garner story, Morrison introduces important philosophical dilemmas that still remain contemporary issues for African Americans. It is not just a story of a reclaiming of history; it has very much to do with a palpitating, pulsating dilemma for African Americans. When I teach classes in which there are many African Americans, this novel is the most moving for them of any novel that I think I've ever taught, even if they cannot articulate precisely how. In writing from an African American perspective, in writing about an African American experience, Morrison writes them through the healing process.

Morrison sees this healing process as having something to do with the crux of mothering itself, so one of the ways I also approach teaching *Beloved* is to explore the fact that none of the major characters in the novel had been mothered. This novel questions the concepts of mother and motherland—Africa. But this theme is also embodied within the story of Sethe. We have the whole issue of mother love; does she have the right to kill her child for love? For Morrison, there is a learning process in becoming free to mother; one reason Sethe's response is so extreme is that she knows what it is "to be without the milk that belongs to you." She is overly possessive in relationship to her children, some people might say, because she was not mothered. This is true of all the major characters.

I heard from Morrison while she was working on this novel, and I remember one time I asked her, "What are you doing? What are you writing?" and she said, "Girl, I'm writing an opera." That is, whether you've read it or you've listened to a program about it on television, you already know what the event is: Sethe kills her child. That's not the issue. Most of the time when you go to the opera, you know the plot. Then you have monologues, duets—as in the Paul D and Sethe scene when they make love—and the three women forming a kind of tableau very often, a gesture, a chorus, the voices that come on and out and speak at the same time or sing at the same time, and, of course, in this section, we have a space in the clearing, if you can imagine it that way. I think it helps students really get into it. We are going to read the following passage because it includes so many of the voices that Morrison uses so much throughout the novel, beginning with the very first line: "It was time to lay it all down."

It was time to lay it all down. Before Paul D came and sat on her porch steps, words whispered in the keeping room had kept her going. Helped her endure the chastising ghost; refurbished the baby faces of Howard and Buglar and kept them whole in the world because in her dreams she saw only their parts in trees; and kept her husband shadowy but *there*—somewhere. Now Halle's face between the butter press and the churn swelled larger and larger, crowding her eyes and making her head hurt. She wished for Baby Suggs' fingers molding her nape, reshaping it, saying, "Lay em down, Sethe. Sword and shield. Down. Down. Both of em down. Down by the riverside. Sword and shield. Don't study war no more. Lay all that mess down. Sword and shield." And under the pressing fingers and the quiet instructive voice, she would. Her heavy knives of defense against misery, regret, gall and hurt, she placed one by one on a bank where clear water rushed on below.[6]

Now, I know where that line "It was time to lay it all down" comes from, because it's a part of my tradition. Where does it come from? From the spiritual, "Down by the Riverside." In other words, it comes right out of the African American spiritual tradition. It was time to lay it all down. Of course, within the line, even if you didn't know that, the issue of time is crucial, central to this novel. Time, in fact, is continuously disrupted or, we might say, informed by memory. The ideal time to "lay it all down," the meaning of that phrase, has something to do with precisely the work of the novel. What does she mean by "It was time to lay it all down?" Notice the way Morrison puts these next lines together: "Before Paul D came and sat on her porch steps, words whispered in the keeping room had kept her going." Of course, the alliteration moves into a kind of healing process, and then the words helped her endure the "chastising" and "refurbished the baby faces of Howard and Buglar and kept them whole in the world." We really have the novel again in those four or five lines. The verb, taking control, helped her keep going.

Now, since we don't have time to discuss the whole novel, at this point, when I use this excerpt (pages 86–89) in class, I usually ask students, "Well, who is Paul D in the novel?" The name Paul, of course, reminds us of the Biblical Paul. His name before was Saul. One of the suggestions I have for people who are really interested in Morrison and what I always tell my students is that it's absolutely necessary to have your Bible by your side. The Bible is central to African American culture since it was the only book that one was often allowed to have access to during slavery. Many people could not read; they memorized whole sections of the Bible. That is, of course, the African American tradition; the oral tradition uses the literary text. Morrison sees the Bible, a written tradition, as one that has been transformed by the oral tradition in the African American culture. In fact, one of the goals of contemporary African American writers is the negotiation between oral and literary traditions. I don't know if negotiating is the correct word, but the way in which they interrelate them.

Morrison is also very much involved in myth, from Greece, from Africa, Native American myth, and, of course, African American myth, which she views as being intersections from the world of African Americans as it evolved. Some scholars argue, in fact, that Greece got much of what it got from Africa, and that's part of the point that Morrison is making. Now in her work, there are always, in the center of the novel, three-women households. Three-women-headed households. Three. Three women representing the trinity, but also the cycle of life. The three-women households serve almost as a signature in her novels. Most of us are used to the Christian concept of the male trinity. But, of course, preceding Christianity, there was a female trinity: after all, it's women who give life, and, for Morrison, that is a much more natural situation than a male trinity. I think it's also her way of saying that African Americans have been criticized for women-centered families (what we call matrilineal and matrifocal but not matriarchal), families that take a different form from your nuclear Western family, where the father is the head. In her households, it is women-centered, and then you spiral out to the men.

For example, through the character of Denver, Morrison comments on the existence of women-centered relationships, even across lines of race, space, and personal freedom; Denver is the transitional figure from slavery to freedom. She is the one who is born on the way from slavery to freedom, and, interestingly, Morrison brings in the whole dilemma of sistering through sisterhood with Amy Denver. Morrison treats the issue of sisterhood across races because Aimée means, in French, "beloved." Denver not only represents a geographical space; she comes out of these two women who do something very good together on the Ohio, which is giving birth to her. On the other hand, even though Amy is a young girl, she sees herself as a daughter of an indentured servant, bringing up that whole history in relation to whites. She does feel superior to Sethe. Nonetheless, Sethe, in naming Denver, recognizes the role of Amy Denver in bringing Denver into the world and thereby investigates all of these issues of kinship.

Related to these concerns is Morrison's exploration of women preachers. Baby Suggs is similar to another character in African American literature, but shown from a very different perspective. Baby Suggs is a preacher, a female preacher. Those of us who have studied African American literature and history know there were many, many women preachers, black women preachers, in the nineteenth century (Sojourner Truth, for example). In fact, Margaret Garner's mother-in-law was a preacher. The fact that there were many itinerant women, black women preachers, is often repressed; in our telling of this, we usually focus on the men and think of this as a male prerogative. But, in fact, this was one of the ways in which women could free themselves from the dictates of what black women were supposed to do. Women, too, could say: "God called me. I transcend the laws of man because God called me to do this work, so I can go out traveling on the road because this is something that God has given me to do." And there is a whole tradition of these preachers within which Baby Suggs falls, and they often preached not in churches, but in the African way, in clearings. That is, they preached in the space of nature itself, which partially has to do with being able to allow the spirit to come in, to be in the context of nature, nature and the spirit being interrelated. So Morrison, then, is able to use this character, Baby Suggs, again partially because historical data has freed her to tell that such women existed and also because they were called upon to do, of course, what Baby Suggs was doing.

One could consider why it is that the female preachers have dropped out of our histories and that the male preachers are the ones which remain. And very often, it is because women preached in the clearings and the natural settings, rather than in the institutional churches, partly because they couldn't enter them. Morrison is recalling an African orientation, because in many African orientations, churches are in nature; you stand under a tree, you're in a clearing space, and so on, because you must be in touch with that natural environment in order to get into yourself. In Morrison, it is consistent in all of her novels: she uses nature as the context for healing.

Morrison is revising tradition and looking at the way in which women are central. She's also turning traditional understandings around because the character who is really raped sexually in this novel is Paul D. In most of the literature and criticism that's being written, rape has been the central symbol of African American women's condition in slavery. This is the first novel in which a writer has willingly, consciously, looked at what we've known all along from studying about slavery: the sexual violation of men. One of the questions we talk about in classes is why it is that we're so much more willing to discuss the sexual violation of women than of men. This is because men are then put in a "female position." Now it's being written about in Charles Johnson's *Oxherding Tale*. He has just won the National Book Award for *Middle Passage*. *Oxherding Tale* is one of the first novels written by a black man in which he looks at the slave man as concubine, if you can put it that way. In *Dessa Rose*, Sherley Anne Williams looks at the relationship between Nathan and Miz Rufel, who was a slave mistress in a somewhat different way. But this is the only novel I know of that looks at it from the point of homosexual violation, rather than heterosexual.

In this context, I would suggest that African American literature has tended to get a bad rap in relation to men. If you really look at the novels, if you really read them, the fact that they're female-centered seems to generate a kind of anxiety, but, in fact, the men do quite well in most of these novels. Paul D, for example, has to go through a different kind of healing process, which is what you hear about from Sethe's perspective. One of the processes of healing is to be able to tell her that he wore that bit, that he had got that neck collar around him, and that Sethe would look at him and still regard him as a man. What black men have had to go through is that their women have seen them "powerless." That is the limit, and that's what keeps Paul D on the run. He's running; he can't stay anywhere. His own fear is that he is not all that he is, so when she returns that look, that's partially what he needs.

Sethe needs something else. She needs to reenact the ritual of killing the baby, and she needs to turn the pick or the saw in the right direction. Instead of turning it in on herself and her children, she turns it out. That is healing. I taught this whole book for a long while in a hospital in San Francisco with emotionally disturbed black people, and it was wonderful because the problem these people were having was that they didn't want to remember. They remembered in fragments because they didn't want to remember the terrible things that had happened to them and the terrible things they had done to others. The novel seemed to them to be quite normal, the way it's written. It is about their pattern of remembering and what they need to do to heal, to go through, that is partially what this novel is all about.

Let me just conclude with some reflections on how gender issues are worked out in this novel. Consider this passage:

> After situating herself on a huge flat-sided rock, Baby Suggs bowed her head and prayed silently. The Company watched her from the trees. They know she was ready when she put her stick down. Then she shouted, "Let the children come!" and they ran from the trees toward her.
>
> "Let your mothers hear you laugh," she told them, and the woods rang. The adults looked on and could not help smiling.
>
> Then "Let the grown men come," she shouted. They stepped out one by one from among the ringing trees.
>
> "Let your wives and your children see you dance," she told them, and ground-life shuddered under their feet.
>
> Finally she called the women to her. "Cry," she told them. "For the living and the dead. Just cry." And without covering their eyes the women let loose.
>
> It started that way: laughing children, dancing men, crying women and then it got mixed up. Women stopped crying and danced; men sat down and cried; children danced, women laughed, children cried until, exhausted and riven, all and each lay about the Clearing damp and gasping for breath. In the silence that followed, Baby Suggs, holy, offered up to them her great big heart.[7]

Note what happens to these categories: "laughing children, dancing men, crying women." In the process of going through this ritual, they also intersect with one another and interact so that they begin to change. Everyone begins to do what everyone else is usually associated with; black women are often associated with crying, black men with dancing, and so on, and then they begin to change. The movement into this life is what African American literature is about, "She told them that the only grace they would have was the grace they could imagine. That if they could not see it, they would not have it."[8] Morrison here, herself, is working an intersection of the physical and the spiritual in the language, in the way in which it's written. And it is this that is central to the African American literary tradition: the intersection here of the erotic and sensual, of the body and the spirit. For me, it is these things that lie at the core of literature.

PART 2

Reading Black Women Writers

Introduction

M. GIULIA FABI

It is quite difficult for many of us today to remember or even really imagine a time when African American women's novels were largely out of print and hard to find, when they were simply and systematically unavailable. The national and international success of some African American women writers during the past four decades, the rediscovery and republication of many nineteenth- and twentieth-century black literary works, and the critical interest that has been both a cause and an effect of these publishing practices tend to mitigate the memory or weaken the awareness of the two centuries of editorial and critical neglect that preceded the black women's renaissance of the 1970s. Yet, such neglect is still very recent history, as Barbara Christian repeatedly reminds us in her critical readings of black women writers of the present and the past.

Profoundly convinced of the intellectual import and the political significance of the "power of memory"[1] and of the need to remember also what we may want to forget, Christian consistently emphasizes the relative novelty of the present interest in African American literature, and especially in African American women's literature. She remembers that still in 1967, as an English instructor in the SEEK program at the City College of New York, in order to use African American literature in the classroom she had to go "on regular treks to black bookstores where [she] could sometimes find out-of-print books, the category it seemed to which most African-American books then belonged."[2] She remembers and reminds us also that "to give primary significance to a brown girl as the protagonist of a novel [as Paule Marshall did] was practically unheard of in 1959";[3] that the paucity of historical information on slavery and reconstruction obliged writers like Margaret Walker in *Jubilee* (1966) "to give . . . history lessons . . . to convince her reader that a viable culture and community existed among slaves";[4] and that for Toni Morrison in the 1950s, and even a decade later in the 1960s, Faulkner was "a code . . . for those of us who wanted to study blacks in literature."[5]

In forcing us to remember what we might have "wished to forget,"[6] Christian cautions her readers against feeling complacent in the present improved situation: she warns against the possible precariousness of the current interest of critics and publishers, and urges us not to take it for granted as a phenomenon necessarily expected to last. She underlies, instead, the limits and the selectiveness even of the present interest in African American women's literary works, emphasizing the racialized cultural politics that continue to influence the publication and reception of these works, the "longevity of . . . taboo[s]"[7] and of cultural stereotypes about black women and gender roles.

Christian's deeply felt awareness of the significance of this *recent,* it deserves repeating, history lends great insight into her critical approach to the works she analyzes, and especially into her care in handling them. Her essays communicate her appreciation for the resiliency of literary works that have survived in hostile cultural soil, her sense that they are precious and that they are to be nurtured actively (i.e., read, written about, discussed, promoted) if we want them to continue to "live" (i.e., to remain in print, to be adopted for courses, to enter and remain in the canon).

Not surprisingly, for the critic who is thus invested with the scholarly, cultural, and political commitment and responsibility to preserve the memory and transmit knowledge, reading black women writers is a "visceral" as well as an intellectual pursuit. In fact, what Christian wrote about Toni Morrison's novels can be applied to her own criticism. Christian wants to involve herself and the reader in such a way as to feel the experience of a text "both viscerally and as an idea."[8] On the one hand, her pioneering work, from *Black Women Novelists* in 1980 to her last essays, has consistently expanded the boundaries of the field of African American studies through the articulation of innovative critical readings of the works of African American artists who would later become generally celebrated. On the other, Christian's criticism has always retained the quality of being for "everyday use," to quote a phrase she borrowed from Alice Walker and used in her own criticism. As her critical writings celebrate the beauty and complexity of the literary works she analyzes, Christian also insists on the relevance of that beauty for the lives of people and on its political importance for planning a different tomorrow and inspiring social change. "Fictions can be beneficial, imaginative, even transforming,"[9] writes Christian; they are empowering in that by breaking silence they become weapons against one of the means "by which the powerless are kept powerless . . . through the distortion of words, of naming, that is imposed on them."[10] They remap "the historical terrain for blacks . . . from the inside of their experiences"[11] and "remind us that if we want to be whole, we must recall the past, those parts that we want to remember, those parts that we want to forget."[12] Like the literary works she studies, Christian's criticism validates and gives scholarly visibility and voice to African American women who, as writers and characters, have long been marginalized and disregarded, who have felt "bereft" and "'needed' [themselves] in language."[13]

Insisting on the everyday use of literature does not mean providing simplified, "functional" or sociological readings of literary texts. Quite the contrary. To avoid misinterpretations, Christian warns her readers explicitly that while Marshall's *The Chosen Place, the Timeless People* (1969) does address "one of the most pervasive problems of the contemporary world, neocolonialism," her novel "is not a political tract; rather, it carefully explores the ways in which people's relationships are critical to historical process."[14] Similarly, even as she examines how Gloria Naylor explores the possibilities of social change in her fiction, Christian stresses that we are not dealing with sociology but with a creative work of literature and explains that "Naylor does not so much give us solutions as she uses her knowledge of Afro-American women's literature to show how complex the conditions of powerless groups are."[15] From this vantage point, foregrounding the everyday uses of art means showing its beauty, its complexity, emphasizing the writer's "craft" since, as Christian already argued in her groundbreaking *Black Women Novelists,* "little attention is ever paid to the creativity and artistry of the black woman writer."[16]

Christian foregrounds and explicates the reciprocal interaction of forms and themes, analyzing the "nuance, windings, shifts, the turning of the music that is this literature,"[17] exploring the writing as an "experimental act,"[18] showing how by "carefully sculpting her characters' forms within the space in which they actually moved, [the writer] illuminated the intricacy of the reality behind their apparently simple appearances,"[19] thus celebrating and making universal the significance of the specific human experiences these forms portray.

Aimed at striking this balance between scholarship and social relevance, Christian's criticism exhibits methodological continuities and scholarly rigor, even as it strives to adapt to the individual voices of the different writers "without mutilating them."[20] Consistently, in her essays Christian points out with philological accuracy the importance of the literary tradition of African American women, of inserting the individual writer within a vast community of earlier, contemporaneous, and later authors, of exploring the intergenerational dialogue with her antecedents and her impact on later artists, foregrounding how each individual author participates in the concerns of "other Afro-American women writers, even as she extends their analysis."[21]

Tradition is an empowering construct in these essays. For Christian, recovering the oft-neglected tradition to which the writer belongs makes it possible to appreciate more fully the individual voice of a specific author, while stimulating at the same time a more pronounced sense of the continuing relevance of certain themes, dilemmas, or literary "tactics to overcome racial stereotypes."[22] Inserting writers within a broader community of authors makes them come to new life, allowing the critic to notice continuities and changes in their "trajectories of self-definition," increasing her sensibility to the writer's experimentation, refining her capacity to evaluate these works on the basis of literary strategies that have developed over time and in a diasporic context where, for instance, Western and African aesthetic concepts continue to influence each other. This dialectic between uniqueness/innovation and tradition/continuity can be sustained best through close readings, one of the strengths of the essays in this section. Christian's eloquent, engaging close readings put forth the writer's own voice, the specificity and meaning of her literary choices. She guides her readers, but also lets them experience firsthand the pleasures of the text through quotations and detailed interpretations of the text's structure that lead to a new, more informed reading experience.

While stimulated to listen to the writer's own voice, to her "craft" and "complexity" (which are keywords in Christian's criticism), the reader is systematically compelled also to reflect on the broader multicultural context from which the unique voice of the individual writer emerges, to explore the "political-literary context within which these writers were constructing their novels."[23] This is an often embattled context that provides an indispensable background to reconstruct and interpret the author's artistic choices, her possible strategies of literary camouflage, her thematic concerns, her omissions, or what she took for granted. While this contextualization is more obviously necessary in the case of early writers like Amelia E. Johnson, it becomes very useful and enlightening in the case of more contemporary authors as well. Christian's firsthand knowledge of the African American cultural movements of the 1960s and 1970s and of the impact of feminism provides illuminating insights into the original context of production and reception of the early works of now-celebrated African American women writers like Alice Walker and Toni Morrison; into the constraints faced by pioneering black women writers like Paule Marshall and Margaret Walker, who addressed gender issues that would emerge as legitimate literary concerns only in the 1970s; or into the impact that the new "intense interest, among scholars, in the history of African-American women from their point of view" has had on the thematic and aesthetic choices of writers like Morrison and Sherley Anne Williams, who are now relatively more free "to remember that which could not be precisely recorded but which continues to exist in storytelling, cultural patterns, and in the imagination."[24]

The eminently readable voice that characterizes Christian's essays is forceful, compelling, strongly individualized. The critic enters into a one-to-one relationship with the texts that is informed by the scholar's analytical tools and broad knowledge of the field, while she also communicates the sense that her work, like the literature it discusses, is supposed to affect her readers "not only in intellectual terms but . . . in feeling ways."[25] This becomes particularly clear in the essay "Layered Rhythms," where her relationship with the text structures the very form of the essay, which turns into a "fiction about you [Toni Morrison] and Virginia Woolf,"[26] a dialogue where Christian expands traditional academic practices as she enters her essay and experiments with the orality and the creativity she values in the works she studies. More generally, as Christian shifts from the intellectual's more neutral stance to the use of "I" or "we" in her essays, so does the relevance of her comments reach out to the present extratextual reality of the reader, making the black diasporic woman a key figure in the critical analysis of literature, politics, culture.

Aware of the scholarly resistance and suspicion against the "personal," in "Being the Subject and the Object" Christian addresses that issue directly, cautioning against superficial readings of that particular quality of her essays as stemming simply from an autobiographical interest:

> While some may say that the reason I responded to *Brown Girl, Brownstones* as I did was due to the West Indian origin I share with Paule Marshall, I did not have that same kind of connection with the characters of *The Bluest Eye,* the first novel by

an African-American woman about which I wrote. I'd never been to Lorain, Ohio, nor had I migrated from the Southern United States to the Midwest. As with *Brown Girl, Brownstones,* however, reading Morrison's first novel was for me intense, emotional. That was due, of course, to Morrison's remarkable language, which sounded so much like black music, and to the themes she chose to craft.[27]

At the same time, however, Christian does not give in to similarly superficial indictments of the supposed theoretical inadequacy of affirming the epistemologic relevance of her being a black woman reader and scholar. She *does* claim the special and specific relevance that this literature has for her, she acknowledges that when she "saw the image of a brown girl on the cover of a cheap paperback and noticed its title, *Brown Girl, Brownstones,*" her curiosity was aroused "precisely because [she] was a brown girl."[28] In doing so, she, as an established critic and scholar, forcefully validates the subject position of black women that has historically been devalued, marginalized, and seen as irrelevant, as intellectually invalid. While celebrating it as special and specific, Christian does not present her relationship with these texts as exclusive, or as the only possible "authentic" one. Christian's literary political focus on "black women in this hemisphere" acquires universal import as it foregrounds dilemmas and dynamics that, while specific, can relate "to all women."[29]

These characterizing qualities of Christian's criticism emerge very vividly also from her book reviews, which she saw as "the testing of an initial response."[30] In 1985 she wrote in *Black Feminist Criticism:* "Book reviews are an immediate, succinct response to a writer's work, quite different, it seems to me, from essays in which one has the time and space to analyze their craft and ideas."[31] What is striking in her reviews is the critic's enormous sensitivity to the individual writer's voice and to the unique characteristics of a specific literary work, as well as her openness to literary experimentation and departures from tradition that can be best evaluated because she is so profoundly conversant with that tradition. For instance, after she contends that *"Living by the Word,* Walker's fourteenth book, cannot be appreciated, *heard,* unless it is set in the context of all of her works," Christian moves beyond the devaluation of other reviewers and brings that volume to life by foregrounding its richness and intertextual echoes, its significance as one of the few available personal journals by a black woman writer, and its variety of topics that she finds "exhilarating . . . as a vivid sign that black women's writing is as wide as the world is wide."[32] As a reader and a critic, Christian is ready to be "dazzled . . . yet profoundly disturbed" by that "extraordinary act of the imagination, of passion" that is a literary work like *Thereafter John-nie.*[33] She writes an eloquent, moving eulogy and tribute to Audre Lorde by addressing her directly and giving us a firsthand sense of the beauty and the importance of her work, making the reader feel how momentous it is that Lorde "championed the complexity of life, named it a blessing and gave that blessing to us."[34]

In her book reviews, tradition, like writing itself, emerges as a "living process."[35] The sense of its being alive, evolving, derives from its being continuously rewritten by writers and rethought by critics in light of new information that is unearthed and made known, as well as from the different everyday uses it serves. In her reviews of Lorde and Jayne Cortez, Christian foregrounds the everyday uses of art through the very structure of the essay, as the critic uses as a refrain the variety of private and public contexts she evokes to exemplify "the life-sustaining force" of literature.[36] Lorde's poetic exploration of the need to transform silence into speech "has ramifications for . . . every area of our lives, from our sexuality to education, from the meaning of our identities to po-litical coalition work,"[37] while Cortez's lines are "not only a battle cry but a powerful cry of hope."[38]

As in her longer pieces, but possibly in even more incisive and en-gaging ways because of their conciseness, Christian's book reviews communicate a strong sense of the craft, beauty, and cultural rich-ness in which the everyday uses of art are grounded. "In love with language,"[39] the critic "revels in the sound and rhythm of words" in her reviews of Cortez's and Lorde's poetry;[40] she approaches with pleasure and scholarly curiosity the experimental qualities of works by Herron and Walker that "reach for understanding and renew the word," finding meaning in "apparent contradiction[s]."[41] At the same time, in her reviews, Christian insistently reminds us of the need to nurture literary works, of the fragility of their bloom, sharing with the readers her concern about how to review a new work without "reducing it to literary formalism, shallow politics or mere entertainment."[42] She "yearn[s] to read more" about early writers like Frances E. W. Harper and is "struck by how the unavailability of a text amount[s] to its erasure,"[43] or she expresses preoccupation because "Despite the existence of many fine black women poets, the publication in America of a selected edition of their poems is still a rarity."[44]

In 1985, in *Black Feminist Criticism,* Christian wrote that book reviews "are necessary to the creating of a wider, more knowledgeable audience for the writer's work—an important responsibility of the critic."[45] What such responsibility may imply becomes particularly clear in her review of Ann Petry's *The Street* (1946). After noticing that "a reissue in a quality edition is long overdue," Christian provides an overview of Petry's "checkered career," recapitulating the critical response to this important work in order "not only to underline its significance but also to sound a cautionary note about our own biases when we read and study African American women's writing: it still seems difficult for readers in this country to comprehend and appreciate that black women can have differing visions at one and the same time."[46] Wondering "why this novel is not better known, more accepted," if only in light of its topical interest in the 1960s and 1970s, Christian shows how, despite widely differing literary-political concerns in the 1960s, 1970s, and 1980s, race and gender assumptions have systematically continued to inhibit an appreciation for Petry's work: "Ironically, while Hurston's novel had been rejected for decades because it was *not* a protest novel, now *The Street* was being criticized because a woman's novel should be affirming."[47] After commenting on the catch-22 situation that characterizes the reception of these writers, Christian, who is writing in the early 1990s, closes on a different note: "Perhaps *The Street* will receive more attention in this era, and find the place it deserves in the literary history of the U.S. For as Petry pointed out in a recent interview, the world it portrays is as real now as it was in 1946."[48]

These closing words, with the words "perhaps" standing out so clearly and "now" so disturbingly, strike a note that is at once hopeful and realistic, wishful and cautionary, in that it reiterates Christian's sense of the scholar's responsibility to be actively involved in realizing the potential of "perhaps" and changing the "now." This is a note that reverberates through Christian's entire work, foregrounding her insistence on the significance and the everyday uses of literary criticism. To borrow her description of Cortez's poetry, Christian's criticism "is a work of resistance."[49] And this, to quote her own words in *Black Women Novelists,* which would later find an echo in Morrison's *Beloved, is,* indeed, a story to "pass . . . on."[50]

6   Introduction to *The Hazeley Family* by Mrs. A. E. Johnson (1988)

Mrs. A. E. Johnson's *The Hazeley Family* (1894) is somewhat typical of the "angel of the home" romances published by American women during the latter half of the nineteenth century—except that the author is a black woman, and her portrayal of the Hazeley family is racially indeterminate, which in this country is generally translated as white. Her portrayal of the benevolent effects of Flora Hazeley's domestic and moral attributes on the well-being of her family reveals no overt signs that the novel's author is black. At first glance, it might seem that Mrs. Johnson has neutralized her tale so as to demonstrate that black women could write a sentimental romance in nonracial terms much the same way that white women did.

But Mrs. Johnson was not alone among Afro-American prose writers of the 1890s in her portrayal of solely nonracial characters. For example, three of Paul Laurence Dunbar's novels published between 1898 and 1901 are about such characters. This choice of character indicates one important aspect of the political-literary context within which these writers were constructing their novels. Afro-American writers used various tactics to overcome racial stereotypes like the smiling plantation darky that white publishers of the era demanded of "colored" writers. Charles Chesnutt, the most important Afro-American prose writer of the period, blamed his retirement from writing on such false stereotyping.

Readers should keep in mind that respectable girls and women of that period were not expected to work outside the home, for they would be subject to attacks on their chastity. Perhaps, then, in order to render her moral story about the qualities that young black respectable women—rather than stereotypical mammies or wenches—needed to keep their families intact

First published in Mrs. A. E. Johnson, *The Hazeley Family* (New York: Oxford University Press, 1988), xxvii–xxxvii.

and flourishing, Mrs. Johnson may have found it necessary to characterize her family in nonracial terms. Nonetheless, her treatment of the male characters in this story—the father who works on the railroad, the older Major Joe who has a modest vegetable trade—makes it obvious that her families are working and lower middle class instead of upper class and as such are subject to the many economic catastrophes that result when one of the breadwinners dies or goes astray. Mrs. Johnson does not portray most of her characters as comfortably well-off, a tendency among nineteenth-century women writers of sentimental romances. Rather, with the notable exception of widows who apparently inherited money from their husbands, her novel portrays families perennially subject to economic trials, a state in which black as well as white working-class families existed, although for blacks it was compounded by the effects of racism.

In her study, *Woman's Fiction: A Guide to Novels by and about Women in America, 1820–1870,* Nina Baym analyzes the fiction of American white women published during the middle of the nineteenth century. Although published in the last decade of the century, Mrs. Johnson's chronicle of the Hazeley family conforms in some ways to the formulae that Baym outlines. *The Hazeley Family* is certainly based on the belief that "a happy home is the acme of human bliss," and that woman is central to the achievement of that acme.

The sixteen-year-old daughter of a small-town railroad worker and a "careless" mother, Flora Hazeley is brought up by her mother's sister, Mrs. Bertha Graham. Mrs. Graham is a kindly well-off widow who decides to train her niece according "to her own idea of what constituted education of a girl" since without it, Flora's situation would be worse off than her brothers'. Mrs. Graham is aware that, unlike Flora's brothers who have a choice of work situations in the world, the young woman will be limited to her role within the home, and that without a proper education in that realm, she will suffer as her mother did. Clearly the concept of an extended family is at work, while at the center of the novel is the theme of education—not only the kind of education a girl should have but also the *necessity* of receiving one if she is to be functional and happy.

Readers might assume that Mrs. Johnson emphasizes a traditional feminine education, and to a certain extent she does. Under Mrs. Graham's care, Flora's time is filled by "school, caring for the flowers in the garden, and dreaming under the old peach tree," in addition to the more mundane tasks designated by Mrs. Sarah Martin, Flora's other aunt, "the details of housekeeping, cooking, sewing, washing." But Mrs. Johnson sees such duties as only half a girl's education. After the death of her Aunt Bertha, and after she is unknowingly cheated of her inheritance by Aunt Sarah, Flora is plunged back into her mother's careless house where the second and perhaps most significant half of her education is realized. It is at this point that the novel begins. Johnson then stresses not only Flora's domestic skill but, more important, the development of her moral fiber.

It is that moral fiber that enables Flora to help keep her family together, a constant concern in Afro-American literature and life. No doubt the American Baptist Publication Society, which published the novel, strongly advocated the message that young black women must develop certain moral qualities in the context of homemaking. An advertisement of this publisher cited *The Hazeley Family* as a "book that should be in every Sunday-School Library." The black church was not alone in advocating this point of view. In preceding generations, black women activists like the ex-slave, Ellen Craft, put much energy into strengthening black families by training black women in domestic skills and homemaking, since the majority of these women had been field slaves and had had no house of their own to maintain before Emancipation. In post–Civil War black society, domestic skills were not only critical to black families' well-being, but were also marketable skills for black women. In this novel, the emphasis is decidedly not on black women as wage earners (although, in a destitute period, Flora and her reconstituted mother do earn their keep by sewing) but on the other important aspect of the homemaker, the capacity to create a nurturing and beneficial space within which the family might flourish.

When Flora is sent back to her mother, she is discouraged by the "neglected and untidy" house where there is no semblance of family. Selfishly, she is not concerned with the people around her, who are *her* family, but is engrossed by the loss of the home in which she grew up. Only when she is encouraged by the example of another sixteen-year-old, Ruth Rudd, and by a minister's homily that "whatsoever thy hand findeth to do, do it with thy might" does Flora find that it is "an actual treat to be busy," her first lesson in the development of her character. Flora takes action. She makes the Hazeley home a place where her father and her younger brothers want to be and thus protects them from the waywardness of the street. Flora affects both the young and her elders. Her example encourages her mother to change her ways while the sixteen-year-old passes on her values of godliness, caring, and homemaking to young girls. By making others happy, Flora becomes happy herself. Mrs. Johnson then makes it clear that a woman's domestic skills and feminine taste are not enough—it is her moral values, her selflessness and devotion that must be at the center of her homemaking.

Mrs. Johnson underlines the theme of Flora's education by including within it the story of another young woman's growth. When her mother dies, Lottie Piper also experiences the loss of her home. She is packed off to her sick aunt, who is cruel and from whom she runs away. Young girls are expected to take care of their older relatives, regardless of how they are treated. With Flora's guidance, Lottie learns not to be a coward, not to run away from her duty. Through gentleness, the young Lottie helps her aunt to change from a miserable old lady to a more kindly one. In both Lottie's and Flora's stories, young girls are mistreated by older female relatives, an indication that family ties do not conquer all. Yet it is through this mistreatment that both girls grow into practical, unspoiled women. At one point in the novel, Flora muses that if it were not for her Aunt Sarah's greediness she would not have returned to her mother's home and been put in a situation where she would become so resourceful and independent. And Mrs. Johnson implies that it is Lottie's service to her aunt that makes her a suitable wife for Alec.

In his introduction to the reissue of Harriet Wilson's *Our Nig* (1859), Henry Louis Gates, Jr., comments that this novel differs from those of nineteenth-century white American women in that Wilson's women characters are not mother figures to Frado, the beleaguered black protagonist—in fact, they are often hostile to her. This hostility is ostensibly due to the fact that the older women in Wilson's narrative are white and see little resemblance, though they are women, between themselves and Frado. Yet in *The Hazeley Family*, which, like *Our Nig*, is set in the North, the friction between the younger and older women is not due to race. Both Flora and Lottie confront older female relatives who are not nurturing figures. However, the reasons for their hostility seem to be societally determined. In both situations the older women are frustrated and fear for their own well-being. Flora's Aunt Sarah is concerned with her own economic fate, while the misery of Lottie's aunt stems from illness and loneliness. What Mrs. Johnson implies about both these women is their lack of security and their alienation in a society that has little space for them. The author underscores this theme by having Lottie's aunt, once she learns that the young girl will be married, express her fear that she will be left alone, the fate of many elderly women. Young girls, then, are subjected to the effects of the societal restrictions imposed upon older women.

While the older women in *The Hazeley Family* are not always good guides for the younger women, they are at least substantive characters. In contrast, the fathers are shadowy figures. We know little of Flora's father except that he works for the railroad and then dies. Lottie's father goes West when her mother dies, leaving her to be taken care of by her aunt. Major Joe is an important older father figure in the novel, but even he is estranged from his daughter when she marries a man of whom he does not approve.

Family unity is not easily maintained and must be carefully nurtured. Mothers and fathers die and children are scattered about. Fathers, brothers, and sons move away to find work. Female relatives cannot always be relied on to nurture the young. Older women languish, ill and alone. The need to secure the family is presented as an urgent one in this novel. Society does not provide any institutions to aid in the solution of some of these problems; hence the importance of the individual's role, that is, of Flora's role in reuniting Major Joe with his granddaughter Ruth Rudd, as well as Joel Piper with his sister Lottie. By becoming a selfless and resourceful woman, Flora effects not only the unity of her own family, but also that of other families. Thus she is not merely a homemaker but a social housekeeper, a role of increasing importance in black Northern communities that was often neglected by society in general, and one that women activists, black and white, undertook in their respective club movements of the 1890s.

But Flora is not the only one in the novel whose moral development is traced. In a subplot, Mrs. Johnson demonstrated how young men are threatened, when they leave home to work in other towns, by social vices—drinking, gambling, petty crimes. It is significant that just as the author focuses on younger women who lack older female guides because their mothers die or their female relatives are not nurturing, she also pays attention to young men who lack father figures. The story of Flora's brother Harry outlines his departure from home to work in another town after the death of his father and traces his fall into the sins of the street and his return like a prodigal son to the bosom of his family. His story parallels that of Joel, Lottie's brother, who also has left home, fallen, and repented. It is Joel, rather than an older man or a young woman, who helps Harry return to the path of virtue, just as it was Ruth Rudd who inspired Flora to become a dutiful daughter. Peers, rather than parental figures or romantic relations, help each other achieve adult development.

Johnson's exploration of the dangers of alcohol was not unusual among women activists of the late nineteenth century. Many of the temperance movement's constituents were women, black and white, who saw drinking and other aspects of city life as corrupting young men and threatening family life. Religious teaching as well as a rendition of the unhappiness caused by such a life are arguments that Johnson uses against these evils, and she emphasizes how family feeling is a bulwark against irresponsibility and waste.

In telling the respective stories of Flora's brothers, it is noteworthy that Mrs. Johnson contrasts the city-dweller Harry with Alec, the brother who becomes a farmer. He does have a father figure, Major Joe, from whom he learns farming. As a result, he remains throughout a sturdy figure who does not submit to the debauchery of city life. His portrayal points to the major positive imagery throughout the novel—that of nature. Clearly Mrs. Johnson is imbued with the sense that being in touch with nature is essential to social well-being.

At every turn, the author weaves flowers, fruit, and vegetables into her narrative. The novel begins with such an image: the sweet potato that Lottie gives to Flora and the growth of which becomes for her a talisman. That potato vine is replaced by more luxurious growth—the geraniums in Ruth Rudd's yard, Major Joe's vegetable trade, Alec's farm—as the author indicates how Flora is flourishing. Flora's name, of course, also participates in this schema. A beautiful and strong flower, she inspires others to grow. In contrast, when Mrs. Johnson wants to emphasize that something is awry, nature is bereft or neglected. Thus the yard of Lottie's aunt is brown and ugly; when the young girl runs away, she weeps under the long bare arms of an old poplar tree. In the writings of women in the nineteenth and twentieth centuries, especially Afro-American women, nature cannot be separated from human society. These two constructs, though apparently different, are interrelated. One has only to think of the titles of major Afro-American women's novels, from Jessie Fauset's *The Chinaberry Tree* to Alice Walker's *The Color Purple,* to realize how pervasive this tendency is in the literature of black women.

Of course, nature imagery is used in various ways by different writers. In many women's novels, nature is related, among other things, to sexuality and is sometimes even a code through which writers, hampered by social constraints, might indicate the sensuality of their characters. But Mrs. Johnson's chronicle of the Hazeleys does not dwell on any aspect of sexuality either in a natural or distorted state. There are no scenes of attempted or covert seduction, as might be implied in scenes in *Our Nig.* Even the men do not have sweethearts, angelic or otherwise. Only at the end of the novel is sexuality hinted at, but only in the context of marriage, and even then, both Alec and Lottie characterize their marriage in practical terms. Nor is bountiful nature in this novel associated with children. None of Mrs. Johnson's young people become mothers or fathers during the course of the novel. Perhaps Mrs. Johnson felt the constraints of stereotypes associated with black women—that they were wanton and constantly bore children—even as she wrote a novel using racially indeterminate characters. Also, Victorian concepts about fecundity, as well as the fact that her novel was published by the American Baptist Publication Society, might consciously or unconsciously have restrained her from dealing with these two significant aspects of woman's development.

Instead, Mrs. Johnson emphasizes through her imagery the natural-ness of family and home and woman's place in it—that God and nature intended this to be the seed from which society proceeds. Without the careful nurturing of the family, human beings lead unhappy, fruitless lives. Perhaps the most succinct declaration of this point of view is found in Flora's thoughts when she must leave her Sunday school class: "Surely, the seed she had sown in their hearts would spring up, blossom, and bear fruit for the Master's kingdom."

In a more or less secular vein, Alec's closeness to the earth, his choice of farming as his profession, results in the financial stability that enables him to buy a house and begin a family. From that seed will sprout the continua-tion of both the Hazeley and Piper families. In the final scene of the novel, which takes place on Christ's birthday, the families have a reunion and Alec and Lottie are married. The various themes of the novel converge in this scene. Harry, the prodigal son, has become a minister; Flora and her mother prosper by helping him save souls; Ruth Rudd raises eggs, a symbol of birth, and gives joy to her half-sister Jem (whose name provides the only hint of blackness in the novel) and to her grandparents whose farm is prospering; Alec buys a house and not only marries the practical Lottie but is able to take care of her aunt. Over this joyous union and rebirth, Flora, who has helped to bring all these people together, presides in happiness and peace.

In calling this chapter "A Homely Wedding," Mrs. Johnson eschews the conspicuously sentimental, romantic imagery of orange blossoms and satin that are desired by the comic Jem and that many young girls might associate with marriage. Instead the author highlights the solidity, godli-ness, and love at the Hazeley family core. She leaves us with the message that such a family can transcend misfortune and guarantee the happiness of its members. Mrs. Johnson, a Northern black woman living during the hard times of Reconstruction when hope might have been in short sup-ply, might have chosen to make her message as palatable and available as possible to both black and white readers by relating it in an apparently race-free novel.

7 "Somebody Forgot to Tell Somebody Something": African-American Women's Historical Novels (1990)

The title of my essay is taken from a radio interview Ntozake Shange did with Toni Morrison in 1978, just after she had published *Song of Solomon*.[1] Morrison's comment referred to a generation of Afro-Americans of the post–World War II era who had seen the new possibilities that period seemed to promise for their children and who thought that knowledge of their history—one of enslavement, disenfranchisement, and racism— might deter the younger generations' hopes for the future. As Morrison put it, the older generation of that era sometimes X'd out the Southern grandfather who had been a sharecropper and tried to forget the brutality of the African-American past. In *How I Wrote* Jubilee (1972) Margaret Walker tells a similar story of how her mother resented the stories about slavery her grandmother told the young Margaret, and how she admonished the older woman not to tell the child those "horrifying lies."[2] Alice Walker tells us in a 1986 BBC documentary on *The Color Purple* that her family spoke "in whispers" about certain parts of their history, whispers which she said fascinated her.[3] These African-American writers, as well as many others, comment on the ambivalence their families felt toward the African-American past.

In the eighties, Morrison, Alice Walker, as well as Sherley Anne Williams, previously a poet and playwright, have written African-American historical novels, a sign of these writers' desire to re-vision African-American history from their imaginative and informed point of view. This trend, I think, indicates the fascination not only of novelists and scholars but also of many other women who share the experiences of African-American women in

First published in Joanne M. Braxton and Andrée Nicola McLaughlin, eds., *Wild Women in the Whirlwind: Afra-American Culture and the Contemporary Literary Renaissance* (New Brunswick, N.J.: Rutgers University Press, 1990), 326–41.

the nineteenth and early twentieth century, the very periods that Morrison characterized as being X'd out by upwardly mobile African-Americans of the forties and fifties.

This is not to say that, as a group, contemporary African-American women writers had not previously recalled the past. However, generally speaking, they had reached back to the period of their mothers' lives, from the 1920s to the 1960s, to a past that often involved shifts of values in African-American communities, sometimes migration from the rural South or West Indies to the small-town or urban North. So, for example, Morrison's first three novels, *The Bluest Eye* (1970), *Sula* (1973), *Song of Solomon* (1977); much of Walker's short fiction as well as her novels; Paule Marshall's *Brown Girl, Brownstones* (1959); and Gloria Naylor's "Mattie Michaels" section of *The Women of Brewster Place* (1982) explore the twenties, thirties, and forties from the African-American women's perspective. As Marshall, Morrison, and Walker have told us, in the process of consciously imagining their novels, they were propelled by the stories their mothers told them about their lives.

During the last decade, these writers have also probed their own contemporary context. Toni Cade Bambara's *Gorilla, My Love* (1972) and Alice Walker's *Meridian* (1976) ask pivotal questions about girls and women who were living in the decade of the intense "black consciousness," the 1960s. Morrison, in *Tar Baby* (1981), Bambara in *The Sea Birds Are Still Alive* (1977), and Shange in *Sassafrass, Cypress, and Indigo* (1982) explore the relationships of women and men as affected by the second wave of feminism, although from very different points of view. Marshall in *Praisesong for the Widow* (1983), Morrison in *Tar Baby*, and Naylor in *Linden Hills* (1985) examine the effects of middle-class mobility among some blacks during the 1960s and 1970s, while in *The Women of Brewster Place* (1982), Naylor tells the story of underclass contemporary African-American women. African-American women have even extended the present into the future, as Susan Willis pointed out in her study, *Specifying* (1982), the most overt being Bambara's *The Salt Eaters* (1980). As a group then, contemporary African-American women have written about every decade of the twentieth century, and about every region of this country — the North, the Midwest, the South, and the West, the country, small town and inner city — as well as the underclass and the middle class. And they have even traveled in their fiction beyond the geographical borders of this country to the Caribbean, to Europe, and to Africa.

Yet, even as many of these writers have, in their earlier novels, focused on the twentieth century, they have, in these same novels, taken us back in time — perhaps because, as Alice Walker has pointed out, "anything of the immediate present is too artificial, one needs historical perspectives to give resonance and depth to a work of art."[4] So Morrison's Pilate tells us the story of her father, an ex-slave—a story which his grandson Milk-man must discover through his travels in time and space to be a part of his own being. The Bottom, the land in which *Sula* is situated, is payment to a slave from his master, while Linden Hills in Naylor's novel of that name is Luther Nedeed's legacy from his ex-slave ancestor. Meridian, in Walker's second novel (1976), must look back to her ancestors of the nineteenth century to understand the meaning of black motherhood, while the mud mothers of Bambara's *The Salt Eaters* continually remind us of the mythic past. Even when major characters resist the past, as Macon and Milkman Dead do in *Song of Solomon,* or Avey Johnson does in *Praisesong for the Widow,* it intrudes itself upon their consciousness through dream and/or song and especially the sense of dis-ease they feel in the present. The use of history in the novels of contemporary African-American women writers, then, is constant and consistent.

Although previous novels have used history within the context of the present and the future, however, most of them would not have been prop-erly called historical novels. In the last few years, novels by African-Ameri-can women have explored those very periods that some post–World War II African-Americans had attempted to erase. So, *The Color Purple* (1982) is set in Reconstruction Georgia, *Beloved* (1987) in the post-slavery years, and *Dessa Rose* (1986) in the 1840s at the height of American slavery. These three novels are historical in that they recall a life which no longer exists and re-create societies that are apparently past. In examining this trend in African-American women's writing, I am not only interested in the novels themselves but also in why they are appearing at this particular time.

In order to understand the ways these contemporary novels revision history, first it is necessary, I think, to emphasize that historical novels by African-American women have appeared before and that there are pieces written by African-American women during the periods about which these three contemporary novels are written.

There is a small but important body of female slave narratives in which successful runaway slaves record aspects of their experience. Perhaps the most notable of these is *Incidents in the Life of a Slave Girl* (1861) written by Harriet Jacobs under the pseudonym Linda Brent. For much of this century, questions of authorship camouflaged the significance of this narrative. It is only recently that Jean Yellin has proven beyond a shadow of doubt that Harriet Jacobs did exist, that she was a slave, that she did escape slavery only by hiding out in an attic for seven years, and that she did write her own story. Yet, despite the fantastic incidents she tells us about her experi-ences in slavery, Jacobs codes her narrative and often tells the reader that because of modesty, a specifically female term, and her desire not to offend her audience, a specifically African-American consideration, she had to omit certain details of her life story.

In the introductory remarks to her reading of *Beloved* at the University of California at Berkeley in October 1987, Toni Morrison emphasized the consistency with which the slave narrators made such statements.[5] Morrison pointed out that their omissions were partly due to the fact that these ex-slaves addressed a white audience. Even more important, she suggested, they omitted events too horrible and too dangerous for them to recall. Morrison went on to state that these consistent comments made by nineteenth-century ex-slaves about the deliberate omissions in their narratives intrigued her and that this was the initial impulse for her writing the novel that would become *Beloved*. Clearly one of the major themes of this masterpiece is the paradox of "re-memory." Morrison emphasizes this theme throughout the novel and reiterates it in the last words of *Beloved*: "This was not a story to pass on."[6] In a different way Sherley Anne Williams, in her preface to *Dessa Rose,* echoes Morrison's idea about her impulse to write *Beloved.* Williams tells us: "I loved history as a child, until some clear-eyed young Negro pointed out, quite rightly, that there was no place in the American past I could go and be free. I now know that slavery eliminated neither heroism nor love; it provided occasions for their expressions."[7]

Not only were the slave narrators restrained by "modesty" and by "audience" from not passing on some stories, so were African-American nineteenth-century novelists. In *Clotel* (1853), the first novel published by an African-American writer in this country, William Wells Brown made palatable the experience of his quadroon slave heroine by fashioning her character according to the acceptable ideal image of woman at that time. Thus, Clotel is beautiful/fair, thoroughly Christian and European upper class in her demeanor and language. African-American women writers also used this construct, most notably Frances Harper in *Iola Leroy* (1892), which was thought, until the rediscovery of *Our Nig* (1859), to be the first novel to be published by an African-American woman.

What is *not* focused on in these novels is as important as the images these writers emphasized. For in these novels, little light is shed on the experiences and cultures of "ordinary" slaves like Sethe or Paul D, Dessa Rose or Kaine, or on their relationships or communities. Clotel grows up with her mother who, because she is the "natural wife" of her master, lives in a fairy-tale-like cottage completely apart from other slaves. Nor is she subjected to the hard labor usually exacted from slaves. Iola Leroy is a slave, but only for a short time and had, as a "white" woman, been educated in fine schools. While Brown and Harper give us hints through some minor characters of the physically and psychologically harsh conditions under which most slaves lived, they reserved privileged positions for their heroines, thus exhibiting even more modesty than the slave narrators. For the sentimental romance form demanded not only a beautiful refined heroine but also that the story be entertaining and edifying.

An idea such as the one which generates *Beloved*, the existence of a "haint," a visitor from the past in which the major characters naturally believe, though an important belief in African-American culture, could not possibly have been seriously considered by these nineteenth-century novelists. They would have been fully cognizant of the detrimental effects that such a "superstitious" or non-Christian concept would have had on their own people. Nor could nineteenth-century audiences react favorably to a contrary slave like Dessa Rose who attacks her master and leads a slave rebellion which results in the death of many whites. Such audiences would have been even more alarmed by the presentation of a "crazy" slave like Sethe who would kill her own child rather than have her returned to slavery. Clearly Brown and Harper, leading activists of their day, would have heard about such events — certainly, the story of Margaret Garner, on which *Beloved* is based, was sensational enough to be known by Harper.[8] But she, as well as other African-American writers, could not muddy the already murky waters of sentiment toward the Negro by presenting characters who might terrify their readers.

That these nineteenth-century writers were constrained by the socio-political biases of their time is graphically demonstrated by the disappearance of Harriet Wilson's *Our Nig* (1859). Although Mrs. Wilson wrote a fluent, strong-voiced novel which is obviously autobiographical, although she employed a form which fused elements of the slave narrative and sentimental romance that readers expected in works written by Blacks and by women, *Our Nig* did not cater to the accepted mores of the time. By emphasizing the racism of Mrs. Bellmont, her Northern white mistress, by exposing racism in the North, as well as by ending her story with her desertion by her fugitive-slave husband, Frado, the protagonist of *Our Nig,* questioned the progressive platform of her time — that white Northern women were the natural allies of blacks, that the North was not racist, that all Black men were devoted to the women of their race.

Equally important, Frado herself is the result of an interracial marriage between a white woman and a Black man, a type of union that was simply not supposed to have existed. Readers could cope with Clotel and Iola's ancestry — that their father was white, their mother Black. But acknowledging that white women would willingly be sexually involved with Black men was opposed to white women's sacred position — that they were a treasure to be possessed only by white men. The reception of *Dessa Rose* in this decade illustrates the longevity of this taboo. For many readers, Black and white, are stunned, sometimes offended by the sexual relationship between Miz Rufel, a white mistress, and Nathan, a runaway slave, despite the historical evidence that such relationships existed.

The disappearance of *Our Nig* for some one hundred years was also due to doubts raised about its authorship. Like *Incidents in the Life of a Slave Girl, Our Nig* was thought to have been written by a white woman because of its point of view and its excellent style. So, in his 1983 introduction to this newly discovered classic, Henry Louis Gates had to spend many pages establishing Mrs. Wilson's existence, that she was a free Black woman, and that the incidents in *Our Nig* are based on her life. When nineteenth-century African-Americans wrote in a manner that did not correspond to deeply held opinions of their time, their very authorship was put in question. Such a restriction, the ultimate one for writers in that it obliterates their very existence, would certainly have affected the way they wrote about African-Americans.

One critical area in which these writers were restricted is their very medium, that of language. Since slaves were hardly conceived of as human beings who had a culture, their language was emphatically discredited. Such a devaluation is central to what experiences could be passed on, for language is the repository of anyone's point of view on experience, whether it is that of oppression, resistance to it, or a value system. Yet African-American language could not be seriously fashioned by nineteenth-century writers to dramatize their characters' essence; for that language was considered at best to be comic, at worst, a symbol of ignorance. Nineteenth-century writers like Brown and Harper imbued their heroines and heroes with a language that indicated their superiority, a language that in no way was distinguished from the language of well-bred white Americans. When these writers do use "dialect," minor characters employ it for comic effect. If one compares Celie, Dessa Rose, or Sethe's language to the language of Clotel or Iola, one immediately feels what is missing. For it is difficult to communicate the authenticity of a character without investing her language with value. If there is any one false-sounding note in nineteenth-century novels about slavery and reconstruction it is the language of the characters, the way the imagination of the authors is constrained by the language their characters use.

Language is not only an expression of one's everyday experience but also of those deeper labyrinths of dream and memory, dimensions to which nineteenth-century slave characters had little access. If memory were central to Clotel or Iola, it would take them back to the past, beyond their personal history to stories their mothers told them, possibly back to the Middle Passage, so horrendous a memory that Morrison dedicated *Beloved* to those anonymous "60 million or more." Memory might take them even further back to an African man, like the one who taught Kaine, in *Dessa Rose,* to play the banjo. To acknowledge that slaves had memory would threaten the very ground of slavery, for such memory would take them back to a culture in Africa where they existed, as June Jordan invoked in her essay on Phillis Wheatley, "in terms other than the ones" imposed upon them in America.[9] Specifically, for Black abolitionists like William Wells Brown, allusions to Africa were politically diverting and provided support for the Resettlement Movement which sought to correct the moral problem of American slavery by sending the enslaved and displaced Blacks back to Africa.[10]

So, memory when it does exist in nineteenth-century African-American novels about slavery goes back but one generation, to one's mother, but certainly not much further back than that. Slaveowners were aware of the power of memory, for they disrupted generational lines of slaves in such a way that many slaves did not *know* even their own parents or children. Nineteenth-century writers like Brown and Harper, too, were certainly aware of the power of memory, for their protagonists, above all else, cling to the memory of parent, child, loved one. In Brown's first version of *Clotel,* he has his heroine give up her freedom to search for her child, only to have her drown herself rather than be re-enslaved. Her story is the other side of Sethe's action in the shed, in that one mother kills herself for her child, while the other mother "saves the best part of herself" by freeing her child through death. Brown does not linger long on the personal and emotional aspects of Clotel's suicide for his purpose is to illustrate the evils of the *institution* of slavery. Morrison, on the other hand, is riveted on the use of memory in all her characters' search for self-understanding. Nineteenth-century novelists could not be as much concerned with the individual slave as a subject as they were with the institution itself. They therefore had to sacrifice the subjectivity and, therefore, the memory of their characters to an emphasis on the slaveholders and their system.

Re-memory is a critical determinant in how we value the past, what we remember, what we select to emphasize, what we forget, as Morrison has so beautifully demonstrated in *Beloved.* But that concept could not be at the center of a narrative's revisioning of history until the obvious fact that African-Americans did have a history and culture was firmly established in American society, for writers would be constrained not only by their readers' points of view but also by the dearth of available information about the past that might give their work authenticity.

In her essay on how she wrote her historical novel, *Jubilee* (1966), Margaret Walker pointed to these difficulties. On the one hand, she made it clear that memory was the impetus for her novel, since it grew out of her promise to her grandmother to write *her* mother's story. On the other hand, as an African-American in the 1940s who wanted to write a historical novel about her past, she knew that few people, black or white, were informed about slavery and early Reconstruction, the contexts in which Vyry, her great-grandmother, lived. She tells us that she found in her research at least three historical versions of slavery: the Southern white version in which the institution was benevolent, necessary, and paternalistic; the Northern white version, which often emphasized the horrors of slavery but was not particularly interested in the lives of the slaves; and the African-American version, of which there were few accounts, and which tended to focus on the lives of extraordinary slaves, almost always men.[11] In each version, the institution of slavery, meaning the slaveholders themselves, was pivotal, while the slaves were reduced to a voiceless mass. How, then, was Walker to write a novel which gave sufficient information about slaves to the reader who was either ignorant about the period or believed in false myths such as the ones featured in *Gone With the Wind?* How was she to do that *and* focus on Vyry, an ordinary slave woman who knew little about the larger political struggles that determined her life—a woman who could not read or write, and who had not been more than twenty miles from the place where she was born?

Margaret Walker decided that her historical novel would take the form of a folk novel. It would emphasize the fact that African-American slaves had a culture and a community, even as it sketched the outline of more specifically historical data, like the Fugitive Slave Law, or the legal conditions that determined a free Black's status in early-nineteenth-century Georgia. She would have to give readers history lessons; she would have to invest with meaning the apparently mundane everyday experiences of her protagonist; and she would have to convince her reader that a viable culture and community existed among slaves.

Confronted with needing to cover so much territory to render Vyry's story, Walker, not surprisingly, created characters, Black and white, who are not subjects so much as they are the means by which we learn about the culture of slaves and slaveholders and the historical period. Vyry, for example, hardly speaks in the first half of the novel, although she becomes more vocal in the Reconstruction section. Despite the many historical details about which she informs her readers, her characters have little internal life, perhaps because Walker, who is writing her historical novel in the forties and fifties before the rise of the black culture movements of the sixties, could not give slaves the right to claim those events they do not want to remember—not only what was done to them but what they might have had to do, given their precarious context. So Vyry is not complex in the way that Sethe and Dessa Rose are, for we are seldom privy to her internal conflicts and to the doubts she might have about her relations to others. Interestingly, one of the few times when we do feel her ambivalence about what she should do is when she must choose between escape for herself and leaving her children behind in slavery. As in *Beloved* and *Dessa Rose,* motherhood is the context for the slave woman's most deeply felt conflicts.

What Walker accomplished so effectively in *Jubilee* is the establishment of an African-American culture which enabled the ordinary slave to survive. In building her novel around Vyry, a hard-working mulatto slave, she revised the image of the beautiful, refined mulatto heroine of the nineteenth century, an image that her grandmother's stories refuted.

That image is further revised in Barbara Chase-Riboud's *Sally Hemings* (1979), a fictional biography of the African-American woman reputed to be Jefferson's mistress for some forty years.[12] Brown's first version of *Clotel,* which was sensationally subtitled "The President's Daughter," was based in part on the fact that Hemings was Jefferson's mistress. But Brown used this slave mulatta's existence to cast shadows on the great Jefferson who, at once, had a black mistress and children he would not free and who nonetheless championed freedom and democracy. In contrast to Brown, Chase-Riboud uses a romantic frame to dig into the myth of Sally Hemings and to reveal this complex woman's bond to her master both as a slave and as a lover. Because Chase-Riboud is interested not only in the contradiction between Jefferson's personal and political life, and in the institution of slavery, but also in the way the nineteenth-century definition of love is related to the definition of enslavement—she revisions Brown's sentimental romance. Still, Chase-Riboud has her protagonist tell her story to a white man who is trying to rationalize slavery so that at times Sally's narrative seems as censored as the slave narratives of the nineteenth century.

Because of the historical information available to her, not only about Jefferson himself but also because of the work done in the sixties about African-American slave communities, Chase-Riboud could free her narrative from some of the history lessons that Walker was obliged to give her reader. However, in a telling moment in the novel, Chase-Riboud has Sally Hemings burn all her records—her diaries that proclaim her existence and her life with Jefferson which she no longer wants to remember. Chase-Riboud is faced with a dilemma: Hemings, the main character, is encased in myth; yet she lingers in the margins of historical records. Because Chase-Riboud must rescue her heroine from myth, she cannot completely free herself from the conventional trappings of the historical novel, trappings which constrain her imaginative use of historical data.

Not so with Morrison's *Beloved* and Williams's *Dessa Rose,* both of which are based on historical notes yet are not controlled by them. Although *Beloved* is based on the sensational story of Margaret Garner, a runaway slave woman who attempted to kill herself and her children rather than be returned to slavery, Morrison leaves the historical facts behind to probe a not easily resolvable paradox—how the natural and personal emotion, mother love, is traumatically affected by the political institution of slavery. Morrison has said that she did not inquire further into Garner's life other than to note the event for which this slave woman became famous.[13] And indeed Margaret Garner did not achieve freedom as Morrison's Sethe does. Instead she was tried, not for attempting to kill her child, but for the "real crime" of attempting to escape, of stealing property, herself, from her master. For that crime, she was tried, convicted, and sent back to slavery, thus restoring his property. But Morrison takes us beyond the world of the slaveholders into the world of slaves as complex human beings. In creating Sethe, who must remember her killing of her own child and must reflect upon whether she had a right to commit so destructive an act against her child which also, paradoxically, is for her an expression of her love for her child, Morrison raises disturbing questions about mother love. And in giving Sethe her legal freedom, Morrison is able to explore the nature of freedom—for "freeing yourself was one thing; claiming ownership of that freed self was another."[14]

Sherley Anne Williams also based her novel on historical notes. As often happens in historical research, the discovery of one source leads us to another. *Dessa Rose* originates with two brief notes about a Southern woman, one a Black slave, the other a free white woman who lived in the first half of the nineteenth century. Williams discovered in Angela Davis's "Reflections on a Black Woman's Role in the Community of Slaves" a pregnant slave woman who helped to lead an uprising and whose death sentence was delayed until after the birth of her child. That note led Williams to another source, Herbert Aptheker's *American Slave Revolts,* in which Williams learned about a white woman living on an isolated farm who was reported to have given sanctuary to runaway slaves. In response to these two women, whose actions appeared to refute what we have been told about both African-American and white Southern women of the nineteenth century, Williams refined her point of view. Like *Beloved, Dessa Rose* is based on recorded historical facts but is not determined by them. "How sad," Williams comments in her introduction to the novel, "that these two women never met."[15]

As important to the structure of the novel as the discovery of these two historical sources is Williams's rage at the credibility given to William Styron's *The Confessions of Nat Turner*, which she points out is an indication of how "African-Americans remain at the mercy of literature and writing."[16] In emphasizing her rage, she highlights another aspect of the slave narrative tradition—one on which Morrison also commented—a tradition which continues unto this day in the form of novels like Styron's. For these narratives were often told to whites, who did not necessarily understand or sympathize with the slave's experience but who, because they were the writers of the narrative, passed on in history the slave experience. To use a title from Valerie Babb's essay on *The Color Purple, Dessa Rose* is a novel which attempts "to undo what writing has done."[17] For in her novel, Williams demonstrates the substantive difference between Dessa Rose's memory of her experience, her telling of it to a white man, and Nehemiah's interpretation of her story, which is of course affected by his desire to write a sensational bestseller.

In *Beloved*, Morrison underlines the way that literary tradition is buttressed by an intellectual one. Schoolteacher not only exploits slaves, he is fascinated by the intellectual arguments he constructs to rationalize that exploitation. Throughout the nineteenth century, American intellectuals performed this function—that of providing intellectual arguments for a profitable legal *and* dehumanizing institution. Nehemiah and Schoolteacher's curiosity about the slave was indeed "scientific"; their historical counterparts did measure the various parts of the slaves' bodies, did observe their "characteristics," did interpret their behavior, and did write serious treatises on them. Morrison stresses these activities—the apparently neutral ways in which intellectuals and "scientists" were fascinated with slaves—by having the most terrible act done to Sethe, the milking of her body for Schoolteacher's scientific observation, be a bleeding wound in her memory.

Williams and Morrison then indict the American literary and intellectual tradition. And clearly, neither of their novels would be what they are if it were not for previous historical fiction by African-American women. Nor, paradoxically, would their novels be as vivid as they are if during the last decade there had not been an intense interest, among scholars, in the history of African-American women from their point of view. In recent years we have seen the publication of works—from the heretofore forgotten female slave narratives to analyses by women historians with different perspectives, such as Gerda Lerner, Paula Giddings, Angela Davis, Deborah White, Rosalyn Terborg-Penn, Jacqueline Jones, and Dorothy Sterling—reclaiming that neglected past. Such publications have grown out of our increased awareness that women's experiences are integral to

African-American history. Paradoxically, such an awareness not only restores historical data, it frees the novelist from that data, to remember that which could not be precisely recorded but which continues to exist in storytelling, in cultural patterns, and in the imagination.

In both these novels, such remembering, such re-imagining centers on motherhood, on mothering and being mothered. On the one hand for slave women, motherhood was denied, devalued, obliterated by slavery since it was considered to be breeding, while on the other hand, it was critical to the concept of self and to the very survival of one's self. It is through the memory of *their* mothers, their reflections on that precarious role, and whether they themselves were able to be mothered, that Sethe and Dessa Rose delve into themselves as subjects. In *Beloved,* this is true of all the major women characters: Baby Suggs, Sethe, Denver, Beloved, even Amy Denver the white girl, who helps Sethe give birth to Denver. Sethe knows "what it is to be without the milk that belongs to you; to have to holler and fight for it."[18] Denver knows what it is to see her mother in a terrible place, for she drinks her mother's milk with her sister's blood. Beloved yearns for complete union with her mother, the mother who kills her and saves her in one stroke. For her, her mother's face is her face and without her mother's face "she has no face."[19]

While Morrison moves us into the chaotic space of mother-love/mother-pain, daughter-love/daughter-pain, a space that can barely be sketched in terms of historical data, Williams takes us in another direction: she explores the concept of that double-edged term "mammy," which slave-owners used for African-American mothering. By reversing the usual image, that of the black mammy nursing the white baby, Williams creates a different context for that term. Rufel, the white mistress and the only nursing woman on her neglected farm, feels obliged, because of her own womanhood, to nurse the baby of the ailing darky, Dessa Rose. But the white woman would not have felt she had permission to do such a thing if she were under her husband's control and not isolated from other whites. As she nurses that Black baby, she dreams aloud about what she considers to be the source of her own mother-love, her mammy, who is not her mother but her darky slave. In an exchange that emphasizes the way these two women interpret that love, Williams shows us how power relations affect mothering. When Rufel claims that *her* mammy loved her, Dessa Rose retorts, "You ain't got no mammy . . . What her name then? . . . Child don't know its own mammy's name?"[20]

In listing the names of *her* mammy's children, names she can remember, Dessa Rose also establishes the existence of a slave community with relationships that provided occasions for the heroism and love that Williams reminds us about in her preface. Her novel opens up the spaces in which that heroism and love can be explored. So Dessa Rose attacks her master because he has killed her lover Kaine. She and the men on the coffle are able to plan an uprising together and that action binds them forever in friendship. Later they are able, in an adventure as exciting as any in American lore, to free themselves and go West. Nevertheless, when she tells her story, many years later to one of her grandchildren, the freed Dessa Rose recalls her mother braiding her hair and her love for Kaine, events that precede the escape adventure. Williams ends the novel with this focus on re-memory, for Dessa Rose insists on having her story written down: "'Oh,' she says, 'we have paid for our children's place in the world again, and again. . . .'"[21]

But while Dessa Rose may remember her mother's name, Sethe, Paul D, and Baby Suggs cannot. For Sethe, her mother is a mark, since she knows her only by the circle with a cross branded into her skin, a sign Sethe cannot even find when her mother's rotting body is cut down from the hanging rope. Morrison's novel, then, moves us into those spaces that we do not want to remember, into the spaces where there are no names *but* Beloved—those forgotten ones of the past even to the sixty million anonymous ones of the Middle Passage, those terrible spaces, those existing spaces which for slave women, men, and children can divide them as much as they can bring them together. So in her novel, the adventure is not an exterior one, but the more dangerous internal one of the self remembering and even understanding its past—of Paul D who lives through the terror of a chain gang which almost distorts his manhood, of Sethe who kills her own child which almost distorts her womanhood. Of Baby Suggs who cannot remember her own children, of Denver who does not want to remember her mother's act, of Beloved who *is* that part of their past that they all attempt to forget.

In the last pages of the novel, Morrison leaves us with that Beloved, "a loneliness that roams" . . . "that is alive on its own," but "by and by is gone," for "remembering seems unwise." "The story of Beloved, of all the beloveds, was not a story to pass on," or one that could be passed on in the records of historians or the slave narrators. And yet it remains in dream, in the "folk tale," "in the wind," in the imagination, in fiction. Paradoxically, only when history is explored and evaluated is memory free to flow. Then, although "somebody forgot to tell somebody something," the past finds its way back into our memory lest, like Beloved, we risk erupting into separate parts. Perhaps that is one reason why African-American women writers are now writing African-American historical novels. As we move into another century when Memory threatens to become abstract history, they remind us that if we want to be whole, we must recall the past, those parts that we want to remember, those parts that we want to forget.

8   Gloria Naylor's Geography: Community, Class, and Patriarchy in *The Women of Brewster Place* and *Linden Hills* (1990)

1

Like Toni Morrison, Gloria Naylor is intrigued by the effect of place on character. Perhaps Afro-American writers have been particularly interested in setting, because displacement, first from Africa and then through migrations from South to North, has been so much a part of our history. Because of the consistency of forced displacement in our collective experience, we know how critical where we are is to the character of our social creations, of how place helps to tell us a great deal about who we are and who we can become. Perhaps place is even more critical to Afro-American women writers. For women within the Afro-American community have functioned both inside and outside the home, have been conservers of tradition (if only because we are mothers), while we have had to respond to the *nuances* of a changed environment. How we negotiate the relationship between the past, as it has helped to form us, and the present, as we must experience it, is often a grave dilemma for us.

The setting of *Linden Hills*, Naylor's second novel, makes it clear that she is creating a geographical fictional world like, say, Faulkner's Yoknapatawpha county. Her first novel is set in Brewster Place, her second in Linden Hills. Brewster Place and Linden Hills are geographically in the same area; both are inhabited by blacks, and in both novels, characters refer to each of these places as proximate neighborhoods, though quite different in their orientation. Linden Hills is a posh upper-middle-class settlement, Brewster Place the last stop on the road to the bottom in American society, where you live when you can't live anywhere else. The outside world perceives Linden Hills as a symbol of black achievement while Brewster

First published in Henry Louis Gates Jr., ed., *Reading Black, Reading Feminist: A Critical Anthology* (New York: Meridian, 1990), 348–73.

Place is seen as a manifestation of failure. Ironically, through her two novels' respective characters and structure, Naylor portrays Brewster Place as a black community (though flawed and vulnerable) held together primarily by women, while Linden Hills is characterized as a group of houses that never becomes a community, a showplace precariously kept in place by the machinations of one wealthy black patriarchal family.

A single writer's juxtaposition of two Afro-American neighborhoods, different in values, separated by class distinctions, yet located in the same geographical area, is an unusual one in Afro-American literature. Afro-American writers have tended to portray black communities as distinct from white society. There have, of course, been novels about upper-middle-class Afro-Americans such as the works of early twentieth-century writer Jessie Fauset, or more recently Andrea Lee's *Sarah Phillips* (1984). But when contrasts in class are discussed in these novels, they are usually in relation to the white world. There have been many novels about urban ghetto blacks such as *The Street* by 1940s writer Ann Petry. Again class distinctions are usually presented in relation to white society. There have been novels about small-town blacks such as Toni Morrison's *The Bluest Eye* (1970), which indicate through their variety of characters that class distinctions among blacks do exist. But these characters are presented in relatively few situations. And there have been works about rural Southern blacks such as Alice Walker's *The Third Life of Grange Copeland* (1970) and *The Color Purple* (1982). But in these novels, the primary point of contrast in terms of class is decidedly the white world that tragically imposes its values on black people as a race.

Most Afro-American writers have tended to focus either on middle-class blacks or poor blacks and have tended to feature their protagonists as belonging to a black community which is distinct, if only because of the threat of a racist white society. When class distinctions are commented on, as they are, for example, in Zora Neale Hurston's portrayal of Jody Stark in *Their Eyes Were Watching God* (1937), Paule Marshall's portrayal of Jay Johnson in *Praisesong for the Widow* (1983), and Toni Morrison's portrayal of Macon Dead in *Song of Solomon* (1977), they are located in the conflict between that one character and others, and on the price he pays for social mobility, or sometimes, as in Grier Brown of Shange's *Betsey Brown* (1985), in that character's allegiance to his less fortunate brethren. Even when the novel is decidedly about class distinctions as in Morrison's *Tar Baby* (1981), conflict is gauged by individuals, in this case, the upper mobile Jadine and the underclass, Son. Neither are presented as having viable communities to which they belong. Marshall's monumental *The Chosen Place, the Time-*

less People (1969) does present a black world in which class distinctions are extensively explored, but this society is emphatically Caribbean.

Gloria Naylor's two novels, when looked at as the developing opus of a single writer, are unique in that together they offer us a graphic depiction of Afro-American groups, physically close, yet so distant because of their class differences. However, as my overview of recent Afro-American women novels indicates, Naylor's novels have been preceded in recent years by an increasing concern among these writers, Morrison in *Song of Solomon* (1977) and *Tar Baby* (1980), Marshall in *Praisesong for the Widow* (1982), Andrea Lee in *Sarah Phillips* (1984), and Shange in *Betsey Brown* on the issue of a distinct Afro-American middle class and on the implications of such a dimension in the Afro-American worldview. As such, Naylor both participates in this concern of other Afro-American women writers, even as she extends their analysis.

2

In the geographical world Naylor is creating, Brewster Place and Linden Hills coexist, and persons from each place have attitudes about the other. So touched by the revolutionary fervor of the 1960s, Melanie Browne of Linden Hills changes her name to Kiswana and goes down to live with "the people" in Brewster Place, much as some whites in the sixties went to live in black communities. The people of Brewster Place wonder what this privileged black woman is doing living in their midst, even as Melanie's family in Linden Hills is hurt, for they have made sacrifices so that she would never have to be associated with the kind of people who live in Brewster Place. The class distinctions between the people of Brewster Place and Linden Hills are clearly perceived by each group and make for a great distance between them even as they both are black.

That is not to say that Gloria Naylor is unconcerned with race as a determining factor in her geographical world. It is precisely the fact that Naylor's two neighborhoods *are* black which causes them to so clearly perceive their difference. Importantly, Naylor locates their similarities and differences in a historical process. Both Brewster Place and Linden Hills have been created by racism, or more precisely, as a result of the effects of racism on their founders. Linden Hills is literally carved out of a seemingly worthless soil by ex-slave Luther Nedeed, who in the 1820s has the secret dream of developing "an ebony jewel," a community of successful blacks who could stave off the racism of America and exhibit through their fine houses that members of the race can be powerful. In contrast, Brewster Place is "the bastard child of clandestine meetings" between local white politicians, at first to satisfy expected protests from the Irish community over the undeserved dismissal of their too honest police chief. Later Brewster Place becomes the neighborhood of successive waves of European immigrants, unwanted Americans who finally become, over time, the black poor.

The origin of communities and their historical development are critical to the structure of Naylor's novels as they are to Marshall's and Morrison's. These two writers, Marshall particularly in *Brown Girl, Brownstones,* Morrison particularly in *Sula,* begin their narrative, not with the introduction of their characters, but with the history of their characters' natal communities. In many ways, Naylor's recounting of the immigrant waves which precede the coming of blacks to Brewster Place echoes Marshall's rendition of the history of the Brooklyn brownstones. And Naylor's chronicle of the history of Linden Hills is similar to Morrison's tale of the Bottom on the top, for both communities are originated by ex-slaves in the nineteenth century. The differences between these authors' respective treatments, however, is instructive, for Marshall's West Indian immigrants see their brownstones as places they can eventually own, as a step up, while Naylor's blacks of Brewster Place are at a dead end. Morrison's ex-slave earns his "bottom" as payment from his ex-master and is cheated in the process, for he is given the worst land in the area. But Naylor's Nedeed carefully *chooses* his site, outwitting everyone who sees his plateau as having no value.

Although Naylor characterizes one neighborhood as held together by women and the other as controlled by a family, she stresses that both are started by men for the purpose of consolidating power. The intentions of these men are evident in the geographical choices they make. Nedeed's choice of "a V-shaped section of land," "the northern face of a worthless plateau," indicates his direction. Not only is his site so clearly visible; even more important, its V-shape allows his land to be both self-enclosed yet situated in the world. And since Nedeed lives on the lowest level of "the hills," he stands as a sentry to his private development. The shape of Brewster Place too is self-enclosed, for a wall is put up, separating it from other neighborhoods and making it a dead-end. Ironically, what is positive in one context is negative in another, depending on who has power. For black Nedeed uses his enclosed V-shape to select those who will be allowed to live near him, while the people of Brewster Place have a wall imposed on them by white city officials who want them separated from more "respectable" folk.

Although the wealthy Luther Nedeed appears to have power and the residents of Brewster Place do not, they are both immeasurably affected by their race, if only because they are separated from other Americans.

The physical separation of Brewster Place and Linden Hills from the surrounding areas—one imposed, the other chosen—is itself symbolic of Afro-Americans' dilemma in the United States. Race and class distinctions are intertwined in Naylor's geography, for in attempting to transcend the racial separations on streets like Brewster Place, her middle class separates itself from less fortunate blacks. They shut themselves in, so that they might not be shut out from the possibility of achieving power in white America. And as Naylor's narrative in *Linden Hills* suggests, they also separate themselves from each other and are not able to become a community.

In keeping with the contours of this geography, Naylor uses quite different forms in her two novels, forms that demonstrate the relationship between the shapes of her two neighborhoods and the ways in which power relations affect them. Because women usually have little access to power in the larger society, it is not surprising that black women, doubly affected by their racial and gender status, are the central characters in poverty-stricken Brewster Place, while the apparently powerful Luther Nedeed is the kernel character in Linden Hills. Yet, in dramatizing the stories of the women in Brewster Place, who seem to be in control but are not, and in analyzing the precarious position of Luther Nedeed, Naylor shows the inaccuracy of such terms as *matriarch* or *patriarch* as they apply to Afro-Americans.

The Women of Brewster Place begins with an introduction about the history of that street, which is followed by a series of stories, each about a particular woman who lives there. The novel concludes with Mattie Michaels' dream-story about a block party in which all the women appear, as well as a coda which announces the death of the street. Created by city officials, it is destroyed by them. Although each of their narratives could be called a short story, the novel consists of the interrelationship of the stories, as a pattern evolves, not only because the characters all live in Brewster Place but also because they are connected to one another. With the exception of the lesbians in "The Two" (a point to which I will return), Naylor emphasizes the distinctiveness of each story by naming it after the specific woman on whom she is focusing, even as she might include that woman in another's story. By using this form, one that heightens the individuality of her characters so that they are not merely seen as faceless "female heads of households," while stressing their interrelationships, Naylor establishes Brewster Place as a community in spite of its history of transients—a community with its own mores, strengths, and weaknesses. Even when that specific Brewster Place is destroyed, its characteristics remain, for most of its inhabitants must move to a similar street. Brewster Place, then, stands for both itself and other places like it.

Linden Hills also begins with the history of this place, which is really the history of the Nedeed men for they *are* Linden Hills. That history is followed by sections, headed not by names but by dates, December 19th to the 24th, this in spite of the many residents of Linden Hills we meet in the course of the novel. Ostensibly the story line is the winding of Lester, a recalcitrant Linden Hills resident, and Willie, his street friend from nearby, poor Putney Wayne, through the affluent neighborhood of Linden Hills as they do odd jobs to make some money for the holidays, which ironically commemorate giving.

Although we meet many Linden Hills people, at the center of the story is Luther Nedeed himself, for he has power over the individuals who live in this settlement. His story includes within it the story of his wife, and the wives of the Nedeed men who precede him. For his story is all of their stories, the present Mrs. Nedeed's, the story of all the Mrs. Nedeeds that preceded her except that this Mr. and Mrs. Nedeed will be the last of their kind. What Naylor presents is the hidden history and herstory that has made Linden Hills possible, at least as it now exists. Hence, in contrast to *Brewster Place,* the process of time, rather than the character of distinct personalities, is the formal structural element of Linden Hills.

What is interesting to me is how many layers of stories Naylor attempts to weave together in Linden Hills, layers that finally do not hold together. For although the persons focused on in stories within the story overlap, they never connect with each other. Like *The Women of Brewster Place, Linden Hills* does conclude with a scene in which all the residents appear, a scene which signals the end of this place as we have known it. But while the residents of Brewster Place are getting together to have a block party, the residents of Linden Hills unilaterally ignore the burning down of the Nedeeds' house by putting out their lights. Hence, the wall that separates Brewster Place from the outer world becomes their mark of community as well as their stigma, while the houses of Linden Hills are critical to the concluding section of that novel precisely because they are the measuring stick of these people's wealth as well as their unwillingness to interact with one another. Only Lester and Willie, outcasts from Linden Hills, are "hand anchored to hand" in those last days of the year.

3

While Linden Hills destroys itself from within, Brewster Place is ostensibly destroyed from without. But Naylor's stories of the women there, usually characterized as strong, matriarchal, enduring by media, scholarship, government policy, emphasize their powerlessness. Most of her central women characters, Mattie Michaels, Etta Mae Johnson, Lucielia Louise

Turner, Cora Lee, live in Brewster Place because they must. Their possibility for controlling their own lives has been blocked by societal mores about women's sexuality and their individual responses to these restrictions. So, although poverty is a condition that they all share, they have been condemned to that state because of society's view of them as women, and their response to that view.

These four women, Mattie Michaels, Etta Mae Johnson, Lucielia Louise Turner, and Cora Lee, are presented as sets of counterpoint, so that Naylor can demonstrate how individual personality is not the determining factor that brings them to this street. Both Mattie Michaels and Etta Mae Johnson come from the same Southern community. But while Mattie is a sweet girl, domestic in her orientation, Etta Mae Johnson is rebellious, yearning for adventure. Still both women are wounded by the fact that they *are* women. Mattie Michaels is "ruined" by a single sexual encounter; her pregnancy results in her estrangement from her doting, then enraged, father who feels she has betrayed him. Mattie makes up for that loss by doting on her son Basil, only to receive from God what she prayed for, "a little boy who would always need her." The son's betrayal of his aging mother depletes her savings and precipitates the necessity for her move to Brewster Place. Etta Mae, too, is estranged from her community. Whites force her to leave because she is too uppity. She lives, however, primarily through hitching her wagon to a "rising black star," to a succession of men; she too never discovers that she can live through herself. Naylor's comment on the effect of sexism and racism on her is so astute: "Even if someone had bothered to stop and tell her that the universe had expanded for her just an inch, she wouldn't know how to shine alone."[1]

Although they have had opportunities to avoid a dead-end street like Brewster Place, both Mattie and Etta Mae end up there because of their concept of themselves as women. Mattie sacrifices herself to her son. Etta Mae will not put up with the nonsense that men bring with them, but neither is she able to see that she can make up her own life. As a result the sweet Mattie and the adventurous Etta Mae arrive at a certain period in their lives without sufficient economic or psychological resources.

Both these middle-aged women live through others; but that is also true of the younger Lucielia and Cora Lee. Their lives complement Mattie's and Etta Mae's. For Lucielia will do practically anything to maintain her relationship with her husband, while Cora Lee is obsessed with having babies. Their stories are counterpoint to each other in that Lucielia's relationship with her husband is damaged because she does get pregnant, while Cora Lee does not care about men except to get pregnant. Lucielia's husband sees her womanhood as a trap: "With two kids and you on my back, I ain't never gonna have nothing." Children for him are a liability since he is a poor man. When Ciel aborts her second child only to lose her first while she is pleading with her husband to stay with her, she almost loses all sense of herself. On the other hand, encouraged by adults in her childhood to desire baby dolls, Cora Lee wants nothing more than to take care of babies. No longer concerned with her children when they naturally grow beyond babyhood, Cora Lee lives in a fantasy world, interrupted only by the growing demands of the human beings she has birthed.

Because of their lack of economic resources, these four women *must* live in Brewster Place. However Kiswana Browne and "the two" choose to live there for different reasons. Kiswana feels repressed, both communally and sexually, in her natal home, Linden Hills. She sees her sojourn in Brewster Place as bonding with her true people, black people. As well, her interaction with her mother, the major event in her story, demonstrates quite clearly that Kiswana sees Linden Hills' morality as hypocritical and narrow-minded. Her prim mother characterizes African sculpture, the heritage Kiswana proudly displays, as obscene, too blatantly sexual. Yet these two women have much in common in that they both enjoy their sensuality, the younger quite openly (at least in Brewster Place), the older more covertly. Naylor's use of their adornment of their feet, a part of the female body that is usually hidden and which is not considered particularly sexual, is an indication of their own pleasure in themselves. But finally it is Mrs. Browne's willingness to visit Kiswana in Brewster Place, the fact that she is concerned about her daughter's welfare despite their disagreements, that is an indication of the strength of their bond. Like the daughter in Carolyn Rodgers' poem, "The Bridge That Is My Back," Kiswana understands that "irregardless" *her* mother is there for her.

Kiswana's meeting with her mother is an amplification of a major chord sounded throughout this novel, for Brewster Place women mother one another. Perhaps these women are sometimes labeled "matriarchs" because together they are able to endure so much. There is no question that their stories in this novel are interconnected because of the caring bond they assume for one another, a bond that does not, however, preclude disagreements, falling-outs, even ineffectiveness.

So although Mattie's mother is ineffectual in her dealings with her father, it is she who, through threatened violence, prevents him from beating the pregnant girl to a pulp. And it is a stranger, Miss Eva, who mothers Mattie and her son, giving them a secure and happy home. Miss Eva may, as she says, be partial to men, but in the novel it is Mattie she treats like kin. The same attitude is evident in Mattie's friendship with Etta Mae Johnson. First mothered by Billy Holiday's music which articulates her spirit for her,

Etta may believe that men are her means to success. But it is to Mattie she perennially returns for renewal. Just as Kiswana is mothered, she also mothers. She takes Cora Lee and her children to see Shakespeare in the park, and it is on that occasion that this lover of babies begins to think about possibilities for her children who are no longer babies. Ciel as well mothers her child Serena and in turn is mothered by Mattie. In one of the most moving scenes in the novel, Mattie bathes the numb grief-stricken Ciel, bringing her from death into life as she reawakens her senses in a ritual of shared womanhood much like Rosalee's bathing of Avey Johnson in Marshall's *Praisesong for the Widow,* a ritual still practiced in voodoo and derived from African religions.

Women mothering other women is consistent throughout this novel as they hold each other in survival. Such mothering, though, does not extend to "the two," the lesbians who for most Brewster Place residents do not even have specific names. The community of women in Brewster Place cannot approach even the thought of sexual love between women, partly because so many of them have had such close relations with each other. As always, Mattie puts the community's fears into words. When Etta Mae says how different Lorraine and Theresa's love must be from the love so many of them share, Mattie responds: "Maybe it's not so different . . . maybe that's why some women get so riled up about it 'cause they know deep down it's not so different after all . . . it kinda gives you a funny feeling when you think about it that way, though."[2]

Unlike Celie and Shug in *The Color Purple,* Lorraine has no community and very much wants one. It is her tragedy that she believes because she is black, she is in the same boat as the other residents of Brewster Place. She learns too late that the effects of racism on this black community exacerbates the homophobia so rampant in the outer world. Although she is killed by men, the women of Brewster Place too share the blame for her death. They do not mother her; instead, they reject her.

Ben, the wino who had lost his crippled daughter, is the only one who befriends Lorraine. Ironically, it is Ben who Lorraine kills in her frenzied effort to defend herself from her attackers. Ben is the first black resident of Brewster Place, and his death at the wall is a sign of Brewster Place's death as a community, of its inability to hold together much longer. Even as the women in the final scene of the novel chip away at the wall that imprisons them, we are aware that this is someone's dream, for such an act would be the prelude to a community rebellion, a step that these nurturing restricted women cannot take if they are to survive as they have. Before such a route can be explored, Brewster Place is condemned by politicians, forcing its people to disperse. As nurturing as Brewster Place

"Afric women" may be, the community cannot withstand the power of those in high places. So Brewster Place residents are displaced again, just as they had been before. They are as powerless as they were when they first came to Brewster Place.

4

While Brewster Place is a community of transients, Linden Hills is a secure settlement with a long history. And unlike the people of Brewster Place, Luther Nedeed has access to people with power. In fact, because of careful planning and sacrifice, his family becomes one of those with power, at least in relation to Linden Hills. The Nedeed men caress, cultivate their dream of an ebony jewel community as if it were a woman they are wooing. Naylor's use of a V-shaped piece of land suggests the female body even as Nedeed's house situated at the entry suggests the male who wishes to take possession. The land is, for succeeding generations of Nedeed men, their love. They carefully select the families who are allowed to live on it. For *their* people, "are to reflect the Nedeeds in a hundred facets and then the Nedeeds could take these splintered mirrors and form a *mirage of power* to torment a world that dared to think them stupid—or worse totally impotent."[3]

But even the Nedeeds, gods that they are, cannot live forever. It is necessary that they have heirs in order to continue to cultivate their dream. Wives then are necessary to their plan, the choice of a wife critical. Naylor gives us the outlines of a developing patriarchy in her description of the way the pursuit of power affects the relations between men and women. In order to serve the dream, the women must be malleable (grateful to be the wife of a Nedeed); they must look like a prize, hence their light skin, but not be demanding beauties. They must bear a son as close in nature as possible to their father, and of course the life of a Nedeed's wife must be submerged in the life of her husband.

It is this flaw in their century-old plan, critical to the development and maintenance of Linden Hills, which generates the novel. For the present Mrs. Nedeed does not give birth to a Nedeed boy that resembles his paternal ancestors. Nature triumphs over planning, for this son harkens back to his maternal ancestors, as the too-long submerged blood of the Nedeed women finally manifests itself. Unwilling to believe that this could happen, that his father's genes could be superseded by his mother's, Luther Nedeed convinces himself that his wife has been unfaithful, for he will not recognize even his own mother's face in his son's features.

At the very core of patriarchal myth, as Naylor presents it, is the idea that the son must duplicate the father, and that he must be separated from the mother. In an attempt to restore order in the world he has created, Nedeed imprisons his wife and child in the cellar, causing the death of his motherlike son, hence ending the heretofore unbroken line of descent. He also precipitates his wife's discovery of the Nedeed women who preceded her, the final blow to his kingdom. In refusing to accept a variation in the pattern his father had decreed, Luther Nedeed destroys all that his forebears had set in motion.

But of course it is not only this individual Nedeed that causes the destruction of this artificial world; for years Linden Hills has been rotting from the inside as Nature refuses to succumb indefinitely to even his family's iron will. The imprisoned Mrs. Nedeed remembers *her* real name because she discovers the records left by her predecessors, letters, recipes, photographs—as the mothers cry out to be heard, to be reckoned with, to exist. As Willa Prescott Nedeed relives the herstory so carefully exhumed from the Nedeeds' official records, we realize how the experiences of the women are a serious threat to the men's kingdom.

Naylor's rendition of this herstory emphasizes one element—that once these women had produced one male, once they had carried out their function for patriarchy, they are isolated from life until they no longer exist. They however leave some record of their presence, their lives, in their own individual feminine forms. Through letters to herself, the first Mrs. Nedeed, the slave Luuwana Packerville, tells us how she is silenced to death; through her recipes, Evelyn Creton demonstrates how she had eaten herself to death, and through the family photograph album, Patricia Maguire graphically displays that she is gradually disappearing. In an act of defiance, in the last photo of the album she scrawls the word "me" in the place where her face should be.

None of these women can fight back effectively, for at first they do not know what is being done to them. When they do begin to discover that *they* are not wrong, that they are being erased not because they have lost their charm, or do not fix the right meals, it is too late. Since she has been systematically isolated from the world, no one questions the absence of the present Mrs. Nedeed, for no one knows her well enough to realize that she has not gone away for the holidays. By emphasizing the Nedeed women's ignorance of their own herstory, Naylor shows how the repression of women's herstory is necessary to the maintenance of patriarchy, and why it is that History is so exclusively male.

Naylor does not present Willa Prescott Nedeed's meditation on her dead child and on the herstory she discovers in a straight line. Rather she juxtaposes it to her presentation of other Linden Hills residents who also must erase essential parts of themselves if they are to stay in this jewel neighborhood. Most of these characters are men: the lawyer, Wynston Alcott; the businessmen, Xavier Donnell and Maxwell Smyth; the Rev. Hollis; the historian Braithwaite; and one woman, Laurel. Each of their lives has been damaged by the pursuit of wealth and power that Nedeed embodies, though some do not even know it. They distort their natural inclinations, introducing death into their lives, even as the Nedeeds, who make their money as funeral parlor directors, have distorted their families in order to create Linden Hills.

Naylor shows us the different currencies in which these characters pay for their ascent to Linden Hills—usually it is their deepest natural pleasures that they give up in order to "make it." So Wynston Alcott gives up his lover David and marries, for homosexuality is not allowed in Linden Hills. Xavier Donnell gives up his idea of marrying Roxanne, a black woman who lives in Linden Hills, because she is so much herself, she might drain him of the energy necessary to reach the top. Maxwell Smyth becomes totally artificial. Everything—his diet, his clothes, the temperature in his house, sexuality—is regulated so as to eliminate any funk. The pressures of his fraudulent job leave Rev. Hollis without the wife he loves and he becomes an alcoholic. Laurel puts everything into becoming a successful business-woman, sacrificing her relationship with her friends, her love of music and swimming, even her concern for the grandmother who brought her up. Her relationship with her husband is described as an ascent up "two staircases, that weren't strictly parallel," and whose steps "slanted until even one free hand could not touch the other's." She finally breaks into a million pieces.

Important among Linden Hills folk is Braithwaite, the historian who separates himself from life, in order to chronicle the comings and goings of the Nedeeds. His view of historiography is that of detachment and dis-involvement for only then, he thinks, can he be objective. He believes that he cannot participate in life if he is to observe it. As a result he does not get to know history's cunning passages—the letters, recipes, the photographs of the Mrs. Nedeeds—since only interest and concern could lead him to them. Through this character, Naylor critiques the intellectual version of Linden Hills where official history-making and an obsession with objectiv-ity means that men like Braithwaite are not concerned with human life.

What Braithwaite does not know and does not wish to know are the very things that cause destruction of Linden Hills. On December 24th, the final day of the book, Nedeed insists on carrying out the family tradition of decorating the tree. He pays those Linden Hills handymen, Lester and Willie, to help him, for his family is supposedly away. By refusing to vary tradition one iota, Nedeed continues to effect his own downfall. He must have the homemade ornaments his family has always used. The closed door is left open so that Willa Prescott Nedeed can ascend, her dead child in hand, the *net* and *veil* of her predecessors encircling her, to make her own order. The final struggle between Luther and Willa will unite them and their child in a circle of fire: "They breathed as one, moved as one and one body lurched against the fireplace."

Nedeed is not only destroyed by his suppression of his mothers, he is destroyed as well by the Linden Hills residents whom he presumed to create. In an act that reveals their hatred for him as their controller as well as the disinvolvement he has always demanded of them, his neighbors let him and his house burn down. Only Willie from Putney Wayne is willing to try to save the Nedeeds who after all are only flesh and blood to him. Finally as if asserting *her* order, Nature immediately reclaims the Nedeed house. The lake, which served as the barrier between the Nedeeds and the world, pulls the century-old house into itself in one single stroke. The Nedeed tradition is extinguished forever.

I think it is important that Willie, the poet from Putney Wayne, and Lester, a descendant of Grammy Tilson, the only one who did not bend to the first Luther Nedeed's will, are the witnesses to this story of Linden Hills. Too, Naylor may be signaling through Willie's importance in the novel, as well as the story of Wayne Ave. residents, Ruth and Norm, that Putney Wayne, a working-class neighborhood, may be the setting of her next novel. If it is, these Putney Wayne characters have learned much about the folly of trying to be a god and that those who place wealth above human beings cannot create a community that endures.

5

In *The Women of Brewster Place* and *Linden Hills*, Gloria Naylor's portrayal of her two neighborhoods demonstrates the effects of class distinctions on the Afro-American community and how these distinctions are gender-oriented. As well, when read together, her two novels present "solutions" idealized during the last decade by important powerless American groups, solutions which are characterized by Naylor, finally, as ineffectual routes to empowerment.

By creating a tapestry of nurturing women in her first novel, Naylor emphasizes how female values derived from mothering—nurturing, communality, concern with human feeling—are central to Brewster Place's survival. Published in 1982, *The Women of Brewster Place* was preceded by a decade of American feminist writing which responded to patriarchal society's devaluation of women by revalorizing female values.[4] In reaction to the Western patriarchal emphasis on the individual, on the splitting of human beings into mind and body, and on competition, conquest, and power, these writers saw the necessity of honoring female values. If women were to become empowered, it was necessary for them to perceive their own primacy, their centrality to their society, as well as to analyze how dangerous patriarchal values were to a harmonious social order.

Because of their origins and history, Afro-American women could lay claim to a viable tradition in which they had been strong central persons in their families and communities, not solely because of their relationship to men, but because they themselves had bonded together to ensure survival of their children, their communities, the race. Partly because of the matri-centric orientation of African peoples from which they were descended, partly because of the nature of American slavery, Afro-American women had had to bond with each other in order to survive. Afro-Americans as a race could not have survived without the "female values" of communality, sharing, and nurturing.

At the same time, the centrality of Afro-American women in their communities was in such great contrast to the American norm of woman's subordination in the nuclear family that they were denigrated both in black and white society. The Afro-American mother was punished and maligned for being too strong, too central in her family, for being a "matriarch," a vortex of attitudes which culminated in white American government policy such as the Moynihan Report and in black cultural nationalist rhetoric of the 1960s.

Afro-American women writers of the 1970s responded to black and white society's denigration of the black mother and of female values by showing how such a position was sexist, was based on a false definition of woman as ineffectual, secondary, weak. Marshall in *Brown Girl, Brownstones* and Morrison in *Sula* present women who are strong, who believe in their own primacy, and who are effective in some says. But these writers also presented another view—that Afro-American women who internalize the dominant society's definition of women are courting self-destruction. So Morrison's Pauline and Pecola Breedlove in *The Bluest Eye,* and Walker's Margaret and Mem Copeland in *The Third Life of Grange Copeland* are destroyed by their inability to resist society's false definitions of man and woman. It is important to note as well that these novels demonstrate not only how these specific women fall prey to sexist ideology but also that they do partly because black communities themselves are sexist. Thus Morrison in *Sula* and Walker in *Meridian* critique motherhood as the black community's primary definition of woman.

Naylor's rendition of her women's lives in the community of Brewster

Place indicates that she is intensely knowledgeable of the literature of her sisters and that the thought of Afro-American women during the seventies is one means by which she both celebrates and critiques women-centered communities.

The obvious characteristic that her women share, with the exception of Kiswana and the two, is that they *must* live in streets like Brewster Place, that is, that they are displaced persons. Naylor is not the first Afro-American woman writer to present a black community which is *where* it is because of socioeconomic factors. Marshall's Barbadian-American community in *Brown Girl, Brownstones* is in Brooklyn because Barbados offers them little opportunity for advancement; Morrison's Southern folk in *The Bluest Eye* migrate to Lorain, Ohio, because they need jobs. Each of these communities is attempting to forge a new tradition based on the old but related to the new circumstances in which they find themselves. But while they still have some belief in being able to improve their lives, the women who live in Brewster Place are caught in a cycle of never-ending displacement. Thus Brewster Place has got a tradition of mores long before Mattie Michaels or Etta Mae Johnson ever get there. Naylor, then, presents a small urban community of black women who are outcasts precisely because they are poor black women, a type of community that has been a part of black life in the United States for many generations. While the urban Selina of *Brown Girl, Brownstones* and the small-town Claudia of *The Bluest Eye* can look back at their story of growing up as an education, the women of Brewster Place are in a static landscape. They were here yesterday and unless there is some catastrophic change in society, they will be here tomorrow.

The culture of sharing and nurturing in Brewster Place is based on a black tradition in this country that harkens back to slavery. Important contemporary novels written by Afro-Americans have presented women characters who are mutually supportive of one another. Margaret Walker's *Jubilee* (1966) reminds us that it was such values that allowed the ordinary slave to survive. Paule Marshall's *Brown Girl, Brownstones* provides us with the vivid scenes of Silla and her women friends around the kitchen table as they defend themselves against their men as well as white society. Toni Morrison gives us a lyrical account of Southern women like her Aunt Jimmy in *The Bluest Eye* who created communities in their own image, as well as a stunning description of the Peaces' matrifocal house in *Sula*. In these novels, as in *The Women of Brewster Place,* women share common concerns such as the raising of children and, like Brewster Place, these women-centered communities are defenses against sexism and racism; in other words, against the abuses that are inflicted on black women. But while these women may be independent, it is an independence forged from the necessity of having to fend off attack; in fact, some of them would prefer not to have such independence since they have not chosen it. And in all of these novels, the women do not or cannot change their condition, so much as they cope with it as best they can.

So neither the feistiness of Eva Peace nor the persistence of Silla Boyce prevents the destruction of the Bottom nor the tearing down of the Brooklyn brownstones. What does occur in these novels is that someone understands something about her relationship to her community. But Naylor is not only concerned with this relationship. While stressing through the form of her novel that her women have strong bonds with each other, she emphasizes as well that these relationships do not substantively change their lives. Her novel ends not with Nel missing Sula nor with Selina understanding her mother, but with the movement of these women to yet another such street, where they no doubt will relive this pattern as "Brewster Place still waits to die."

By presenting a community in which strong women bonds do not break the cycle of powerlessness in which so many poor black women are imprisoned, Naylor points to a theoretical dilemma with which feminist thinkers have been wrestling. For while the values of nurturing and communality are central to a just society, they often preclude the type of behavior necessary to achieve power in this world, behavior such as competitiveness, extreme individualism, the desire to conquer. How does one break the cycle of powerlessness without giving up the values of caring so necessary to the achievement of a just society? Doesn't powerlessness itself breed internalization of self-destructive societal values? How does one achieve the primacy of self without becoming ego-centered? Further, since the values of these women are necessary to their survival, wouldn't they change if their socio-economic conditions changed? Isn't it the very fact that these women do cope through these values that precludes their destruction of the wall which entraps them? How does one fight power without taking on the values of those who have power?

Two elements in the novel suggest other avenues. One is Mattie's dream at the end of the story in which the women learn that they have participated in the destruction of Lorraine, one of their sisters, and can redeem themselves only if they protest her death—in other words, that their internalization of societal values helps to keep them powerless. Having learned this, the anger of the women erupts against their real enemy, the wall that shuts them in. But Mattie awakens from this dream to a gloriously sunny day on which the community is to have a block party, an event which will take the pain away, at least for a short time, of Brewster Place's inhabitants.

The other element in the novel is Naylor's portrayal of the character

Kiswana. Although she is presented as lacking the grit and humor of the other women who have endured more and lived more deeply, she is nevertheless the only one who attempts to help the community see itself as a political force—that it can fight the landlords and demand its rights. Still she can leave Brewster Place when she wishes. She does not risk survival, as the others would, if they rebelled; nor has she yet been worn down by the unceasing cycle of displacement that the others have experienced. And she has a sense of how power operates *precisely* because she comes from Linden Hills, a place which she leaves *precisely* because it is so focused on money and power.

Naylor's inclusion of Kiswana as a pivotal character in *The Women of Brewster Place* indicates the great distance between women who *must* live in women-centered communities and those who have the option to live in them. For Kiswana's choice to live in Brewster Place is already a sign that, in relation to the other women, she has some privilege in the society. She is an "exception," while they are the majority. And her privilege comes from the fact that she was raised in a wealthy community.

Kiswana is, in fact, the link between Naylor's first novel and her second, *Linden Hills,* in which the pursuit of money and power is a central issue. Given the nature of the power in this society, many powerless groups have experienced the ineffectiveness of sharing and nurturing communities as a means to liberation. They therefore have often idealized another solution in their search for autonomy, that of taking on the values of the powerful. In *Linden Hills,* Naylor analyzes the effects of the drive for power, a drive that originally emanates from Nedeed's desire to elevate black people's status in America.

Just as *The Women of Brewster Place* was preceded by a decade of writing about female values, *Linden Hills,* published in 1985, was preceded by a decade that marked the rise of a more distinctly visible black middle class than had ever existed before in this country.[5] This period was, as well, a time when the goal of women was often portrayed as "making it" in the system. Recent media events such as *Newsweek*'s article on the Black Underclass and ABC's program on the Women's Movement emphasize this orientation. What these analyses often omit, however, is that the rise of the money/power solution among powerless groups in the 1970s has much to do with the character of Afro-American and women's mass movements of the '60s and early '70s when political goals were difficult to achieve, not because they were not vigorously fought for but because of the system's successful resistance to meaningful change. In the '70s, the emphasis on material gain that characterized so much media presentation of these groups' desires is actually a return to an old strategy which has never worked. But since so few of us are aware of our history, it is not surprising that the swing from mass political movements to an emphasis on individual gain as a route to empowerment would occur.

In critiquing the solution of money and status as a means to empowerment, Naylor stresses that it too is part of Afro-American tradition. Unlike Morrison's Macon Dead of *Song of Solomon* who begins his rise in the 1920s, Luther Nedeed's plan originated in the 1820s when slavery was very much alive. By charting the Nedeed generations, she reminds us that a black upper middle class has existed for some time, and that the drive to liberate the race through the creation of an elite group is not unique to the 1970s. Also, in portraying the original Nedeed plan, Naylor points up an abiding element of this "solution," for in choosing those who will be allowed to become a part of this class, Nedeed recognizes that they must deny their history of shared oppression, lest they see structural changes, rather than a duplication of the existing structure, as their goal.

What also distinguishes Naylor's presentation of the black upper middle class is her analysis of its patriarchal position. All the Nedeed men clearly grasp the fact that the subordination of the female to the male is an essential element in becoming a powerful people in America. The first Nedeed buys his wife, a slave, and never frees her and successive Nedeed men imprison their wives through isolating them. As well, the subordination of female to male is, in Naylor's narrative, interwoven with the Nedeed's emphasis on a fixed hierarchy as a necessary characteristic of their domain. So what level one lives on in the "hills" is a sure indication of one's status, and absolutely adhered to traditions determine even the Nedeed men's behavior, as they attempt, through the control of community mores, to obliterate change.

In selecting her essential elements of a developing patriarchy, Naylor has learned more from contemporary Afro-American women's literature, for it has provided her with clues about the dangers to which the creation of a black elite might lead. So Linden Hills is not so much hill as plateau, in much the same way that in *Sula* Morrison's Bottom is actually the top. One means by which the powerless are kept powerless is through the distortion of words, of naming, that is imposed on them. Like Morrison, Naylor emphasizes then how language, in this case the language of one of the powerless, is distorted to camouflage truth. And like Morrison, Naylor also uses dates to name her chapters, as if the march of time is the determining factor in her narrative. Naylor's dates are not only ironic in that they are the days of giving and of peace; they also emphasize the Christian and therefore Western orientation of Linden Hills. So while Morrison's chapters emphasize that time for the folk is not so much chronology as it is significant action, Naylor's chapters are a means by which we discover the tension between Nedeed's Western patriarchal orientation toward time and the difficulties such rigidity imposes on even his most willing residents. As has been true of so many monarchs, his inability to change is one major cause of his downfall in those last days of the year.

Naylor also revises Morrison by having Luther Nedeed, her ex-slave, become financially successful, because he, unlike Morrison's nameless ex-slave, excludes from his settlement those blacks who refer to a collective history. While Morrison's Bottom, then, is a distinctly Afro-American community with a distinct Afro-American culture, Linden Hills residents reject black culture. It is no wonder that Luther Nedeed sees that his ancestors' plan has failed. For though Linden Hills residents have money and status, they are no longer black. They have lost their identity, the identity which was the source of Linden Hills' origins. They therefore cannot create a community, and worse they hate their controller, Nedeed himself, who has so conditioned them as to be interested only in individual gain. By placing the pursuit of money and power above all else, the Nedeeds fragment the black community and destroy the goal for which they have sacrificed family feeling, love, fraternity, pleasure, the very qualities that make life worth living, qualities which are central to liberation and empowerment.

Ironically, not only have Linden Hills residents lost their identity, neither have they gained power. Nedeed perceives how his showplace is threatened by the proliferation of Brewster Place, those who have been excluded from money and status. To the larger world, Linden Hills' image is affected by Brewster Place's image, just as the status of the black upper middle class today is affected by the fact that during the '70s there was a corresponding rise in poor blacks, particularly poor black women. The creation of an elite class has not empowered the race, nor has it resulted in the existence of a group of blacks unaffected by racism. The distance between Linden Hills and Brewster Place, then, is not as great as it might appear to be, and Nedeed is not so much a patriarch as a manager, who must hold to rules that are actually determined by whites.

Naylor recalls, as well, Marshall's depiction of her Barbadian-American community in *Brown Girl, Brownstones* by demonstrating their desire for property and status as a bulwark against failure. But while Marshall's Silla belongs to a distinct woman-community and passes on some of its values to her daughter, Selina, the Nedeed women are isolated from other women as all traces of female values or of a distinct woman community are erased from Linden Hills. Like Marshall's Avey in *Praisesong*, the Nedeed women lose their identity and sense of community. But while Avey is able to retrieve her true name because of her experience with her maternal ancestors, the Nedeed women are cut off from their own herstory and have no daughters to whom they can bequeath their own personal experience. By emphasizing these women's ignorance of their herstory as well as their sons' separation from them, Naylor revises Marshall's emphasis in all of her novels, of the continuity of community values, of "female values," among New World Blacks. Naylor suggests then that such values can be obliterated by the predominant class distinctions inherent in the urge to develop a patriarchy.

In many ways, the Nedeed women more resemble Jadine of Morrison's *Tar Baby* in that they themselves believe in the primacy of material success and place little value on the ancient women-properties of sharing and nurturing. But Jadine does sense, through her obsession with the African woman in the yellow dress and her dream in Eloe of her maternal ancestors, that she may be giving up something of incalculable value. However the Nedeed women, as well as Laurel, the successful businesswoman of Linden Hills, do not sense this until it is much too late. Like the tragic mulattoes of the nineteenth- and early twentieth-century literature, they are trapped by their own adherence to class values which demean them as women without their even being aware of it. Unlike Hurston's Janie Stark, who too experiences the trap of ladydom, they find, too late, the language to give a name to their condition. Nor given the lack of a community, which has got a tradition of pleasure as an important value, do they encounter a woman friend, as Walker's Celie does, who might enable them to challenge the Nedeed patriarchy.

What is also interesting about Naylor's account of Linden Hills as opposed to recent Afro-American women's literature is her presentation of central male characters. In her development of Nedeed characters, she not only gives us their attempt to develop their patriarchy but their failure as well. That failure is due to their inability to create a community, which Naylor suggests must be the source of any route Afro-Americans take to empowerment. A community does not exist if it is rigidly controlled nor can it exist without a shared history or without shared values. But Naylor also presents male characters who experience the restrictions of Nedeed's vision. Like Son in Morrison's *Tar Baby,* Willie in *Linden Hills* values fraternity above money, but significantly unlike Morrison's refugee, Willie is still a viable part of a working-class community, Putney Wayne. While her first novel focuses on women friendships, *Linden Hills* emphasizes the friendship between men, Willie and Lester. And in contrast to one other such friendship in contemporary Afro-American women's fiction, the friendship between Morrison's Milkman and Guitar in *Song of Solomon,* Naylor's Willie and Lester are not opposed to each other's values. In so tenderly portraying the relationship of these two, Naylor may be suggesting that genuine friendship between men who share similar values, as well as friendship between women, is critical to the Afro-American community's search for empowerment.

Like Kiswana, who is the transitional character between *The Women of Brewster Place* and *Linden Hills,* Willie may be the transitional figure between Linden Hills and Naylor's next novel. Like Kiswana he is interested in and knowledgeable about the history and literature of Afro-Americans. But he is also educated in one respect that she is not. He comes from a living working-class Afro-American community with a deep cultural past that is as old as Linden Hills. Through his friendship with Lester, he learns about Linden Hills from the inside and thus knows that the solution of the creation of an elite class fragments and destroys the community. As a person intensely involved in the direction of his folk's future then, he is not as likely, as have some upper-mobile working-class men, to repeat Nedeed's error.

What he and others like him can do to empower their communities is not solved for us in either of these novels. For Naylor does not so much give us solutions as she uses her knowledge of Afro-American women's literature to show how complex the condition of powerless groups is. She may be the first Afro-American woman writer to have such access to her tradition. And the complexity of her two novels indicate how valuable such knowledge can be. In doing her own black feminist reading of her literary tradition so as to dramatize the convoluted hierarchy of class, race, and gender distinctions in America today, she has begun to create a geographical world in her fiction, as varied and complex as the structure of our society.

9 Being the Subject and the Object: Reading African-American Women's Novels (1993)

If memory serves me right, the first novel by an African-American woman I'd even held in my hand came from a second-hand bookstore in Harlem. It was 1967. I was a graduate student at Columbia, and an English instructor in the SEEK program at CCNY, a program designed to uplift apparently uneducable black and Puerto Rican youth by giving them the skills to enter city colleges. In ways I'd not consciously calculated, I was pursuing two different tracks of training. At Columbia, I was working on a paper on Wallace Stevens, a concession to me from my professors who, mostly, were immersed in British literature and who barely touched on American contemporary writers, the writers in whom I was most interested. At SEEK, I was fast discovering African-American writing (in response to which my students suddenly exhibited the writing capacity they were not supposed to have) and was planning classes on *Invisible Man*. Using African-American literature in the classroom sent me on regular treks to black bookstores where I could sometimes find out-of-print books, the category it seemed to which most African-American books then belonged.

So it was, that I saw the image of a brown girl on the cover of a cheap Avon paperback and noticed its title, *Brown Girl, Brownstones*. I'd been in this country, and had studied literature long enough to know that brown girls did not usually appear on book covers nor did they figure prominently in novels. My curiosity aroused, precisely because I was a brown girl, I bought the book for fifty cents, and put it away until at some future date, after I'd completed the Stevens paper, I could read it.

The world I entered into in Paule Marshall's brownstones was unlike any other I'd encountered in books, not even that of James Baldwin or Richard

First published in Gayle Greene and Coppelia Kahn, eds., *Changing Subjects: The Making of Feminist Literary Criticism* (London: Routledge, 1993), 195–200.

Wright, LeRoi Jones or Ishmael Reed. Perhaps because I am a Caribbean woman living in the United States, *Brown Girl, Brownstones* resonated for me on many levels, some of which I cannot yet articulate. Reading this novel was, for me, an intensely personal and emotional experience. It was not that I'd grown up in Brooklyn, as Selina had, for I'd spent my childhood in the Caribbean. Nor that my mother and father resembled Silla and Deighton—quite to the contrary. Yet I recognized, *knew* Marshall's characters—the Boyces, the Chancellors, Suggie, Clive; I spoke their language with its *Wunna's* and *beautiful-ugly's*. I'd experienced their cultural context without being able to really articulate it, for it was the worldview in which I was raised. I'd tasted every day the gritty dilemmas with which they were contending—without having named them. Marshall's first novel insinuated itself into my emotional psyche and compelled me, in spite of myself, to remember the rich, sometimes frustrating complexity of my own people, a complexity many of us wanted to ignore, forget about in the black revolutionary fervor of 1967.

In particular, Silla's woman-voice constantly interrupted my mind-voice. Her anguish-rage warned me of trials I might have to face. Like a lioness she stalked the corridors of my imagination even as she challenged the ideal of black womanhood enunciated by ideologues of the sixties. Her fate called on me to act, lest my life resemble hers. Her wonderful and terrible deeds mocked the simplicity of many of the views I held.

For at that time, many young black women like myself thought ourselves free enough to be all we could be, at least in the Struggle—only to find that we were enclosed, even in our own communities, in cages of misrepresentations as to who a black woman should be. As many of us were beginning to value, to celebrate the black culture our mothers had been instrumental in creating and passing on, we found ourselves entangled in contradictions about black motherhood, and silenced by versions of history in which we were said to have undermined our own.

Supposedly we'd been domineering matriarchs, powerful furies who'd brought the race down and who needed to come down off our high horses so that our men could ascend to the throne—in much the same way that the ancient mother goddesses of pre-history had had to be tamed by the enlightened male gods who vanquished them. How else were black people to survive in the male-centered world of America? As Selina tossed one of her silver bracelets, the symbol of her West Indian heritage, on to the American landscape, I fondled the bracelets I still wore and wondered what my fate would be.

Whether or not we young black women subscribed to the ideals of womanhood in this society, we could not achieve them and survive, given the racism we daily encountered. In fact, rather than being powerful matriarchs, we made "our mouths a gun" precisely because we were the least of the powerless, caught up as we were by the demands of survival for our families, demands which were sometimes in conflict with our own desires and personalities. We were often blamed for the sacrifice of self even as we were called upon to make the sacrifice. No wonder, like Silla and her women friends, we'd traditionally sought the company and solace of each other, for which we were again criticized in this Western society focused on the male/female couple.

Marshall did not resolve our dilemmas. What she did was to name them, embody their complexity in the language, the gestures of her characters, in their relationships with one another. By carefully sculpting her characters' forms within the space in which they actually moved, she illuminated the intricacy of the reality behind their apparently simple appearances. Why, for example, did so many of the black men I knew appear to be hedonistic, irresponsible ne'er-do-wells? Marshall's deft analyses of Deighton and Clive's characters exposed the rage, the aura of deep-felt impotence behind their pose. Why did so many black women appear to be hard, scheming, embittered bitches? Marshall's tender but precise probing of Silla and her women friends revealed the vulnerability of their existence, the woman-impotence and rage with which they contended. What could brown girls like Selina, like myself, *become,* given the society's view of who we were? Could we disentangle ourselves from the intersections of oppressions we moved in, or were we doomed to relive the life of Silla?

For me, *Brown Girl, Brownstones* was not just a text, it was an accurate and dynamic embodiment both of the possibilities and improbabilities of my own life. In it I as subject encountered myself as object. In illuminating so clearly, so lovingly, the mesh of my own context, Marshall provided me with a guide, a way to contemplate my own situation and gave me back the memory, the embodied history of women like myself who had preceded me. *Brown Girl, Brownstones* was not a book I read in order to write about, or to answer smart questions about. It was crucial to a deeper understanding of my own life.

When I met Paule Marshall a year after I'd read her novel, I was not surprised to hear her say that she'd written *Brown Girl, Brownstones* not so much with publication in mind as to unravel her own knots. Years later when I read an interview with Toni Morrison, in which she said that she wrote what she did because *she* needed to read it, I recalled Marshall's comment about her reason for writing *Brown Girl, Brownstones* and my response to it. If there is any one reason why I write literary criticism (and there are times when I wonder why I do), it is because of the need

I feel in African-American women writers to craft experience informed not only by their intelligence but also by *their* imagination and *my* need to respond to that crafting. African-American women interpret, create their own experience even as that experience might have been critically affected by forces outside them.

For although the *idea* that there is a shared experience between African-American women's history and the reality of African-American women's lives is now being challenged, *my* experience is that we have known both a collective life as well as individual variations that are ours and ours alone. That both these ideas are true does not mean that either is not true.

While some may say that the reason I responded to *Brown Girl, Brownstones* as I did was due to the West Indian origin I share with Paule Marshall, I did not have that same kind of connection with the characters of *The Bluest Eye,* the first novel by an African-American woman about which I wrote. I'd never been to Lorain, Ohio, nor had I migrated from the Southern United States to the Midwest. As with *Brown Girl, Brownstones,* however, reading Morrison's first novel was for me intense, emotional. That was due, of course, to Morrison's remarkable language, which sounded so much like black music, and to the themes she chose to craft.

If there is any experience black women in this hemisphere have in common it is the way our physical appearance, our bodies, have been held against us—how the norms of beauty as self-worth for a woman have systematically been denied us. When Pecola sees the disgust in the eyes of the Polish storekeeper when he tries not to look at her dark face, her kinky hair, her Negroid features, I know what she is feeling. That look is a look that was burnt into my psyche from my youth and embellished even by my own community's comments about "good" and "bad" hair. As late as the 1980s the usually astute Stevie Wonder could use as one of his lyrics in a popular song: "She's dark *but* she's pretty." Every black girl in this hemisphere *knows* the feeling of schism from watching the fly-a-way hair and true blue-eyed imitation blonde TV icons of beauty. And despite the "black is beautiful" slogans of the late sixties, one can open up any popular black magazine today and *see* the unbelievable ways in which black women are still drastically altering their physical selves.

What Morrison dramatized so beautifully in *The Bluest Eye* was the relationship between the value of woman's physical self and philosophical concepts about the society's definition of the good and the beautiful. How societies are fixated on *The Body* rather than valuing the fact that there are many bodies. How we create hierarchies of worth based on *The Body* as a manifestation of class, wealth, virtue, goodness. And because black women's bodies have been the object of systematic abuse for all of this century's history, it stands to reason that our bodies would be placed lowest in the hierarchy. Although Pecola is a tragic victim, Morrison achieves a triumph in giving her, who has never had a voice, a story in her own right, in situating her who has been the margin of the margin, at the center of a narrative. In doing that, Morrison challenged the concept of physical beauty as monolithic, and as an ideal, not only as it relates to brown girls but to all women, to her fair-skinned Maureen Peal, and to societal icons of beauty such as the Shirley Temple girl doll of her novel.

In one of her talks, Morrison said that she created Pecola because she'd known Pecolas—the ones with no voice whose stories are not acknowledged, and that she'd written *The Bluest Eye* partly because she did not recognize the black people in much of the literature of the 1960s. For many of us at that time wished to forget about the Pecolas—those who had not survived the madness of this society—and preferred to focus on the Afro-coiffed beauties of the time.

Interestingly, *The Bluest Eye* was published at the end of that decade, in 1970, a date it shares with another pivotal African-American women's novel for me—*The Third Life of Grange Copeland*. Alice Walker's first novel shares with *The Bluest Eye* a focus on types of black people hardly mentioned in the literature of the decade that preceded it. In dramatizing the life of a family of black sharecroppers that moves in time from the 1910s to the 1950s, Walker reminded us that all blacks did not live in the Northern urban ghettoes. For her rural blacks, the "violent" revolutionary rhetoric of the period had little meaning. Yet violence was very much a part of her characters' lives—not only the institutionalized violence of racism and segregation that contained them, but violence within their own families.

In the sixties of my youth, the black family was one of the most idealized icons of the movement—from the Muslim messages to the cultural nationalist images of the neo-African family. Yet I wondered, as Walker did, "why people in [black] families are often cruel to each other and how much of that cruelty was caused by outside forces such as various social injustices, segregation, unemployment, etc." That question was not an abstract one for me. I'd lived in Harlem where one could nightly hear and sometimes witness the rage and violence that black men and women, often in families, turned on each other. And as any West Indian can tell you, the Saturday night yard fights of husbands and wives were common occurrences of communal life. I did not want to remember the *internal* violence we inflicted on one another for it led so easily to racist stereotypes about the innate violence of black people. Yet in trying to forget it, not speaking about it, I ignored the destruction of so many people, particularly of women I knew.

What I responded to most personally in *The Third Life of Grange Copeland* were the many black women who were destroyed within their own families, Mem and Margaret Copeland, Josie—and how that destruction went against the monumental image of the strong black woman who could bear anything, would bear anything, an image so often invoked by black society. Because I am a black woman, that quality of indomitable strength had often been attributed to me, more accurately laid on me sometimes as an excuse as to why I should put up with, endure that which no one should have to endure. Why could we not be like other human beings who could only bear but so much? Why were we not valued? Walker's graphic portrayal of Mem Copeland reminded me that we did not always endure—that many of us were destroyed within and by our own families.

For it seemed to me in 1970 that Walker was directly asking us, black women of my generation, whether women were valued in the idealized black family that political ideologues promoted, where the black man was head of the house, the black woman, the black madonna, clearly an imitation of the Western Christian family. I knew that American society promoted power and money as the measuring sticks of manhood, attributes to which few black men had access. And that, like Grange Copeland, in believing in this conception of manhood, many black men too felt powerless and vented their frustrations on us, the only ones over whom they felt the could exert some power. In not understanding this situation, in acquiescing to that control, black women participated in the destruction of themselves and their families. I did not acknowledge what I knew was happening all around me until I read Walker's spare incisive analysis of Grange Copeland's first two lives. Walker's novel was a novel, to use one of her own titles, "for everyday use."

Walker's novel reminded me how important family history was—not the abstract history of textbooks, but the remembering those who came before us, the means they used to hold on to their humanity, and the ways in which they failed. Even as many of us in the sixties invoked images of a romantic Africa that never existed, we tended to forget those who'd recently preceded us, the sharecropping grandmother, the uncle in the sugarcane plantations, the generations who'd preceded us in this new place of pain and had something to tell us that we needed to know. Grange's conversations with her granddaughter Ruth about their family history, the land they cultivated, the dances they danced, were conversations *with me* as well, about the recent past and the wisdom embodied in it.

Like Marshall and Morrison, Walker both criticized and celebrated those who came before them, before me, and in languages that my ancestors, I myself, had helped to create, languages that were ours and affected me not only in intellectual terms but in that deep part of myself—in feeling ways. Their voice, their many voices sounded so authentically like mine, like ours, like the calypso, like jazz, like country blues, and their different uses of tone, pitch, timbre emanated from a deep part of themselves as women. They dared to remember the recent past, and show how it continued to affect the present, the history we are now making, not only through intellectual concepts but through those shared sounds, gestures, nuances that cannot be completely dissected. Like Claudia and Frieda as they listened to the grown-up women in *The Bluest Eye,* we not only hear the words but sense the "truth in timbre."

How does one respond to a language that is tonality, dance, to these voices without mutilating them and turning them into logical progressions, mere intellectual concepts? How does one shimmy back to forms that soar beyond philosophical discourse or jargon? How does one respond to the nuance, windings, shifts, the turning of the music that is this literature? That is the goal I am still seeking.

Writing and reading are not all that distinct for a writer. Both
exercises require being alert and ready for unaccountable
beauty, for the intricateness or simple elegance of the writer's
imagination, for the world that imagination evokes. Both require
being mindful of the places where imagination sabotages itself,
locks its own gates, pollutes its vision. Writing and reading
mean being aware of the writer's notions of risk and safety,
the serene achievement of, or sweaty flight for, meaning and
response-ability.[1]

I see your face, Toni Morrison, possibly the best novelist in America today, when people ask, "What does it mean that you wrote your M.A. thesis
in the early fifties, on *suicide* in the works of William Faulkner and Virginia
Woolf?"[2] Do such people want to inflict the "anxiety of influence" on you?
Or perhaps, is it that they want to be sure that your writing will be seen as a
part of the Great Western tradition? What is the purpose of securing a link
between you and William Faulkner, as Harold Bloom did in his introduction to his edition of collected essays on your work?[3] Or between you and
Virginia Woolf, as the program of this conference suggests? Why must you
be studied in relation to such writers, icons of twentieth-century European
and Anglo-American literature? Is it that as an African American woman
writer, clearly a "genius," you must have a Western white literary father and
mother—not just any white father but one such as Faulkner who, as Ralph
Ellison has put it in *Shadow and Act,* was one of the few Anglo-American
writers to fight out "the moral problem [of Negroes in America] which
was repressed after the nineteenth century."[4] Not just any white mother,
but one such as Virginia Woolf who is now clearly situated in the canon,

First published in Mark Hussey and Vara Neverow, eds., *Virginia Woolf: Emerging Perspectives* (New
York: Pace University Press, 1994), 164–77. This paper was originally written to be the featured
event at the Third Annual Conference on Virginia Woolf that took place at Lincoln University,
Jefferson City, Mo., June 10–13, 1993.

as Modernist, satisfying the twentieth-century Great Books requirement,[5] as Feminist, satisfying the needs of twentieth-century women scholars?[6] You have commented on this tendency among critics. Your own words are a cautionary preface to our project:

> My general disappointment in some of the criticism that my work has received has nothing to do with approval. It has something to do with the vocabulary used in order to describe these things. I don't like to find my books condemned or embraced as good, when that condemnation or that praise is based on criteria from other paradigms. I would much prefer that they were dismissed or embraced based on the success of their accomplishment within the culture out of which I write.[7]

I am an African American woman critic who wrote about your work before you were celebrated and who has, despite critical trends, maintained my sense of your writing as an African American woman. Please allow me to invent, as you do in your novels—in this case, a fiction about you and Virginia Woolf—for fictions can be beneficial, imaginative, even transforming. Because I know this is an invention and I worry about "notions of risk and safety," I will rely primarily on your words and Virginia's in the charting of my invention. I am inspired by your and Virginia's different related projects, layered rhythms I call them.

I see you in the early fifties, a colored graduate student when colored meant black, pacing yourself through Cornell, squinting your eye at that famous suicide point on the campus where too many students took their lives. I see you, a colored girl who, a few years before, had changed her name from Chloe (a name in America associated with blacks) to Toni (an androgynous name), because even folk at Howard U had trouble pronouncing it. I find that an instance of serendipity for Virginia Woolf used the name Chloe in her fictional representation of Mary Carmichael's novel in *A Room of One's Own,* "Chloe liked Olivia," pointing to Shakespearean characters, even as she disrupted bourgeois heterosexuality.[8]

Yes, yes, I do see you, assessing the wintry whiteness at Cornell. But you are used to whiteness. You are from Lorain, Ohio, where possibly your father, like Claudia's daddy in your first novel, *The Bluest Eye* (1970), became, in the winter, a "Wolf killer turned hawk fighter, [who] worked night and day to keep one from the door and the other from under the windowsills."[9] Yet how different this wintry whiteness is in this New England enclave of privilege. A graduate student, a black graduate student, a black female graduate student—what was there for you at Cornell? Years later, you would say about your stay there that "if [your] ancestors could go through slavery, you guessed you could get through that."[10]

I understand what you mean. For I went to one of those graduate schools in English. But at least Columbia U was in New York City, with its many colored folk, and I was there in the mid-sixties. Still I was one of a few blacks, possibly the only woman (oh no, a black female West Indian, are you from Jamaica? No—from the V.I. graduate student). So I can see you pondering wintry Cornell. What do we want in these places to which we came, so far away from home—from Lorain, Ohio, from St. Thomas, Virgin Islands, from wherever, a black wherever?

Why are you, in 1953, majoring in English. I can see your parents asking you, "What are you going to do with that degree? To study English at Cornell? You're so bright. Why don't you become a doctor, a lawyer, a Credit to Your Race?" But, on some visceral level you can't explain, you love language, the shapes of stories, ironically, an inheritance from your parents, who were great storytellers, but did not necessarily understand themselves as artists, nor what they bequeathed to you.[11]

You want—what do you desire? Chaucer, Shakespeare certainly, but where do you dwell in their words? You'd certainly heard of African American writers. You'd taken a course at Howard during your undergraduate years with Alain Locke, that elder African American critic, who'd helped to make the Harlem Renaissance, who'd seen the beginnings of the Richard Wright era.[12] You would say, in one of your interviews, that reading much of the African American literature you encountered in classrooms had left you feeling bereft, for it did not seem to be directed to you, a black person, but seemed to be addressed to an other. You felt bereft.[13] You "needed yourself" in language. How else to fulfill that need, and still be a Credit to The Race, except to go to Graduate School in English.

1953 is New Criticism at its height: the text is all. No world lies outside the text. The text has nothing to do with race or even cultural specificity. You are reading not only Chaucer and Shakespeare, those ancient venerables from Europe, but also American writers, Hawthorne, Melville, for the American academy is finally admitting American writers into the Canon. Even Faulkner, though he is still alive, might just have made it into the curriculum. Like so many of the few African Americans in Literature, you will focus on Faulkner's words, a code, even 10 years later in the 1960s for those of us who wanted to study blacks in Literature. There was no such thing as African American Literature—studying Faulkner was what they call in the music business a cover. Still, although blacks appeared to be absent from "American" literature, you sensed the ways in which the African presence in America erupted in the works of Hawthorne and Melville, a subject you would write about in 1992, in your book of criticism, *Playing in the Dark*.

But what about Virginia Woolf? Not an American who had been confronted with a black presence, whether she repressed it or not? (Although her antics in the Dreadnought Hoax, so much discussed by Woolf scholars, need to be thought about from a Black perspective.)[14] Not a venerable British ancient, but an early-twentieth-century British woman who, after all, had insisted in an essay that the reason why there was no female Shakespeare was because Shakespeare's sister did not have 500 pounds a year, or a room of her own. Mrs. Woolf did not come to a writing career easily. As was true of her times, her so educated father, Leslie Stephen, discriminated between her and her brothers. While they were allowed to go to Cambridge, she had to stay at home. But you, Toni Morrison, in the tradition of black families, precisely because you were a daughter, were encouraged to go to college. How else might you survive, without the brawn of a black man, the sentiment that circumscribed white women?[15] Like so many black women, "[you] had nothing to fall back on: not maleness, not whiteness, not ladyhood, not anything. And out of this profound desolation of [your] reality [you] may very well have invented [your]self."[16]

Unlike Virginia, you would become a mother, and for much of your adult life, a single mother, who would write, not in a room of your own, but with the interruptions of children and the jobs necessary for your and their survival, writing on scraps of paper at subway stops. You would see motherhood as liberating, as "your best self," for your children respected those parts of you that had little to do with society's demands, since they were fresh, not yet quite socialized. And through their eyes, you could see the world through an imagination not yet tainted by stereotypes.[17] So different from the Virginia you would meet in 1953 who was concerned that having children would stifle her creativity, and exacerbate her bouts of depression.[18] One of the major themes of your work would be the complexities of motherhood, the liberation and restrictions of that role for African American women: how thick that mother-love was, and yet how complex, how beautiful, even monumental that role could be. So different from Virginia who was living every day with her fecund sister, Vanessa, a source of some sibling conflict. Although from different cultures and times, you and Virginia did face problems as women writers. While Virginia had to "kill the Angel in the House,"[19] you, Toni, had to "kill the mammy in the Big House." Virginia was responding to the fact that women were not expected to write, and that when they did write, their tone "admitted that [they] were only women or protesting that [they] were as good as any man."[20] When women wrote, they were still expected to write in specific ways about specific themes—that is, in the romance genre—about love, marriage, manners. Virginia did have some women writers to whom she could refer: Jane Austen, for example, who had brought the comedy of manners to a peak of perfection. But you, Toni Morrison, could not, in 1953, in spite of society's stereotype of the black woman as a mammy, know about any African American women writers of any substance. Before the 1970s few scholars, even of African American literature, saw women as writers or even knew that there existed a strong line of African American women. In fact, it is unlikely that you read inside or outside the classroom any African American women of the past, except perhaps Gwendolyn Brooks, who won a Pulitzer in 1951. You had not read the domestic allegories, as Claudia Tate called them, in the sentimental fiction of nineteenth-century African American writers like Frances Harper and Pauline Hopkins,[21] or that great African American romance, Zora Neale Hurston's *Their Eyes Were Watching God* (1937). You could claim no maternal ancestors, although, of course, the stereotype of black women when they did appear would be as mammies in white fiction,[22] "mammies" of a sort in the black fiction of Du Bois, Wright, or Ellison.

What did Virginia mean when she used the term "woman writer"? Was she speaking about you? No wonder, in order to write as a woman, you would focus so much on the subject of mother-love, while Virginia, because of her specific cultural inheritance, had to disrupt the European script of romance imposed on women.[23] Because of your folk's history, you did not have the same need as Virginia to "kill the Angel in the House." In contrast to Virginia's deconstruction of the nuclear family, your novels usually include a three-woman-headed household recalling an older mythic familial structure. Thus, you would say in an interview that

> It seems to me that there's an enormous difference in the writing of black and white women. Black women seem able to combine the nest and the adventure. They don't see conflicts in certain areas as do white women. They are both safe harbor and ship; they are both inn and trail. We, black women, do both. We don't find these places, these roles, mutually exclusive. That's one of the differences.[24]

How to find a sentence for that difference in representing gender would become one of your abiding theoretical concerns.

But I've gone ahead of myself. What I want to know is how you got to know Virginia? Today, everyone reads her. But this is 1993, 20 years after the Virginia Woolf Fever of the 1970s.[25] And you are going to graduate school in the 1950s. Did someone just happen to mention her? Did you have one of those crazy teachers who insisted on exposing his students to odd writers? How would I know? I'm reaching across time from 1993 to you in 1953. Even in 1965, some 10 years later when I was a graduate student at Columbia, Virginia Woolf was still a suspect writer. Certainly her books were, mostly, out of print in the early fifties and were included in few college syllabi. Yet, in 1955, you completed a thesis on an aspect of her work.

Wait a minute—you are in graduate school at Cornell in 1953. That was the year the critic Erich Auerbach's classic *Mimesis: The Representation of Reality in Western Literature* was translated into English. In it he included a long critique of an out-of-print book called *To the Lighthouse* by Virginia Woolf, an upper-class British woman who killed herself. Maybe one of your teachers' discussion of Auerbach's book in one of your classes led you to Virginia Woolf's book. After all, a twentieth-century woman writer was a relatively unusual item in your curriculum.

But what did you want with the work of a woman who killed herself? You know the way Black people feel about suicide. As your narrator commented in your novel *Sula,* the black people of the Bottom feel that suicide is "beneath them" (90). Yet you were obviously intrigued by the idea of suicide, for that's what you focused on in your thesis. You'd clearly read *Mrs. Dalloway* which was published in 1925 in which Septimus Warren Smith kills himself, a victim of shell shock in World War I. So like, yet unlike Shadrack in your novel *Sula*, published some fifty years later, who too is suffering from World War I shell shock. But your Shadrack does not kill himself. Rather, "Blasted and permanently astonished by the events of 1917, he had returned to Medallion handsome but ravaged," not so much afraid of death or dying

> but the unexpectedness of both. In sorting it out, [your Shadrack] hit on the notion that if one day a year were devoted to it, everybody could get it out of the way and the rest of the year would be safe and free. In this manner he instituted National Suicide Day.[26]

Shadrack turned shell shock, and the possibility of suicide, into a rite which in turn is adopted by his community so that "they absorbed it into their thoughts, into their language, into their lives."[27] While the Bottom might not understand Shadrack's experience in the War, ironically a position which in the modern world will ultimately result in their extinction as community, they do understand the workings of rituals in staving off irrational catastrophic events like racism and war.

Like Virginia's works, your novels are bracketed by war—in your case the major wars in which America engaged—the Civil War in *Beloved,* World War I in *Sula* and *Jazz,* World War II in *The Bluest Eye* and *Sula.* None of your works is specifically about the action of war itself so much as they are about the effects of such tumult on the psyches of your respective communities. Virginia was an adult during World War I and experienced firsthand the devastating effects on her generation—on dazzling young men like Andrew Ramsay in *To the Lighthouse* (1927) whose death from an exploded shell she literally recorded in brackets.[28] You were not born until 1931, but you must have early on known about the Civil War which changed the very status of your black being. Your childhood memories must have included stories you heard about World War I, the war to end all wars, a war that ushers in a new period in African American history, the Jazz Age, when a flood of blacks migrated North to work at those jobs the soldiers had left. Your narrator in *Jazz* experienced the effects of the war quite differently from Virginia's characters, for that war is followed in America by the development of this whole new feeling among African Americans about themselves—that of experiencing the freedom and danger of The City, where one might be:

> Alone, yes, but top-notch and indestructible—like the City in 1926 when all the wars are over and there will never be another one. The people down there in the shadow are happy about that. At last, at last, everything's ahead. The smart ones say so and people listening to them and reading what they write down agree: Here comes the new. Look out. There goes the sad stuff. The bad stuff. The things-nobody-could-help stuff. The way everybody was then and there. Forget that. History is over, you all, and everything's ahead at last.[29]

How wrong your narrator is, as Virginia Woolf would come to know in 1941, when partially as a result of depression about the news of World War II, she took her life.

But perhaps Virginia Woolf's works were not included in any of your classes. Maybe you, Toni, ran into her works in an avant-garde bookstore, and someone told you that her grandfather was a staunch abolitionist who married the sister of Wilberforce, the major speaker in the House of Commons against the slave trade;[30] here, your two apparently disparate cultures and histories cross and you are not as distant from one another as it might seem. Or perhaps some crazy too-advanced graduate student, who'd been to England, talked incessantly about this innovative, what is the word, experimental woman writer—check her out—not like those too-old guys you're reading in class.

In an interview published in 1983, you made an observation:

> My sense of the novel is that it has always functioned for the class or group that wrote it. The history of the novel as a form began when there was a new class, a middle class to read it, it was an art form that they needed.[31]

You see your writing of novels as related to the needs of your group, African Americans. An English major, you knew the novel came out of an historical context, that as a form like any other that is not "natural," it was constructed in relation to the needs of a class. So you would state in that same interview that "the novel is needed by African Americans now in a way that it was not needed before," since "we don't live in places we can hear those stories anymore, parents don't sit around and tell their children those classical mythological archetypal stories that we heard years ago." In order to create a novel that would accomplish these goals, that would be not only beautiful and powerful but would also "work," you asserted, one needed to incorporate "unorthodox novelistic characteristics." You did not "regard Black literature as simply books written *by* Black people, or simply as literature written *about* Black people or simply as literature that uses a certain mode of language in which you just sort of drop g's." You saw your struggle as "the struggle to *find* that elusive but identifiable style" that is Black Art.[32]

Virginia Woolf would seem to be coming from the other side of that problem. But she too had to define what she was doing—what it meant, assured as she was of the British tradition, to be a woman writer. She saw the British tradition of novel writing as being so fixed, so focused on the conventions of her ancestral class, the class which had created it for different purposes, precisely because it was a different time, that the genre had not adapted to the catastrophic changes that her generation was experiencing in the early twentieth century. Freud's theory of the unconscious brought into question the nineteenth-century European idea of characters who had total control over their knowledge of themselves. The Great War had wiped away any sense of European cultural coherence; the Bolshevik revolution had transformed world politics. Woolf would speak for a whole generation when she asserted, in her essay "How It Strikes a Contemporary," that in contrast to the novelists of the nineteenth century, contemporary writers are beset by the dilemma that they "cannot make a world, cannot generalize. . . . They cannot tell stories, because they do not believe that stories are true."[33] Yet as Ralph Freedman pointed out in his book *The Lyrical Novel,* Virginia Woolf saw that in order to write lasting, generally accessible works, the writer needed to find appropriate avenues of escape. "[Woolf's] attempt to translate the traditional forms of the novel into organized explorations of consciousness represents her contribution to this task."[34] But her concerns were not only and precisely with the traditional forms of novel, but with what these forms meant, for a woman writer in that tradition. So, Virginia saw that women writers, as she knew them in

1925, needed to "[break] the sentence, [break] the sequence," the subject of Rachel Blau DuPlessis's study *Writing Beyond the Ending: Narrative Strategies of Twentieth Century Women Writers.*

You, Toni, would also see the need for inventing "unorthodox novelistic characteristics." Your reasons, though related to Virginia's, were also different from hers, as indicated by your differing use of the concept of "stories," your inheritance from quite different cultures. For Woolf's contemporaries, it is novelists who tell stories; the novel as a genre developed out of a particular class in Europe as a means to creating a sense of coherence. For you, however, stories refer to a racial group who have maintained coherence by passing on their communal memories, often different from those of the dominant group. While Virginia's "stories" are print and class-based, your stories, Toni, are oral and folk-based. Early-twentieth-century British novelists were stifled by the novel of manners that Jane Austen had brought to a peak of perfection, a construct of conventions that had been wiped away by the intellectual and social events of early-twentieth-century European societies. But African American writers had been stifled by the necessity to write primarily to audiences other then themselves, restricted as they were by an American master narrative. So Virginia would question the existence of a coherent narrative while you would feel "bereft" when you read literature that was supposedly about yourself.

As was true of Virginia's context in the 1920s, monumental social events in your time opened up a space for your development of "unorthodox novelistic characteristics." As a result of the African American cultural movements of the 1960s, African American culture would begin to be conceptualized as a culture by intellectuals rather than a pathology of or a deviation from Euro-American culture, as it was characterized in the works of possibly the most visible of pre-1960s African American writers, Richard Wright. Increasingly African American writers would characterize their primary audience as that of African Americans. Oral storytelling, which had been one basis of the persistence of that culture, was increasingly recognized as "legitimate" conventions capable of being refigured in a literary genre such as the novel. So while Virginia could redefine the traditional concepts of British fiction in the 1920s, you could, in the 1970s, recuperate traditional concepts of African American linguistic expression, considered "unorthodox" in the Euro-American novel.

For while you saw the novel as valuable for its ability to carry on the tradition of African American oral storytelling, that it could be "both print and oral literature," that the novel could harken back to an older communal tradition even as it was very much of the modern world, Virginia doubted the "truthfulness" of stories. While your writing is clearly concerned with expressing the communal quality of African American life, its myths, beliefs, dreams, Virginia wondered about the idea of a communal narrative.

Yet, although your and Virginia's views of the novel might seem to be worlds apart, both of your writings are riveted on the relationship between the inner life of your characters and the world within which they find themselves, the object in fact of their consciousness. In this regard, I remember the talk you gave at UC Berkeley about your novel *Beloved* in 1987, when it had just been published. You stressed that one of your interests in writing it was that much of what had been written about American slavery ignored, repressed the inner lives of slaves, sometimes for very good reasons, such as the fact that nineteenth-century African American writers had to be primarily concerned with the *institution* of slavery, with the abolishment of that institution, a concern which often precluded the exploration of their characters' psyches. The slave's narrative used a narrative formula based on the Biblical story of the Fall and the Resurrection to engage the largely Christian white audience. Slave narrators had to hold back memories which might alienate their white readers.[35] But you were not so much interested in what happened: you already knew the Margaret Garner story. In fact, in every one of your novels, the reader knows what has happened on practically the first page. What you wanted to do was to fill those silences and to involve yourself and the reader in such a way as to feel the experience, both viscerally and as an idea.

As Virginia's works so amply demonstrate, memory is a central aspect of the inner life, one means by which we interpret the present as well as remember the past. How does one express that inner life without completely losing sense of the world in which characters in a novel must move, that is, the specificities of time and place. Virginia solved that tension between the inner and the outer life in the construction of what Ralph Freedman calls "formal monologues," where psychological drama and common speech are replaced by lyrical drama and inner speech."[36] Unlike the stream-of-consciousness technique of writers such as Joyce, which Woolf criticized as being "too centred in a self which in spite of its tremor of susceptibility, never embraces or creates what is outside or beyond,"[37] her monologues were carefully crafted to not only reveal the quality of that particular character's mind, but also his or her ways of perceiving the world. In *Mrs. Dalloway*, we are in the minds of Clarissa Dalloway, Septimus Smith, Mr. Dalloway, Peter Walsh, importantly during one day, a day framed by the tolling of Big Ben, clearly situating us in high-society London. Even as the reader is experiencing reality in terms of the characters' inner lives, we are anchored in some time and place.

As a reader of Virginia Woolf, you, Toni, were clearly alert to the world evoked by her imagination. As a writer, you were confronted with some of the same issues of narrative technique with which she had to contend. In your first novel, *The Bluest Eye*, you would use soliloquies as she had, in order to capture the inner lives of your characters. However, you had to deal with an additional problem, for readers were not used to focusing on the inner lives of black characters. Racism, after all, affected the social lives of African Americans in such a way that the external social world had taken precedence over the inner lives of characters. How stunned I was when I first read Pauline Breedlove's soliloquy in *The Bluest Eye*, possibly the first evocation of a black domestic's inner voice. Although the omniscient narrator focused on Pauline's social situation, her inner voice allows the reader to feel her specific dreams, her intense use of images of color, her individual way of perceiving the world in images of color even as it is rooted in her rural Southern upbringing. You established for her a love of order, a sense of design which would have served her well, if she had had the opportunity to become an artist. It was from the African tradition of storytelling, where playing with images is as important as it is in a Woolf novel, that Pauline acquired her voice.

Perhaps your most characteristic transformation of the narrator is your different use of a chorus, a community that includes the reader, in every one of your novels, since as you have said, "[your] audience is always the people in the book [you're] writing at the time."[38] So, there's the choral "I" narrator of *The Bluest Eye*, "the town functioning as a character in *Sula*," "the neighborhood and the community that responds in the two parts of town in *Song of Solomon*," "all of nature thinking and feeling and watching and responding to the action going on in *Tar Baby*,"[39] the chorus of the community, living and dead, in *Beloved*, the City in *Jazz*. In this, your most recent novel, your unnamed narrator admits that she/he does not know everything about the characters in much the same way we do not know everything about someone by looking at a photograph, an aesthetic form that emerged in the 1920s, which seems to mimic life even as it freezes it:

> When I see them now they are not sepia, still, losing their edges to the light of a future afternoon. Caught midway between was and must be. For me they are real. Sharply in focus and clicking.[40]

In her last novels, Virginia too began to use the concept of the chorus, especially in her last work, *Between the Acts*, in which she devises what Rachel DuPlessis calls "a communal protagonist," "where no character in the plot stands above any other."[41] There are real differences between your respective uses of the chorus, however, for while both of you are insisting that there is a communal protagonist, your novels, Toni, still insist upon the tension between individuals, the experimental ones and their relationship to the community, to which, in your work, they return, as a means of testing out the extent difference is allowed, and might even triumph. Although you used soliloquy to express the inner voice, a choral note to express community, both social and mythic, you also needed an omniscient narrator in much of your work, for unlike Virginia, you were not usually writing about characters in the present. Part of your task had to be a remapping of the historical terrain for blacks, a terrain that had been previously charted by a master narrative from the outside, rather than from the inside of their experiences, a history that even African American communities might have begun to forget, or might not want to remember. So, for example, although *The Bluest Eye* is set in 1941, so that the reader might understand Pauline and Cholly Breedlove you had to move back in time to the 1920s of their Southern youth. Even *Tar Baby,* your novel set primarily in the present, draws power from the mythic past of the island on which it is set. As critic Wahneema Lubiano has said about your work, because it "remaps the terrain of African American cultural and social history and allows for a community of the imagination, it interrupts the ideology that produces the kind of world we inhabit."[42]

But while your writing remaps American history, it is not historical in the usual sense of that word; linear progression is not its goal, for as you have so beautifully captured in your rendition of the inner voices of your characters, whatever we consider reality to be, we do not experience it either individually or communally as a march of years. Rather, there is both inner time and outer time. Virginia expressed a similar sentiment, when in her essay "Modern Fiction" she critiqued the thirty-two perfectly balanced chapters of the Victorian novel which emphasized the material world as the real world: "Is life like this? For life is not a series of gig-lamps symmetrically arranged; but a luminous halo, a semi-transparent envelope surrounding us from the beginning of consciousness to the end." Virginia experimented with the formal monologue, as a way of fusing inner and outer time, honing it from novel to novel until in *The Waves* (1931) no narrator intrudes, and the juxtaposition of the characters' inner voices produces its own design of the interrelatedness and separateness of the characters, the waves of lives being the intersections of the private inner voice, the continuity of the seasons with their mythic significance, the traditions and shifts of society. What she wanted to do in *The Waves* was:

> to saturate every atom, . . . to eliminate all waste, deadness, superfluity: to give the moment whole; whatever it includes. Say that the moment is a combination of thought; sensation; the voice of the sea.[43]

In *The Waves,* Virginia eliminated the narrator, the external movement of the narrative being delineated by her juxtaposition of her characters' formal monologues. In contrast, Toni, you wanted:

> to make the story appear oral, meandering, effortless, spoken—to have the reader *feel* the narrator without *identifying* that narrator or hearing him or her knock about, and to have the reader work *with* the author in the construction of the book. . . . What is left out is as important as what is there.[44]

In your work, as in Virginia's, inner time is always transforming outer time through memory. But since memory is not only individual, but merges with others to create a communal memory, outer time also transforms inner time. It is that reciprocity between the individual inner and the communal outer which your work seeks. The folk's time, however, is not mechanical time, the march of years, which your chapter titles in *Sula* mock, but time, as it marks an event in human society but also in Nature, which for you includes the folk, as much as it means the seasons. The mythic quality of your worlds seems to be in opposition to many people's concept of human history, when in fact history and myth have always been related, myth being a central part of any people's history, history itself creating myth, time and timelessness in dialogue. In your work there is a deep relationship between your characters' belief system and their view of Nature. Thus Baby Suggs preaches in "the Clearing," Eva in *Sula* can read the signs of Nature. And in *Song of Solomon,* Milkman learns about,

> what there was before language. Before things were written down. Language in the time when men and animals did talk to one another . . .[45]

and that he has an ancestor who can fly.

Nature in its many aspects is central to your work, I believe, because Nature is one constant, in time and space, for all human societies. As *The Bluest Eye* is structurally arranged in terms of the seasons, Nature responds to the action in *Tar Baby;* Sethe has got a "chokeberry tree" inscribed upon her back. Virginia too felt that deep connection with Nature, that it is a crucial element of that "luminous halo" and is inside ourselves, even as it appears to be outside, thus her desire to fuse "thought, sensation, the sea."

But Myth, Toni, in your work means not only a recognition of the power of primal natural forces, but also the presence of an ancestor. For African Americans, who were torn from their homeland, and for whom migrations have been a constant, the ancestor rather than a particular homeland is the ground of wisdom, the timeless presence. Art, for you, becomes one means by which that ancestor can be invoked. How does Virginia relate to an ancestor figure? Her evocation in *A Room of One's Own* of her father's favorite poet, Milton, critiques that male lineage. Instead she turns to the aunt who willed her money: "My aunt's legacy unveiled the sky to me, and substituted for the large and imposing figure of a gentleman which Milton recommended for my perpetual adoration, a view of the open sky,"[46] a space within which she might create another lineage.[47]

Toni, you have described your own works in terms of rhythmic shapes: *Sula* as a spiral, for example; *Song of Solomon* as "a train picking up speed," for "every life to [you] has a rhythm, a shape" whose "contours you can't see all at once."[48] Virginia wanted to capture "the moment," which reveals that life; you want to revel in the rhythm of that life. Related temperaments yet different in their approach to language and to the imagination. You see the need "to clean the language up and give words back their original meaning," so that "the language does not sweat." In an interview, you set a new goal for yourself—to write novels in which you do not have to indicate that your characters are black or white, by the use of modifiers—but that the reader knows because of the context, your use of language. What, you wondered, would that mean for you as a writer?

Like Virginia, writing novels for you is decidedly an experimental act, a creative one—so that you are always pushing against what you have already learned to do. Increasingly, as in the prose poems of *Beloved*, the painterly prose of the narrator's observations in *Jazz*, your language is symbolic, just as Virginia's language in her last works became more formal, more like poetic drama.

Novelists, you have said, are always influenced by the moral currents of their world. It is not surprising then, because you and Virginia come from different cultural cosmologies, that the moral questions you pose in your work are somewhat different, even as women. While you both clearly acknowledge the imagination as central to your temperament, while you have used some similar narrative strategies, what strikes me as your major difference is your relationship to the idea of love in your novels. You have so many times said that love is your major theme: life is poor, uninteresting, without being able to love somebody; but love is also a dilemma for human beings because like the elements of nature it can run so quickly to excess. All of your novels deal with that dilemma. Virginia, on the other hand, was concerned that women were expected to write about love, love here meaning romantic love; she insisted that women also wanted poetry, dreams, imagination. Without question, so do you, though in a different context. You have said that you "are not interested in indulging [your]self in some private, closed exercise of [your] imagination that fulfills only the obligation of [your] personal dreams—which is to say yes, the work must be political."[49] Virginia, I believe, would have held to that same sentiment, while questioning whether the imagination can be anything but private.

Perhaps, Toni, because you are an African American woman writing in the later part of the twentieth century you can now write about expanded definitions of love, rooted in a tradition of a people who, from their beginnings in this country, have been denied the right to express love, and thus have invented their particular strategies to hold onto it. In your world, love is not so much romance as it is primal "risk," and "freedom," incapable of being completely contained.

In keeping with your open endings of your novels, I hesitate to bring any resolution to my invention. For your work is not yet finished, while Virginia's is there for you to contemplate. In being aware of her notions of "risk and safety" you may well have expanded your own—creating layered rhythms in your fiction, that is both your own personal voice and that of the folk's. I see you, Toni, continuing to write and read, read and write in layered rhythms.

11 There It Is: The Poetry
of Jayne Cortez (1986)

Review of *Coagulations: New and Selected Poems*
by Jayne Cortez

Last spring, when students at the University of California, Berkeley, asked me to speak at a rally opposing the University's investments in South Africa, I chose, without hesitation, to read Jayne Cortez's "For the Brave Young Students in Soweto." The poem became a mainstay in that movement's activities. When Oakland High School students asked me to comment on contemporary world politics, I read to them Cortez's "There It Is," a succinct, powerful analysis of our situation. When a rather hostile group of "hip" black men asked me to speak about "black feminism," I responded with Cortez's haunting "If the Drum Is a Woman." And when I was asked by my students to choose a poem which revels in the sound and rhythm of words, I picked Jayne Cortez's "You Know." Their laughter was knowledge.

Jayne Cortez's poetry has been, for many years, at the cutting edge of black sound—an intense cacophony of experience, commentary, irony, music. Since 1969, she has published five volumes of poetry. When I heard her read from her first volume—"Pissstained Stairs and the Monkey Man's Wares," I scoured bookstores for copies and yearned for a rendition of Cortez reading her jazz poetry. Other readers must have felt the same way. In 1975, accompanied by jazz musicians, Cortez put out an album, "Celebrations and Solitudes." And in 1980 she recorded "Unsubmissive Blues." Now her most recent recording, "There It Is," includes selections from her latest publication, *Coagulations: New and Selected Poems*.

Despite the existence of many fine black women poets, the publication in America of a selected edition of their poems is still a rarity. There are but

First published in *Callaloo* 26 (Winter 1986): 235–39.

a few (Gwendolyn Brooks, June Jordan, Audre Lorde come to mind) who have had the opportunity to put together such an edition. These volumes are especially valuable because they give readers an opportunity to see the continuity and variety of a poet's work even as they give the poet the opportunity to choose poems as examples of that continuity and variety. The publication of *Coagulations,* then, is an important event, for it includes not only new poems but selections from three of Cortez's earlier volumes: *Scarifications* (1973), *Mouth on Paper* (1977), and her last volume *Firespitter* (1982). The result is a powerful collection which charts Cortez's development and merges the qualities of sharp political insight, strong imagery, and intense rhythmic patterning for which she is known. The collection is further intensified by Mel Edward's drawings which complement the energy and insights of Cortez's poetry.

The poems from *Scarifications* are not for the fainthearted. Insisting that we experience our present, where we are, and what is happening to us, they abound with images of New York City where Cortez now lives. Through her precise imagery, the city becomes a living person with "tobacco teeth," "marquees of false nipples," a person "that imitate[s] no one." These poems talk of harsh smells; yet, there is always the miracle of art, of music, song and dance. In "Tapping," Baby Lawrence the tap dancer tells us that "when i dance my spine in a slouch / slur my lyrics with a heel slide / arch these insteps in a free time . . . i am gonna pay my dues / i am gonna 1 2 3 / and let the people in the apple / go hmmp hmmmmp hmmmmmp." Those *m*'s rescue us from the despair that could send us over the edge.

While the poems from *Scarifications* are just that—scarifications, the selections from *Mouth on Paper* are more explicitly political. Included from that volume is one of Cortez's finest poems, "For the Brave Young Students in Soweto," a poem which succinctly dramatizes the connection between apartheid South Africa, racist U.S. and the greedy countries of the West while honoring the courageous students of the world. Built around a refrain, "Soweto, when I hear your name," the poem looks at and smells the terrors of racism and greed visited upon the peoples of the Third World. The last lines are not only a battle cry but a powerful cry of hope:

> Soweto i tell you Soweto
> When i see you standing up like this
> i think about all the forces in the world
> confronted by the terrifying rhythm of young
> students
> and the revelation that it won't be long now
> before everything
> in this world changes

Like this poem, many of Cortez's pieces inform us about the realities of our world, about facts so many of us would prefer to ignore, lest we be forced to respond. "For the Poets," another poem from *Mouth on Paper,* responds to the senseless killing of poets Christopher Okigbo and Henry Dumas, "mugged" by police, while "Give Me the Red on the Black of the Bullet" reminds us that 14-year-old Claude Riece, Jr., was "shot in the back of his head/shot by a police officer/shot for being black." Cortez refuses to ignore the terrors that afflict us; but what distinguishes her sound is the way she makes us respond, through her strong rhythmic patterns. "For the Brave Young Students in Soweto" uses a refrain that always brings us back to the horrors of life in Soweto. And "For the Poets" repeats the sound "ah" as Cortez sounds a ritual chant so much a part of human history:

> i need spirits ah i need ankles ah i need
> hurricanes ah . . .
> to make a delta praise for the poets ah

This quality of using sound and silence to create a rhythm to which we must respond is a strong element of Cortez's work; she practices the *first* meaning of poetry—words as music. Her poetry is a musical blending of words, whether she is informing us of the greedy men that are destroying our lives, our world, or whether she is capturing the feeling of "the people" who speak the *"you know* language." In "You Know," a marvelously humorous poem from *Mouth on Paper,* Cortez celebrates those folks who cannot utter a phrase without following it with *you know.* Her rendition of this language reminds us how a phrase like "you know" gives a certain rhythm to speech, even as it becomes contagious, even addictive:

> You Know
>   I sure would like to write a blues
> you know
>   a nice long blues
> you know
>   a good feeling piece to my writing hand
> you know.

Such a skillful use of rhythm is particularly strong in Cortez's last published collection, *Firespitter.* Inspired by the black poets and artists who traveled to Lagos for FESTAC, the "festival of firespitters," Cortez celebrates these warriors. Like her previous work, this volume is international in scope: she connects the art, experience and resistance of people of color all over the world. She evokes the "bull roarer tongue" of the Red Pepper Poet, Leon Dumas; she connects the oppression of the Crow and the Sioux with the blacks in South Africa; she celebrates the resistance and power of Afro-Cuban musician, Chano Pozo. Cortez has traveled all over the world reading her poetry; and in the process, she has forged those connections in her work that help us see how our histories, whether we live in Chile, Harlem, or Nigeria, are related. The result is a poetry as wide in its scope as it is compelling in its craft.

One of the poems in *Firespitter* is a fine example of Jayne Cortez's ability to use a musical tradition in poetry. The poem *is* the sound of Chano Pozo even as it recalls Cortez's experience of hearing him play: "Is there anyone finer today olé okay / Oye I say / I see Chano Pozo / Chano Pozo from Havana Cuba." The poem skillfully varies intonations of the word *fine,* a word which blacks and Latin Americans use in so many ways and with so many inflections. *And* the poem puts into words the power of music, which we all experience but find difficult to articulate:

> Oye
> I'm in the presence of ancestor
> > Chano Pozo
> Chano connector of two worlds
> You go and celebrate again with
> the compañeros in Santiago
> > and tell us about it
> you go to the spirit house of Antonio Maceo
> and tell us about it

Like any fine musician, Cortez has many styles, and yet a sound that is hers alone. Not only can she capture the Afro-Cuban drum rhythms of Chano Pozo; she can rivet us with a simple (yet complex) question. In "Rape," she asks, "What was Inez supposed to do for / the man who declared war on her body." Her precise naming of rape as a declaration of war on a woman's body reminds us why we also talk of countries being raped: that rape of a woman is as evil an act as an attack on one's country. Her answer is as precise as her question: "She stood with a rifle in her hand / doing what a defense department would do in times of war." It is that clarity about what *is* really happening, that ability to name the truth beyond the muddle of propaganda, that characterizes Cortez's poetry. In "There It Is," one of her most ironic, yet direct poems, Cortez tells us:

> My friend
> they don't care
> if you're an individualist
> a leftist   a rightist
> a shithead   or a snake

They will try to exploit you
absorb you   confine you
disconnect you   isolate you
or kill you

In "Stockpiling," she directly names the greatest terror of them all, "the
nuclear bleach of reality," "the final stockpile of flesh dancing in / the terrible whooping cough of the wind."

But Cortez does not only name the terrors; she also celebrates the means
by which we survive and suggests ways to change our world in her poems
about art, music, song, poetry. In "Rose Solitude" she declares: "i cover
the hand of Duke who like Satchmo / like Nat (King) Cole will never die /
because love they say / never dies." And in "There It Is" she postulates:

And if we don't fight
if we don't resist
if we don't organize and angry and
get the power to control our own lives
Then . . .

There are of course those who do just that. Cortez's body of work is
punctuated with praise songs for those who do resist, organize, unify.
Among her new poems in *Coagulations* are tributes to Michael Smith, the
Jamaican poet-prophet who was killed by "treacherous Black brothers,"
as well as to "Solomon Mehlanga Freedom Fighter from Mamelodi" who
"Became immune / to the compounds used to separate people." As always,
Cortez takes us back to the source of our energy, to the rhythms within us
that can make us, like Chano Pozo, as powerful as "atomic heat." In "Tell
Me," the last poem of *Coagulations,* she implores: "Tell me you really intend
to go forward / Tell me / Tell me / Tell me."

It is eminently clear from her selected edition that Jayne Cortez is a blatantly political poet—that her work intends to help us identify those who
control our lives and the devastating effects such control has on our lives,
and she rouses us to do something about it. As a result, the stories she has
to tell, the images she evokes, are not often pretty; yet her skill with words
and rhythm demands that we listen. When a student at Berkeley asked
her if people who organized readings did not try to *censure* her work, she
replied that people knew what they were going to get when they invite her
to read—that her point of view on the state of the world is clear. Like the
poets and warriors whose words and actions it celebrates, Jayne Cortez's
Coagulations is a work of resistance. So There It Is.

**Review of *Living by the Word: Selected Writings, 1973–1987*
by Alice Walker**

By now, *Living by the Word* has been reviewed in many mainstream journals and newspapers. But many readers may have been misled, as I was, by most reviewers' characterizations of this book. Almost invariably they have read it as a collection of traditional essays and compared it, usually unfavorably, to Walker's 1983 collection of nonfiction, *In Search of Our Mothers' Gardens: Womanist Prose;* but in fact, I think that Walker's careful selection of the writing for *Living by the Word* is a clear signal that she is experimenting with a form she has not used before.

Experimentation is not new for Walker. Every one of her books is both formally connected to, yet distinctly different from, her previous work; in her work, form cannot be separated from meaning. *Living by the Word* is an arrangement of dreams, journal entries, her "letters" to herself, her ancestors, blood and spiritual kin, as well as her responses to her readers and critics. Above all, it is a personal record of her journey, as she says in the book's preface, "to find [her] old planet," and "to coconspire (breathe together) with it."

Although many of the pieces in *Living by the Word* have been previously published, when arranged as they are in this volume each of them does not seem so much a finished product as writing in process. What Walker gives us is an opportunity to enter into the way she lives with words, how words live and breathe for her, and how, for her, writing is a living process rather than primarily the production of artifacts for publication. Walker's writings are a continuing whole; for her, writing is a healing process as well as a communing with various audiences, human and non-human, in

First published in *The Women's Review of Books* 6, no. 5 (February 1989): 9–10.

the past as well as the present. She often explores apparently similar ideas, feelings, images, in various genres; her use of one form, say the essay, is sometimes complementary, in dialogue, with a poem or short story she'd previously written. It is as if she is an orchestral composer who uses different instruments and arrangements to get inside the nuances of an apparently simple sound.

Living by the Word, Walker's fourteenth book, cannot be appreciated, *heard,* unless it is set in the context of all of her works. Her meditation on her father in the essay "Father" recalls, sometimes revises, poems about him published in *Once* (1968), her first collection of poetry, as well as in *Horses Make a Landscape Look More Beautiful* (1984), her most recent. A reminiscence, "The Old Artist: Notes on Mr. Sweet," evokes the personal context for her first published story, "To Hell With Dying" (1967) which has just been released as a beautifully illustrated children's book. "Coming In from the Cold," named after one of Bob Marley's songs, is a sensual analysis (the best I've read by anyone) of Celie's language in *The Color Purple,* while Walker's recounting of her visit to Bob Marley's grave in "Journey to Nine Miles," reminds us of her previously published 1975 essay, "Looking for Zora."

Even the form of *Living by the Word* resonates with other Walker works — the arrangement of short stories, many at different stages of development, in *You Can't Keep a Good Woman Down* (1981), the use of short units to create different kinds of quilts, a unique characteristic of her three novels. And in many ways Walker's most recent publication complements *The Color Purple,* for in *Living by the Word* she writes *her* letter to God — to her ancestors, to the trees, rocks, animals, to her sisters and brothers, to all that is the universe she'd so succinctly symbolized by the image of the color purple.

Seeing connections among Walker's many works is not merely formal counting, it is integral to what she calls "living by the word." To live by the word is to be on a continuing journey, exploring oneself as a part of the universe, the universe as part of oneself where one knows "everything is only a human being." Perhaps because so many of us tend to look at writing primarily as an intellectual product rather than as a spiritual journey, it is not surprising that some reviewers devalued Walker's exposing of work not yet finished, still evolving.

The *New York Times* reviewer was particularly annoyed by her inclusion of the apparently unfinished memoir, "The Dummy in the Window," whose title refers to the dummy of an "elderly kindly cottony-haired darkie" that was featured for many years in the window of her hometown's Uncle Remus restaurant. Walker begins "The Dummy in the Window" with the explanation that she was asked to write an essay on folklore and what it meant to her writing; but because her hometown, Eatonton, was also the home of Joel Chandler Harris, author of the Uncle Remus stories, it was too painful for her to write. Instead she shares with us her notes, her research—not the completed essay. And yet it is the piece's unfinished quality that is so meaningful to me. From such sharing have come the narratives of ex-slaves—of Linda Brent, for example, who could write only that which she could bear to remember, to expose, to craft. It is from this apparent contradiction of not being able to *bear* one's "subject matter" that we reach for understanding and renew the word, even history—for example, most recently, Sethe's path to rememory in Toni Morrison's *Beloved.*

While there are unfinished pieces in *Living,* the work is coherent in its tone and meaning. Walker first speaks to us with a journal entry: "The universe sends me fabulous dreams." By beginning with that most private of experiences, the dream, she sets the tone of the intimate, which is the particular sound of this book. And by sharing with us a dream in which she asks a two-headed woman whether the world will survive and what "I/we could/should do," Walker announces the theme that unites the various pieces of *Living:* that the universe responds to what we do and how we do it.

Punctuating her more "public" writing—speeches, remembrances, essays, letters, analyses—"private" journal entries appear throughout the book as conversations with the universe. Even as she records her mundane activities ("I've put a wash in the machine which shakes the whole house"), Walker tells the universe: "There is no doubt in my mind that I am blessed. That you are present in the cosmos and in me and that we are breathing together—conspiracy." Sometimes the entries indicate the attention she pays to even the smallest of living things: "I went to the outhouse where a family of wasps now live." Sometimes her comments are about the writing she is doing:

August 30, 1984
Have finished a typed draft of the "Coming In from the Cold" essay . . . I'm sure I'll want to work on the essay before delivering it at the Writers Union meeting. But I'm *grateful* that it came at all. I've felt so empty, so much as if I might just dive off forever into my hollyhocks.[1]

Dry moments are noted as well as lovely ones: "Just be, Alice. Being is sufficient. Being is All. The cheerful sunny self you are missing will return as it always does, but only *being* will bring it back." There are entries about dreams she's had of her ancestors ("Last night I had the most extraordinary, beautiful and exquisite dream about myself and Langston Hughes"); but we also hear about public events and how they are related to the personal:

The morning of the demonstration [at the Concord Naval Weapons Station] I dress in jeans, sneakers, sunglasses and an old felt hat, and I carry with me a sweet-faced black doll with crisp, shiny hair. I've named her Windela after a newborn niece of the same name I have not yet seen, and because I want to symbolize the connection I feel to Winnie and Nelson Mandela and the common awareness that it is up to those of us who are adults to leave to all children a habitable planet.[2]

Throughout *Living* Walker demonstrates how her "private" and "public" life nourish each other. Although we can assume that this was true of other African-American women writers, we have few of their written journals, partly because they had to code their writings so as not to offend their audiences, or give critics ammunition against them. For many years, the journal of the nineteenth-century abolitionist Charlotte Forten was the only known published journal of an African-American woman. As I read *Living*, I thought constantly of the many black women writers, Phillis Wheatley, Zora Neale Hurston certainly, Nella Larsen perhaps, who'd lived, I believe, by the word, but whose "personal" journals we do not have.

Having read Alice Dunbar-Nelson's diaries which Gloria Hull had the good fortune to find and the good sense to publish, I know that the journal has also been *our* form. Even more, I am struck by Dunbar-Nelson's concern about World War I and her pacifism — issues not specifically about racism and sexism, issues that we supposedly are not to be concerned about. And yet we have always been attuned to the universe and the events that affect it (us) precisely because of our historical, spiritual journeys. So Alice Walker's journals, which record her active participation, her thinking about our most contemporary, live dilemmas, are exhilarating to me, as a vivid sign that black women's writing is as wide as the world is wide.

Walker writes about a variety of subjects that are often labeled topical: animal rights, Our War in Central America, Apartheid, Dessie Woods, homosexuality, vegetarianism. For those who associate African-American women's writing with specifically gender or race issues, or for those who define the political as antithetical to the spiritual, some of these essays may be startling. Has Walker abandoned the political stance she is known for? In writing about animal rights or vegetarianism, has she succumbed to the California New Age diversions of the eighties? What I think is remarkable about these essays is the way she shows that "political" struggle is firmly rooted in the honoring and appreciation of life — a theme some readers may recall as being the focal one in her second novel, *Meridian*.

In heightening through the word the aliveness of all that *is* our planet, Walker reminds us how we supposedly superior human beings objectify and dismiss as unalive that which we do not see as a part of ourselves. The essay "Am I Blue?" is not an abstract analysis of the pros and cons of animal rights; it is a thoughtful story about what Walker learns from the white horse Blue whom she comes to know because he is forced to live separated from his mate in the meadow outside her house. In feeling Blue as alive, as like her, she remembers that black people during slavery were perceived as "animals" and therefore not really alive and capable of feeling:

> I almost laughed (I felt too sad to cry) to think there are people who do not know that animals suffer. People like me who have forgotten, and daily forget, all that animals try to tell us. "Everything you do to us will happen to you; we are your teachers, as you are ours. We are one lesson" is essentially it, I think. There are those who never once have even considered animals' rights: those who have been taught that animals actually want to be used and abused by us, as small children "love" to be frightened, or women "love" to be mutilated and raped. . . . They are the great-grandchildren of those who honestly thought, because someone taught them this: "Women can't think," and "niggers can't faint."[3]

Personal experience *is* connected to one's perception of "issues"; echoing Martin Luther King Jr.'s words, "as long as the Earth is enslaved, none of us are free." That view of life is integral to other pieces in the book, in which Walker traces her interconnectedness with her physical and spiritual family: her father in "Father"; Dessie Woods in "Trying to See My Sister"; the Indian leader Bill Wahpepah in "My Big Brother Bill"; homospirituals in "All the Bearded Irises of Life."

She sounds that chord, as well, in her responses to her readers and critics. In one essay, "In the Closet of the Soul," she answers a critic who had objected to Walker's claiming (in the introductory poem to *Horses Make a Landscape Look More Beautiful*) all that is a part of her—her white Anglo-Irish great-great-grandfather as well as her "part" Cherokee great-grandmother—by quoting the rest of the poem he'd neglected to mention: "Rest in Peace./In me/the meaning of your lives/is still/unfolding."

"The Universe Responds," the last piece in *Living by the Word*, circles back to the beginning of her journey even as Walker has moved beyond that point. There she gives her answer to the question she'd asked the two-headed woman in the dream at the beginning of the book: Will the world survive? "What you ask of the universe it gives"; "Peace will come wherever it is sincerely invited." In sharing with us her journey, Walker invites us to pay attention to our own.

13   Epic Achievement (1991)

Review of *Thereafter Johnnie* by Carolivia Herron

I am dazzled, literally, by the intense light of Carolivia Herron's *Thereafter Johnnie,* a lyric poem in its orchestration of image and song, as well as a novel about the decline of a contemporary middle-class African American family. It is an epic in its contrapuntal use of ancient cultural myths (which are, whether we know it or not, the bases of our deepest-held assumptions), even as its story is grounded in contemporary Washington, D.C. I am dazzled, yes, yet profoundly disturbed, as I am sure its author intended, by this work's prefiguring of the future.

This is Carolivia Herron's first novel and it is obvious that she is a writer to be reckoned with. Its dust jacket endorsements from eminents Carlos Fuentes, Gloria Naylor, and Henry Louis Gates are striking in the claims they make for the novel. Fuentes emphasizes in it a "tragic vision" virtually unique in United States literature. Naylor calls it "a book for the ages." Gates notes its "formal intricacy" and canonizes Herron "a fourth Fury." Yet neither these superlative assessments nor the publisher's succinct jacket blurb tries to or can prepare us for this modern-day *Odyssey.*

For the narrative design of *Thereafter Johnnie* is a labyrinth that intentionally displaces and continually rearranges time and event so that our notions of clearly defined categories — fact/fairy tale, science/poetry, past/present/future, religion/sexuality, family/race/nation — are challenged. Director of the Center for the Study of Comparative Epics at Harvard University, Herron brings to this work prodigious scholarship; yet this novel, first and foremost, is an extraordinary act of the imagination, of passion. To discuss it with those who have not read it seems almost a violation. As reviewer,

First published in *The Women's Review of Books* 9, no. 1 (October 1991): 6–7.

I will try to do just that without, I hope, reducing it to literary formalism, shallow politics, or mere entertainment.

Thereafter Johnnie spans seventy years (from the 1920s to the 90s), but ripples back to slavery and forward into the future, a new millennium. At the book's center is the Snowdon family: its "King of Hearts," John Christopher, a successful African American heart surgeon in Washington, D.C., and his queen, Camille, a light-skinned green-eyed cultivator of roses. In this contemporary "fairy tale" they have three daughters: the dark-skinned Cynthia Jane, a poet who in the course of the novel will become a nun and the repository of the family's linear history; the pet, Patricia the patrician, who studies classical languages and obsessively loves/hates her father; and Eva, the light-skinned woman-loving prophet who is an innocent.

The novel swirls around two traumatic events which occur almost simultaneously. Eva is raped by a white bum, an "avenging angel," on the same night that John Christopher first has sex with his daughter Patricia. The result of the incestuous mating is the conception of Johnnie, a black girl with eyes so blue they appear white. At the novel's beginning Johnnie has become a "light" in Washington, now abandoned by blacks and in the midst of a racial domestic war:

> This is the story. Sing of how it happened. I sing of how it happened.
> Because now she is a light and cannot die. Johnnie. Who never wanted immortality. Alone in the city, alive, who wanted to die forever, who wanted without a dream to sleep forever, condemned to eternal life.[1]

We, the readers, do not know who is singing this epic ballad until it is almost completed. In mythic stories, origins cannot be separated from "what is." *Thereafter Johnnie* is composed of twenty-four parts like Homer's *Odyssey* and like it demonstrates that *sex* is *religion* is *nation,* that, to use a Freudian term, "family romance" is a nation's soul. In the United States that soul originated in bloody sexual violence. Johnnie, the black-skinned, white-eyed maiden who is nursing her wounded father/grandfather, tells Potomac, a Black-Indian woman, why the land is parched:

> This is my father who is the union of 2 brothers who came to America from Europe and Africa. They fought in the Atlantic Ocean, striving and striding Westward through the sea to America until their wrestling bodies became one. Thus they came to the Potomac River basin where by a grave mischance this mourner, my father, fell into a nightmare and cannot awaken, and all this beautiful land and the village that surrounds the basin has fallen by enchantment into a desert.[2]

Because of the nature of its beginning, a great curse descends upon this house/nation: "The females shall be raped and the males shall be murdered." As in the stories of the old gods (Zeus, Jehovah), incest is central to this contemporary family/national romance.

What feminists may find disturbing in this novel is not the theme of incest *per se*. Herron figures different forms of incest, sister/sister, father/daughter, almost as emblems of different mythic structures—one is tempted to say, of a matriarchal vs. patriarchal worldview. But she does not present father/daughter incest, as Alice Walker does in *The Color Purple*, as a powerful father-figure's brutal assault upon a helpless girl-child, or as Toni Morrison does in *The Bluest Eye*, as a powerless father's sense that sexual love is all he can give his wounded daughter. In *Thereafter Johnnie* both father and daughter seduce each other, so that it is difficult to distinguish between "who was the possessor, and who was the possessed." And Herron writes of their sexual intercourse in language so erotic it approaches the divine.

Crucial to father/daughter incest in this novel is not only the father's concept of himself as scientist/god but the daughter/scholar's sense of who she is. "Patricia" means literally "of the father," "of the nation." A scholar of classical languages and myth, she calls herself "an empty skull," "the sign of the fall of Washington," a modern-day Sodom. Succored by such classical and biblical myths as Leda and the Swan, the story of Lot and his daughters, or "the long tale of the wandering god who begot Jesus Christ upon Mary his daughter," Patricia will have god and only god as her lover. She conceives of her union with her father beyond the human realm: her fruit will, she believes, restore the soul of Washington, the light in the skull.

Whether Patricia is an insane woman who, as a result, seduces her father, or whether her obsession with her father is a result of his seduction of her, depends on whose point of view you are hearing. Cynthia Jane insists that Patricia ran after her father, yet she also muses on how her father always preferred Patricia to her. In contrast, her mother Camille insists that John Christopher raped Patricia that fateful night when Eva was also raped. Yet Camille also admits that she knew something was wrong with Patricia when she was two and responded traumatically to a hurricane. "It was after that when [she] started to show those strange feelings for John Christopher. It was as if she had been raped by a hurricane." There are glimmers in the text, particularly in the erotic scenes of Pat and John Christopher's lovemaking, that that "hurricane" might well have been Pat's father's finger on her two-year-old clitoris.

What is significant is that while many other daughters blighted by incest in contemporary fiction are passive victims, Patricia appears to be an active agent. Although Patricia and her father's sexual involvement pre-cipitates the destruction of their family, it is related to, in a sense activated by, another incestuous relationship. It is the erotic bond among the three sisters which threatens the father. As John Christopher witnesses his three daughters, "3 witches" he calls them, dancing and singing in a moonlit circle in the snow, he remembers that "always there are stories of 3 witches and the fourth is always a king who is betrayed to his death." A heart trans-plant surgeon, he decides to "break the affection among [his] daughters, and pull all that affection toward [himself]." Believing his daughters to be incestuous, he begins a campaign to overpower them with his ability to give and take life. For John Christopher the religion of this era is science. Patricia is most vulnerable to that modern deity, her father; yet his two other daughters are also infected by father-myths.

Woman-bonding is primarily associated with Eva, the youngest member of this female trinity. Just as Patricia's name calls up images of patriarchy, Eva's name evokes a period before the Fall into patriarchy. Although she is called an "Eternal Virgin" who renews her virginity with the moon, Eva, like the Biblical Eve, is accused of introducing the serpent into the garden. Eva wants "the family to stand in a circle in love with one another complete and forever." Her love, however, produces opposite results:

> But where does sisterhood end? They said it was not sisterhood but seduc-tion. They said they would have never thought of lovemaking if I had not touched them. They said they knew that my touch was innocent but theirs was not innocent.[3]

A wandering prophet, Eva is raped on "the stone of Washington" (a figure for the city itself, and the empire) by an "avenging white angel." Thereaf-ter, she "dismissed [her] mind," choosing "not knowing" instead. In "not knowing," Eva preserves her innocence, blinds herself to the threat of apocalypse: "Let there be veils," she intones, years after the rape. "Let there be protections and escapes from the knowledge we are condemned to work so hard at discovering."

Rather than "dismissing her mind," Cynthia Jane, the poet and the eldest sister of the trinity, silences herself and literally becomes a Sister, leaving her family, which she calls Egypt, for the promised land of the convent. She is enraged that Patricia has broken their circle of sisterhood by sleeping with their father. Yet perhaps even more than Patricia, it is she who loves the god, the Father—not as human but as divine. She pits "a sanity of fasts and meditations" against "the insanity inside that rages against this house of the damned." Still, it is Cynthia Jane who speaks the word, who in the chapter "Sestren" tells the seventeen-year-old Johnnie who her father is. It is this Sister who hands over Patricia's letters to Johnnie, thus precipitating Johnnie's mission of illumination.

Like so many messiahs of our civilization, Johnnie is a fruit of incest nurtured in isolation, this time completely in the company of women. Diotima, Patricia's Mexican lover, enters the novel as a central figure after Johnnie's birth. She is more mother to Johnnie than her own mother and is more crucial to this tale than readers might at first realize. Reborn into the world as a result of her mother's suicide-drowning in the Potomac, Johnnie will first enter the apocalyptic city of Washington at the age of seventeen and will remain there long after it falls, as its "light," waiting to reverse the great curse on the house so that she can announce "A Happy New Millennium."

But as Alice Walker has succinctly put it, "Only Justice can stop a Curse." Will there be a thereafter? Herron's unrelenting vision illuminates our Western origins, the incestuous nature of the Gods our civilization has created and the consequences of that creation.

Review of a Reissue of *The Street* by Ann Petry

Last February Houghton Mifflin reissued Ann Petry's first novel, *The Street,* which it was fortunate enough to publish to much acclaim in 1946. This work was the first novel by an African American woman to focus on the struggles of a working-class black mother in an urban ghetto, and a reissue in a quality edition is long overdue.

In the 1920s and 30s, African Americans published novels centered on urban women. But these—Jessie Fauset's *Plum Bun* (1929), for example, or Nella Larsen's *Quicksand* (1928)—portrayed middle-class female protagonists, usually childless, whose lives, despite their class status, are gravely constrained by the sexism and racism of urban America. African American male writers—Richard Wright in *Native Son* (1940), or William Attaway in *Blood on the Forge* (1941)—wrote protest novels to dramatize how the lower-class or working-class status of their black male characters determined their tragic fate. Zora Neale Hurston built *Their Eyes Were Watching God* (1937) on a black woman's search for fulfillment in a rural community. But few African American writers in the first half of this century attempted to gauge the effect of the urban ghetto on the sexism and racism that African American women had always confronted.

Ann Petry's graphic portrayal of the inevitable downfall of her character, Lutie Johnson, is remarkable for its intensity of focus. By constructing a proletarian protest novel from the point of view of a black woman, Petry both criticized and developed that genre. Given the fact that millions of African American women live in conditions like those of *The Street,* and when one considers the emphasis on urban racial issues in the sixties and

First published in *The Women's Review of Books* 9, nos. 10–11 (July 1992): 18–19.

on women's issues in the seventies, one has to wonder why this novel is not better known, more accepted.

I first saw a copy of *The Street* in the early seventies. I'd been teaching supposedly "uneducable" Harlem blacks and Puerto Ricans at City College in New York, and had learned what might now seem obvious but was then considered radical—that if my students were presented with books that related to their lives, they "miraculously" became passionate about reading and writing. Because in those times only a few books by blacks were regularly available at "normal" bookstores, I periodically combed Harlem's thrift stores for discarded books.

It was in one of these unintellectual places that I found a dingy copy of *The Street.* I was drawn to its cover—a brash photograph of an attractive black woman in wintry urban clothing framed by bold print: "SHE WAS A SOUL ON ICE IN A BRUTAL GHETTO"—words which gave me the mistaken impression that the novel was influenced by that literary blockbuster of 1968, Eldridge Cleaver's *Soul on Ice.* Unconsciously registering the fact that a woman's book was being authenticated by a man's, I wondered how I could have missed such a rare event—a new novel by a black woman.

I would soon discover that the much-used paperback I'd bought for ten cents was the eighth printing of a 1961 reissue of a novel originally published in 1946. Ann Petry was not a new writer: my Pyramid reissue had been cleverly packaged to take advantage of the country's then-intense interest in the black ghetto, particularly its raging male inhabitants, a result of the response to "race riots" that swept major U.S. cities in the 1960s. That interest was too short-lived to keep many such books in print. The few that did survive were written by men: Richard Wright's *Native Son* (1940), James Baldwin's *The Fire Next Time* (1963), Ralph Ellison's *Invisible Man* (1952). Nor were even these books usually taught in literature classes, since African American literature apparently did not exist; they were more likely to turn up on sociology class lists, where blacks were seen as appropriate objects of inquiry.

No wonder then that *The Street* had its ups and downs. In print and acclaimed in the late 1940s, it was ignored for much of the 50s. Reissued in the early 1960s, it was difficult to obtain for much of the 1970s and 80s. In 1985 it was reissued under Deborah McDowell's editorship in a series of black women's novels that had been long out of print but were brought to light through the efforts of African American women critics. Now Houghton Mifflin has not only reissued *The Street* but intends to add Petry's other works for adults: two novels—*The Narrows* (1953) and *Country Place* (1947)—and her collection of short stories, *Miss Muriel and Other Stories* (1971).

In tracing critical response or the absence thereof toward this novel from the fifties through the eighties, I mean not only to underline its significance but also to sound a cautionary note about our own biases when we read and study African American women's writing: it still seems difficult for readers and critics in this country to comprehend and appreciate that black women can have differing visions at one and the same time.

In the few literary analyses of African American fiction published in the 1950s, *The Street* was usually mentioned, but almost always as a foil to Richard Wright's *Native Son,* whose alienated, angry, male protagonist was seen as more emblematic of the black ghetto than Petry's industrious, upwardly mobile black woman. These novels do have much in common. Both Bigger Thomas and Lutie Johnson are trapped by the physical and social space which their race and poverty condemn them to move in. At a pivotal point in the novel, each is employed as a servant to a wealthy white family whose racial or sexual stereotypes influence their tragic fate. Both Bigger Thomas and Lutie Johnson kill in the course of each novel as a result of the racial or sexual myths imposed on them.

But there are also major differences between the two novels—in their respective authors' philosophical concerns and their delineation of their major characters. While Bigger Thomas does not care about his family or believe in the American Dream, Lutie Johnson, like many other poor mothers, believes—one is tempted to say, *must* believe—that if she works hard enough, is thrifty, follows Benjamin Franklin's example, she might be able to save her son from the degradation of those streets that attempt to destroy or at least entrap anyone who is black and poor. While Wright adopts major Western philosophical frameworks—Existentialism, Marxism—to articulate the psychology of Bigger Thomas, Lutie Johnson is worried not so much about her womanhood as she is about the mundane: about food (for example, the red dye in the meat she and other Harlem mothers are forced to buy); about housing—not only the rent she can barely afford but the claustrophobia of her three tiny rooms; about her son, and whether her attempts to protect him from the dangers of his own street are futile; about her own body as she maneuvers in the terrain of male desire where both black and white men see her as sexual prey.

Perhaps the most telling disparity between these two protest novels arises out of their parallel plots: both protagonists kill, but the conditions and the effects of their acts are very different. Bigger Thomas accidentally kills Mary Dalton, a white woman in whose bedroom he is trapped, because of his fear (a well-founded one) that he will be accused of having raped her. Lutie Johnson, defending herself against being raped, kills Boots, a black man. Bigger is psychologically liberated by breaking the Great American Taboo (that of a black man having sexual relations with a white woman); he is defended by a Marxist lawyer in a trial that is as much about the meaning of oppression as it is specifically about his crime; and he comes to some self-knowledge just before his execution by the state.

In contrast, Lutie Johnson flees to another ghetto after her act of self-defense, leaving her child behind to the white world of the juvenile hall, because she is convinced that he is better off there than with her, his power-less and now criminal mother. Lutie does not draw the attention of Marxist lawyers. She does not become a cause célèbre. After all, how could a black woman be raped? And even if she were, after all, all she did was to kill a black man. While Wright's novel employs the outlines of the crime story intact with a murderer on the run, Petry's novel is not about adventure so much as it is about cramped space, about doors of opportunity that shut one after another in Lutie Johnson's face.

No wonder then that Wright's novel overshadowed Petry's in the 1950s and 60s. The civil rights and Black Power movements emphasized the muscular path of black manhood. Since the U.S. was clearly a patriarchal society, how else could blacks achieve equality? One result of that assump-tion was the much-touted belief that black men had been castrated—not only by white society but by the overpowering black matriarch, the female head of household so domineering she prevented her sons from growing up to be responsible men. It was she who was to blame for the "breakdown" of the black family, for the epidemic of black juvenile delinquents who threatened the order of society.

That perspective was to culminate in the Moynihan Report of 1966. But as public policy it had been circulating among intellectuals and popu-lar commentators since the 1940s. In writing *The Street,* Petry used the mass of detail gathered in the investigative reporting she'd done for the Harlem weekly *The People's Voice* on urban ghetto housing, on black male unemployment and its relationship to "broken" marriages, on education, childrearing and sexual violence in the ghetto, to demonstrate that juvenile delinquency and the breakdown of black urban communities were due not to domineering black mothers but to rampant institutional racism. Petry underlined this point when at the end of the novel Lutie Johnson ironically asks whether there is really any difference between the Southern slave plantation and the urban ghetto.

In the fifties the prospect of integration raised hopes among many that U.S. racism might be eliminated once blacks finally "legally" gained access to the American Dream. But neither Benjamin Franklin's philosophy nor her own literacy, beauty, intelligence and morality save Lutie Johnson. In its scathing critique of the benefits of access, *The Street* might have been seen as a throwback to a less enlightened decade. Too, protest as a literary form was becoming unpopular, not only because it dwelt so heavily on the "grim side of black life," but also because it reduced black characters to types, as James Baldwin would argue so eloquently in his essay "Everybody's Protest Novel."

But what about the sixties, the decade that dwelt so much on urban black America and fostered so much protest? Why didn't *The Street* receive more attention when it was reissued then, since it, perhaps more than any other African American novel I've read, details so completely the conditions that a person encounters every day in the ghetto: the crowded tenements, the smelly streets, the grimy food markets, the hostile police, the indifferent, tired educational system? Why didn't cultural nationalists celebrate this "realistic" novel as they did the philosophical *Native Son?*

Though they valued literature as protest, the Black Power movements of the 1960s portrayed women as adjuncts to men, a perspective that Alice Walker, June Jordan, and Audre Lorde would later come to criticize. One has only to consider the killing of Boots—a black rapist, not a white one—to see the ideological difficulties that cultural nationalists might have with the novel. At a time when Black Unity meant that women should not protest their conditions as women, Petry's analyses of the ways in which black men vented their frustrations on black women must have seemed (at best) strategically incorrect.

When I taught *The Street* for the first time in 1971, many of my students who lived in Harlem were alert to that point—what they called Petry's fostering of disunity. However, as the women's movement gained momentum, students from the same background were intrigued by the fact that a novel written well before the explosion of African American women's literature in the 1970s had attacked sexism in the African American community. Now they objected instead to the way in which the black community was represented as a ghetto, an alienated place where there is no indication that community ties exist. Many of them pointed to Petry's own small-town New England background as a way to justify their sense that a different moral and social ethos was at work: Petry was an outsider who saw the ghetto only as a place of material deprivation, and not as a community with deep cultural vitality.

But why hadn't these same students raised this objection to *Native Son?* Didn't Wright also focus on the black urban environment as a deprived ghetto? Unlike Petry, he came from a devastatingly poor family and had suffered intense racism in his childhood, so what did background have to do with it? Might not Petry's as well as Wright's emphasis on the destructiveness of the ghetto have more to do with the intention of the protest novel—that its goal is to demonstrate the effects of oppression? Would these novels be as effective as protest if rich cultural vitality was their focus? June Jordan pointed out in an essay on *Native Son* and *Their Eyes Were Watching God* that novels of affirmation *and* novels of protest are necessary to African American intellectual and social expression: doesn't that also apply to *The Street?*

As my students examined their criticisms, it became increasingly clear that while they could accept, even applaud, Wright's representation of an urban black man as alienated and angry, they could not accept Petry's representation of an urban black woman as disconnected from the community and angry at the limitations of her environment. Black women, whatever their class or condition, had to be community-oriented, or how would the community survive? What they applauded was Janie in *Their Eyes Were Watching God,* a woman who desired community, was clearly sensual, and achieved her voice. Ironically, while Hurston's novel had been rejected for decades because it was *not* a protest novel, now *The Street* was being criticized because a woman's novel should be affirmative.

While my students' opinions are not exactly a definitive explanation of why *The Street* failed to attract more attention in the woman-centered seventies, I think their responses do indicate the discomfort this novel might have caused in the last two decades among readers who yearned (as we should have) for rebels like Morrison's Sula, or her wise Pilate in *Song of Solomon* (1977), or for political activists like Alice Walker's Meridian or Toni Cade Bambara's Velma in *The Salt Eaters* (1980). Although I do not share Hazel Carby's assessment of our idealization of *Their Eyes Were Watching God* as a return to a pastoral past, I do think we ought to reflect on why so few novels about working-class urban black women were published or celebrated during the 1970s—and why so many prominent African American women's novels of that period were set in small towns, villages of the past.

In the fiction of the 1980s the issue of class became more focal. Yet except for Gloria Naylor's *The Women of Brewster Place* (1982), most of these novels emphasized middle-class black women: Jadine in Morrison's *Tar Baby* (1981), Celie in Alice Walker's *The Color Purple* (1982), Sarah Phillips in Andrea Lee's 1984 novel of the same name. Whether or not that trend was due to a social climate in which working-class lives were less central to intellectual inquiry or to the perceptions of publishing companies, it is nonetheless true that African American women were then and are now a majority of the Black urban ghetto.

In the 1990s a new trend is beginning to emerge. Films like *Boyz N the Hood* and *New Jack City* indicate that the new black ghetto, the "hood," is causing the rest of American society much consternation. Perhaps *The Street* will receive more attention in this era, and find the place it deserves in the literary history of the U.S. For as Petry pointed out in a recent interview, the world it portrays is as real now as it was in 1946.

15   Remembering Audre Lorde (1993)

The phone rings. It is Lisa, one of the graduate students with whom I work: "Barbara, I have bad news." Silence. "Audre Lorde just died in St. Croix." I am stunned, unprepared, though I should not be. Audre has had breast cancer for many years. I know she now lives in St. Croix, my ancestral home, where the sun and the sea are invigorating her. The islands, her mother's islands, would save her body, I had hoped. Lisa repeats: "Audre died in St. Croix." Silence. Then I say, "I will never see her again."

I will always hear her, though. Audre left for us her work—words that many African American women had been too afraid to speak. We had been taught that silence was golden, that it could protect you. Yet, as our daily lives and statistics proclaimed, we were steadily being attacked from within our homes as well as from without. Audre Lorde refused to be silenced, refused to be limited to any one category, insisted on being all that she was: poet, black, mother, lesbian, feminist, warrior, activist, woman.

As I grieve her passing on, I cannot help but think of the irony that we split her into her separate parts: so many white feminist/lesbians respond only to her lesbianism; blacks to her race activism; literary critics to her poetic craft; mother goddess followers to her African goddesses.

Ah—Audre—if there is any tribute we can give you, it is to acknowledge all those parts of yourself without which you would not be you.

> Love is a word, another kind of open
> As the diamond comes into a knot of
> flame
> I am Black because I come from the
> earth's inside

First published in *The Women's Review of Books* 10, no. 6 (March 1993): 5–6.

now take my word for jewel in the
open light[1]

I remember the first time I met Audre. It was 1968. Both of us were
working in the SEEK program at City College, New York, a program designed to prepare apparently uneducable Blacks and Puerto Ricans for college. We were demanding our rights, insisting on structural transformation
of the educational system. I'd read some of her poems and was inspired
by their sinewy sound and honesty. In love with language, we talked about
poetry, about protest, about social change.

I was just beginning to realize the sexism within the Black Power Movement and was grappling for the words to express it. Unity was the call
word of the day, even if it was a false unity. The black revolutionaries we
thought ourselves to be could not be fragmented by such trivia. I did not
then know that Audre was a lesbian. In 1968, to be a black person and to
be a homosexual (James Baldwin notwithstanding) was to be against the
revolution, to be tainted by white evil.

By the time I'd moved to California, in 1971, Audre had published "Love
Poem," which was clearly about sexual love between women. Like Martin Luther at Wittenberg when he'd seceded from the powerful Catholic
Church by tacking his precepts up on a church door, Audre, the librarian,
had tacked her poem up on her office door for all to see. I heard the re-
verberations from coast to coast. Her insistence on speaking as her entire
self, whatever the consequences, became a model for many women who
had begun to realize that when the words "Black Liberation" were spoken
they were not referring to us, precisely because we *were* women.

Like other women, I had been mute, silenced by the black rhetoric of the
period. Audre's courage, her honesty, reminded us that we could not act for
ourselves or others if we could not transform our own silence into speech:

if we speak we are afraid
that our words will be used
against us

And if we do not speak
we are still afraid

So, it is better to speak
knowing we were never meant
to survive.[2]

It is 1978. I am listening to the radio on a Saturday as I clean the house.
I have a child, am married, yet might as well be a single mother. I am writ-

ing a book on black women novelists and am known as a feminist, yet feel troubled about European-American feminism. Its puritanical tendencies do not relate closely enough to many people's lives, our need to *feel* the connection between the pleasure we desire in our everyday life and the political activity necessary to change our lives. I hear a voice I think I recognize, a voice from the "Take Back the Night" feminist rally in San Francisco. It is Audre's voice, articulating for us how the erotic energizes our lives, analyzing precisely how political struggle is connected to our understanding of our desires.

> When we begin to live from within outward, in touch with the power of the erotic within ourselves and allowing that power to inform and illuminate our actions upon the world around us, then we begin to be responsible to ourselves in the deepest sense. For as we recognize our deepest feelings, we begin to give up, of necessity, being satisfied with suffering and self-negation, and with the numbness which so often seems like their only alternative in our society. Acts against oppression become integral with self, motivated and empowered from within.[3]

In her works published during the 1980s—her biomythography, *Zami* (1982), her two collections of essays, *Sister Outsider* (1984) and *A Burst of Light* (1988), her nonfiction, *The Cancer Journals* (1980), her poetry collection, *Our Dead Behind Us* (1986), Audre emphasized the intersections of oppressions—that racism, sexism, homophobia, stem from the same source, from *"the inability to recognize the notion of difference as a dynamic human force which is enriching rather than threatening to the defined self."*[4] Even those in search of social change tend to be intolerant of differences among their own constituents and thus recreate the societal pattern they claim to be opposed to.

What Audre learned from her outsider position in society is that real change cannot occur unless we

> stop killing
> the other
> in ourselves
> the self that we hate in others[5]

Her analysis of this fear has had ramifications for just about every area of our lives, from our sexuality to education, from the meaning of our identities to political coalition work. A poet-thinker, Audre enlarged the race-feminist theory of that period, so much so that the concept of difference as a creative force is today as "natural" a part of our analyses of the world as the notion that oppressions exist.

I last saw Audre at the peak of the divestment movement at the University of California at Berkeley. On May 14, 1985, Sisters Against Apartheid put together a poetry meeting to honor our sisters in South Africa. Together with the Native American poet Paula Gunn Allen, the Japanese American poet Janice Mirikitani, and the Chicana poet Cherríe Moraga, Audre Lorde commemorated the significance of women in the anti-apartheid struggle as well as the life-sustaining force of poetry in social change movements. It was an event that symbolized so much of who Audre was. As she rose to speak with women from all over the world about an issue to which she had been unstintingly committed, she stressed the gift of learning to use one's own power:

> It is important for Black South Africans to know they are not alone. To know that our voices are being raised. It is a very important lesson, too, to know that learning to use your power is not a free lesson; but it is an invaluable one, because to be able to know what it feels like to put all of who you are behind something you believe is a priceless present.[6]

In 1978, Audre learned that she had breast cancer. She could not be silent, as so many women had been. She wrote *The Cancer Journals* some ten years before the media would acknowledge that breast cancer is virtually an epidemic in the U.S.

I last heard her voice in 1988, when she spoke at Stanford University. By then, she knew that the cancer had metastasized to her liver. She spoke not of loss but of blessing: that she had been *"blessed to believe passionately, to love deeply and to be able to work out of those loves and beliefs."*[7] In working out of those loves and beliefs, Audre Lorde clarified for us the multiplicity that each of us is. Rejecting a "mythical norm," she championed the complexity of life, named it a blessing and gave that blessing to us.

> Black mother goddess, salt dragon of
> chaos, Seboulisa, Mawu. Attend me,
> hold me in your muscular flowering
> arms, protect me from throwing any
> part of myself away.[8]

PART 3

Black Feminist Criticism in the Academy

Introduction
GLORIA BOWLES

Barbara Christian wrote these essays a quarter century after her initial years as a teacher and graduate student in New York City. During her distinguished career, she would play a major role in the founding and development of Afro-American studies, ethnic studies, and women's studies. The essays in this section trace the final period of her career, thus long past the revolutionary peak of the civil rights and women's movements and the ethnic and women's studies programs inspired by them. Today these movements and the long struggle to challenge the absences in university research and curriculum are a distant memory for those who participated in change and a historical artifact for the teachers and students who now expect an inclusive education.

It may be surprising to some that a chair of Afro-American studies and one of the founders of the ethnic studies Ph.D. program at Berkeley was also central to the development of women's studies. Always willing to enter into coalitions for common cause, Barbara Christian nonetheless often felt pushed and pulled in various directions. The problem was in part practical; as the first tenured black woman at Berkeley, she was endlessly called upon to represent both "Black" and "Woman." The challenge was intellectual as well, since white women and women of color came to feminist debates with different experiences and thus with different agendas for change. Women had to learn from each other. The solitary black woman at the university was often a bridge between various points of departure.

At Berkeley, Barbara Christian's classes gave many white students their first opportunities to enter through literature into the experiences of blacks in the United States in the nineteenth and twentieth centuries. But this seemed a one-way street. How does one divide one's time between teaching whites and educating students of color, who often have different questions? Many women of color felt apart from women's studies programs dominated in the seventies and eighties by white and lesbian issues. In her teaching and writing, Christian bravely lays out these and other conflicts, not resolving them, but in effect asking us to face up to them. The titles of many of her essays, beginning with a provocative question, capture her method, one of dialogue and conversation. After reading her, we are impressed by the enormous scholarly and pedagogical challenge of keeping race, gender, and class within our sights.

Like the writing of the Afro-American novelists and poets whose work she unearthed, Barbara Christian's criticism was always rooted in historical and political reality. She believed in the relationship between thought and action, community and university. Her essays are expressions of emotion and passion as well as intellectual analysis. She often decried narrow ideas of "political," as in candidates and parties, for she saw politics as an expression of power relations inside and outside the university. Her approach was no longer au courant in the literary criticism of the eighties and nineties, dominated by the sometimes arcane musings of U.S. scholars whose heads had been turned by postmodern French philosophers—read, I might add, in translation and often without a deep understanding of the European context. "I find the narrative theorizing of say a Toni Morrison or an Alice Walker to be far more dynamic, significant, and useful than the majority of lit crit theory being published today," she wrote.[1]

Barbara Christian remained a political thinker long after many had abandoned analytical and practical politics for the more ethereal realms of "high" theory. Toward the end of her academic career (she had intended to retire at 60), she thus found herself swimming upstream yet again. The new struggle demanded a shoring up of critical perspectives based not on rigid categories or fragmentation, but on interrelationships, intersections, and interdisciplinarity. At the same time, her approach entailed an analysis of the realities on the ground. In the late eighties and early nineties, Barbara Christian could often be heard reflecting on what had been accomplished during the movements for change and at the same time wondering whether future generations would carry on the work. This question of legacy hovers over all of the essays of this section. In these later years, she was as interested in teaching her students about the facts of life in the academy as in introducing them to the arenas of study she helped to found. This is the voice we hear in the "intergenerational polylogue" first published in *differences,* where she asserts that power has not shifted in academe, despite the civil rights and feminist movements. In "Diminishing Returns," Christian delivers the startling perception that a Ph.D. is a luxury most black women cannot afford. Moreover, with the demise of affirmative action, she is confronted with the distinct possibility that elite public universities such as Berkeley will enroll many fewer blacks for even a first year of undergraduate study. In fact, in fall 2004, Berkeley admitted 30 percent fewer blacks, diminishing a total that was already small.[2]

It is amazing to hear, as we do in "Camouflaging Race *and* Gender," that a woman as celebrated and accomplished as Barbara Christian should in the mid-nineties feel "alienated from the culture of this university." One who had labored all her adult life for an atmosphere of tolerance, diversity, and a more inclusive curriculum and research agenda felt she was seeing an erosion, even a rejection, of the core of her work.

Nor is it easy to understand, since we now take it for granted, how complex is the task of creating a whole new field. By reminding us of the medieval origins of the idea of canon, Christian forces us into a perception of how deep-seated are the academy's habits of study. She points out that some canons posit a pure, transcendent art, relegating politics and history to a lesser realm. Such narrow definitions can exclude Afro-American literature, which has "tended to be concerned with issues of social justice." Instead, she argues for a more capacious sense of what we call "literature."

Professor Christian understood deeply the power of canon, having been one of the major forces behind *The Norton Anthology of African American Literature,* published in 1997. "A Rough Terrain," which begins to ask the questions that would shape a new field, the study of Caribbean women writers, gives us some insight into the time and thought that are required to create an anthology and thus a new canon. This particular labor would remain unfinished but, in the careful laying out of a path, we can watch just how Barbara Christian worked, step by step over the years, to create new realms of knowledge.

16 Being "The Subjected Subject of Discourse" (1990)

Questions 1, 2, and 5:[1] To cast the history of a feminist presence in the academy as a generational one immediately reminds me of my marginal position as a feminist academic of color born outside of the U.S. For much of my academic life, from 1967 to the present, I was not certain of my status as "sister" either in the feminist or African American academic family. Often I felt myself to be more of a step-sister to my white sisters and black brothers, who were respectively themselves step-daughters and sons in the academy. I wondered then, not about the nature of relationships I might have with academic daughters or sons, but whether I would have any children at all.

Would there be any young women (men were even more unlikely), whether black, colored, or white, who would freely choose a low-status mother and focus on intersections of race, class, gender in Afro-American women's literature, in fact in any literature written by people of color? My position as a potential mother had more to do with the difficulty of getting pregnant, of gaining access to the academy for children, particularly my beleaguered younger sisters of color. In another familial turf, I knew I had potential daughters and sons, those who read my work inside and outside the academy and those who took my undergraduate classes, but who of those had the luxury of becoming feminist scholars of my ilk?

Recently, however, that situation has changed considerably. During the last five years, partially as a result of the academy's growing interest in Afro-American women's literature, in theoretical inquiries into the relationship

First published as part of "Conference Call" in *Differences* 2, no. 3 (1990): 52–108. The editors "thought it a timely project to set up an 'intergenerational polylogue'" between graduate students interested in feminist theory and distinguished scholars in women's studies. The graduate students collaborated in writing questions directed to the scholars (see endnote 1). In *Differences,* these questions are on pp. 54–56 followed by Professor Christian's response on pp. 57–65.

of race, class, and gender (the new Trinity), and institutionally because of the establishment of an Ethnic Studies Ph.D. program here at Berkeley, I find myself an academic mother to more children than I could have possibly imagined, and to types of children beyond my conjuring. This is so because scholars in my version of feminist thought are scarce at my university as well as anywhere else in the country. I have spent some twenty years in the academic feminist and Afro-American family; yet I have become a mother overwhelmed by children at a time when many of my white counterparts are already academic grandmothers.

Perhaps because my "sisterhood" was so precarious, perhaps because I have come so late to the role of academic mentor to graduate students, perhaps because I am a single mother in my other life, I question the familial metaphor as an accurate metaphor for feminist scholars. True we nurture, approve or disapprove of, desire (no matter what we say) to reproduce students much like ourselves; but our love is not nearly as unconditional as a mother's is supposed to be nor is our tenure with our students long enough to entitle us to call ourselves parents. Like other faculty, our relationships with students vary according to our and their needs, temperaments, desires, and are finally concerned with a relatively narrow range as to who we are or they are. Most important, our relationships with students are not necessarily free because students have needs they *must* have fulfilled by us, such as letters of recommendations, grades, etc.; moreover, we are aware that the students associated with us are in some ways a reflection of colleagues' assessment of *our* academic excellence. There are limits then, especially institutional ones, built into the relationship between teachers and students in the university. Being a feminist scholar does not eliminate them; it might at times even heighten the necessity for such limits since our area of inquiry is so beset by stereotypical caricatures of "mothering." Yet, there is a special urgency we feminist scholars do feel towards those students with whom we work.

What I wish to communicate to my students, on the one hand, is the knowledge I have acquired in my field as a result of many years of study, and on the other hand, my history in and reflections on the academy. What I find I gain from students is the opposite, their freshness of approach to both knowledge of my field and to experience in the academy precisely because they are first beginning to encounter both areas. If we are to use the metaphor of the family for this process of continuity, then my students give birth to me as much as I do to them, depending on our mutual needs, desires, temperaments. Whether my "expertise" is useful to them or theirs to me has much to do with our respective starting points and goals—which has little to do with how smart we are at what we do.

Like many feminists of my generation, my starting point in this arena of change was not my becoming an academic. My goals at that time were very much influenced by the Civil Rights Movements of the 60s, which moved me to the study of Afro-American history and literature as one means through which I believed a change in consciousness might occur in this country. Contrary to the question the graduate students in this polylogue asked, the categories of "Difference" as I remember them in my lifetime were not first contested in the academy by feminists but by people of color. My first "academic job" was in the area of "literacy" rather than scholarship; I taught supposedly uneducable blacks and Puerto Ricans to read and write by using literature that was relevant to them. Along with others, I had literally to excavate that literature and in doing so ran up against the obstacle of sexism, as well as racism, in trying to achieve such a small task. Along with others, I entered the academy with a mission many of us believed might not be achieved but which we had no choice but at least to attempt.

In contrast, most of my students come to graduate school with the specific goal of becoming an academic in feminist scholarship, a goal many of them could not have imagined if they had come of age twenty-five years ago. And unlike the atmosphere of economic prosperity and progressive politics during the period when I was going to graduate school, they are preparing themselves for their career during a much more restrictive economic and ideological decade.

As a result, their itinerary is, to my mind, much more planned yet more complicated; they have more choices yet fewer chances of being successful mavericks. In effect, institutionalization of any field seems both to enlarge and restrict its possibilities. Most of my students will, I hope, be revising, even at times opposing, my points of view, since so much more is known in my field than was known twenty-five years ago. Yet at the same time I wonder about whether the institution (my learning aside) produces a climate in which they can produce original, *significant* work without affecting the trajectories of their careers. In other words, if I am an academic mother, I am one with relatively little power to create for my students as much space for free play; that is, space to create work that might be disturbing to the academy itself.

It is for this reason—notwithstanding Barbara Johnson's observation about the often repeated misperception of the "real" world seeming to be the world outside the institution—that I believe the non-academic aspects of my feminist students' lives are as important as their academic ones to the development of feminist scholarship. For me the problem is not so much the split between the real world outside and the unreal world of the institution inside, but that the academy behaves as if it *is* the world, the only world, and that which lies *outside* it is but raw material which it transforms into ideas. It is in reaction to this stance that the academy is often accused of not being "the real world"—a reaction that unfortunately does not pinpoint the issue—that the academy is both *in* the world and *of* it. It helps then for students, as well as teachers, to see themselves as citizens of interrelated communities, which indeed they are, whether they are aware of it or not.

It is the academy's insistence on itself as *the* world which leads me to be so concerned about the feminist students who come after me. At the risk of sounding essentialist, I am alarmed at the few women of color engaged in feminist scholarship even as universities are now rushing out to hire scholars in this field, supposedly at the cutting edge. It is not that I think that, for example, only black women should pursue academic careers in the study of Afro-American women's writings. Certainly the field is rich enough, deep enough to be approached by women and men of all ethnicities—providing of course they do study it with all the respect and thoroughness it deserves. But I do worry about the omission of the perspectives of women of color—not only because I am one but precisely because of the interrelatedness of communities within and without the academy. In many cases, though their experiences vary, these women bring an urgency to insights about their study similar to those which brought me to the academy in the first place.

But of course the academy is *in* the world, and in the world, women of color have few sites of power. Who of us can afford to be a feminist scholar, not only to pay back the loans that graduate study entails but to exist so purely within an institution which distances itself from other "families," "communities," and "cultures"? Clearly many of the few women of color who have access to the academy and who might want to pursue feminist scholarship have decided to go into other fields—such as the professional schools—perhaps because activism in relation to communities outside the academy is more acceptable there or perhaps because the careers pay enough to help one sustain the blows students sustain in the academy.

In the meantime (a phase that resonates for people of color *in* the world), I must be concerned about spending time developing feminist scholars, many of whom do not have a visceral connection to communities outside the university and for whom feminist literature is not so much a prod to change as much as it is an artifact. For one of the academy's major strategies of containment is not only excluding some, but discouraging others who might disrupt and transform it by attempting to incorporate them into an exclusively academic culture so that they become increasingly cut off from the other cultures and communities which nourish them. Those who do not exhibit the correct demeanor, attitudes, manners often do not last long in the academy. Sometimes they are promoted; sometimes they are marginalized and devalued. I find this pattern to be particularly applicable to some lesbians whose behavior may not seem "feminine" enough and to some working-class women whose "demeanor" does not imitate that of the "cultured" scholar. Academics sometimes express their opinions about the competence of "different" scholars in terms that have little to do with intellectual rigor but more with whether the person is "right" for them, an argument that masks the real source of discomfort. The result is that academic culture remains much the same as it was before the second wave of American feminism.

Yet if our work does not substantively change the composition and culture of the academy and the power relations that exclude the very writers of that literature we study, then those of us who see the academy as a *real* articulator of power will have miscarried many times over. Hopefully by the time I become an academic grandmother, my grandchildren will be as varied as the many communities outside the academy. Then perhaps I can face the problem of to what extent we want to keep "it" in the family.

Questions 4 and 8: It is galling to me that after black women critics of the 1970s plowed the neglected field of Afro-American women's literature when such an act was academically dangerous, that some male and white female scholars now seem to be reaping the harvest and are major commentators on this literature in influential though not necessarily feminist journals such as *The New York Review of Books.* Historical amnesia seems to be as much a feature of intellectual life as of other aspects of American society. Since I have already given my version of the history of contemporary black feminist criticism in my essay, "But What Do We Think We're Doing Anyway?", I will not here repeat myself. Still there are some pressing issues that have occurred to me since I wrote that essay.

Not until recently have black male scholars had access to these influential publications. Given the fact that the brilliance of the few who now regularly appear in these pages could not have just surfaced, I wonder why they are now being given access:

Could it be that these scholars are more inclined than their female counterparts to employ the current fashionable linguistic practices of the academy rather than explore the possibility of critical practices that might develop out of Afro-American and/or women's cultural forms? There are a few black women critics who use the preferred language of the academy. Why have they not gotten more play?

Is it that black men are still more titillating to whites than black women? I recall that black female abolitionists complained how even their white sisters paid more attention to black men than they did to them.

Might some critics, because of their collective history and invisibility, black women critics for instance, ask questions and use forms that might be disturbing, even disruptive to certain publishing outlets?

Could it be that black men are just better than black women at the analysis of black women's texts? That inevitably white female and male critics might be better as well?

Could it be that in the academic world, whites are still more privileged than blacks, men than women?

Is it none of these, some of these, all of these?

Ah, I hear the retort that I am being essentialist, that I am using race and gender as some kind of mystical entry to special knowledge from which others are barred. Do I not know that "race" and "gender" are historically constructed systems rather than essential attributes which are unchanging, that these charged words signify different ideas depending on the historical context? Do I not understand that I am reinforcing the very discriminatory practices to which I am opposed?

There was a time, specifically in the 1960s and 70s, when, respectively, race and then gender could be used to justify the claim that some groups because of their collective experience knew more than others about their own history and culture. But those days are gone. We know, in the 80s and 90s, because of our understanding of discursive practices, that people of color and/or women cannot provide any particular insights into the complexities of a text, even if that text is primarily concerned with them.

I do believe that Afro-American women's literature, like any other literature, can be approached from any number of perspectives and by people of different races, ethnicities, cultures, genders. But I do question whether the racial or gender experience of a scholar is an unimportant issue as to what questions she/he asks, what approaches she/he privileges.

I wonder whether the intellectual focus today on race and gender as exclusively historical constructions, though rooted in the abstract sphere of logic, is itself not a historically constructed response to the recent past. That is, that this new contemporary position ignores the power relations in this society which *still* result in a hierarchal structure with regard to the value of different groups, their forms, questions, expressions. What alarms me about our present assessment is that although everything (in the philosophical discussion about race and gender) has changed, everything (as to whose voices are privileged in institutions, publishing outlets, universities) remains the same.

I may not appeal to my race, gender, or ethnicity as critical tools which might give me insight into a text, without risking the damning cry of being an essentialist, even as I continue to live in a world whose institutions still behave as if essentialism were the norm. What, I wonder, is the purpose of this debate? Who benefits from it? Does it contribute to a sharing of power in intellectual and academic institutions of those whose points of view have been traditionally ignored? Or does this new academic position result in the maintenance of the visibility and power of those who have always had it? I suppose I should take it as a "compliment" that at least the literature of some black women is receiving attention. Whether that attention will wane as "new markets" of interest arise will be a telling phenomenon to observe.

Questions 3 and 7: Perhaps one of the most significant developments I see in current feminist academic scholarship is the beginnings of the realization that gender never exists as a pure category, that no woman exists who is not also of a particular racial/ethnic group and sexual preference and who does not belong to one class or another in a specific society. That while gender is critical to the formation of every human society, the way it is constructed is always in relation to these always existing factors. That realization is not a new one in other areas of American feminism outside the academy (as in the works of writers such as Audre Lorde and Adrienne Rich) and in fact is for me the source of 1970s women of color feminisms; it even possibly influenced the character of early white women's liberation groups, since their orientations grew partially out of their experience in the 1960s Civil Rights Movement.

However, during the 1970s, as gender became more of an "intellectual" as well as a social category, it seems to me that it increasingly was studied as an isolated concept. Scholars needed to make generalizations about Who Woman Is so as to articulate theories about Her. Not surprisingly, because female scholars in the U.S. tended to be white, middle class, and apparently heterosexual, that configuration became the norm and all deviations from that norm were seen as pollutants, sometimes important ones, but still pollutants in the pure field of gender. Some might say that such a focus, one of simplistic unity, was a necessary, almost inevitable forced step in the launching of feminist scholarship in the academy. Yet in so doing, feminist scholars often imitated that which had occurred in the scholarship of race relations and class relations, most of which ignored gender, not to mention the celebrated studies in bourgeois scholarship which ignored, altogether discounted, intersections of race, class, and gender as "intellectual" concerns. By imitating the very systems that opposed it, in fact shut it out, feminist academic scholarship undercut itself and did not develop the depth and complexity it could have, and should have, if change in gender relations were to occur. Now the growing tendency among feminist scholars, who still are white, middle class, and apparently heterosexual, to move away from the universal unified simplistic Abstract to more complex inquiries may result in more accurate, exciting, and transformative scholarship.

Such a realization, if accepted and acted upon by the majority of feminist academic scholars, may also release some of the energy women of color scholars have had to expend by having constantly to "correct" the norm and may free *us* so that we do not have to oppose their monolithic norm with one of our own. Even more important, perhaps we might be able to focus on developing new ideas that emanate out of our specific contexts—ideas that might benefit all of us—a focus we might have been able to pursue years ago if we did not have to protect the advance in thought we had already made. Often I find that women of color are represented in scholarship by Afro-American women, as if Chicanas, Asian Americans, or Native American women, not to mention women living outside this country, did not have their own specific contexts. If we are to move beyond a stultifying and false unity toward a more accurate, rich inquiry into the worlds of women, and therefore to new ideas about how liberations might come about, we will have to do more than acknowledge or cite differences; we may have to see the intersections of our many differences as central to the quality of our work.

Such an exploration of our condition(s) will be aborted, I believe, if more than a very few select women of color are not central to its birthing process. As academics (and I include myself among those few women of color at major American universities) use "specimen texts" in their syllabi and extend their analysis of Western feminism to international contexts, I find that rather than listening to multiple voices that theorize in the forms of powerful non-Western philosophical systems, we translate these "others" into the language of our family, the academic language with which we are familiar. By so doing we imply that we do not value those "other" systems and their wisdom, for many of us believe their ideas/language are too underdeveloped for the work of analysis. Why then, I wonder, pay attention to these multiple voices at all?

In an insightful essay, "The Theoretical Subject(s) of *This Bridge Called My Back* and Anglo-American Feminism," Norma Alarcon demonstrates that although Anglo-American feminists often cite *Bridge* as an instance of difference, they consistently subsume women of color into "the unitary category of woman/women." Alarcon astutely points out that Anglo-American feminist theory takes for granted the linguistic status upon which subjectivity is based and "appropriates woman/women for itself and turns its work into a theoretical project within which the rest of us are compelled to fit."[2]

Academic language has become the new metaphysic through which we turn leaden idiom into golden discourse. But by writing more important thinking exclusively in this language, we not only speak but to ourselves, we also are in danger of not asking those critical questions which our native *tongues* insist we ask. Whether anyone in the academy knows it or not, the old Afro-American refrain "God don't like ugly" (note the lack of tri-syllabic words) is very different from its translation into current linguistic practice. Those who study Afro-American literature, for example, and do not wish to know, far less try to understand, the implications of that difference, be it from the perspective of race, class, or gender, may be (to use current/correct language) reifying the homogeneous discourse they desire to decenter.

17 Whose Canon Is It Anyway? (1994)

In the last five years, issues of canonicity, political correctness, and multi-culturalism have been hotly debated in the American popular media as well as in intellectual and academic journals. The debate is often presented as two-sided, with the "pure intellectuals" defending standards on one side and the "politicos" insisting on social justice on the other side.[1]

The intellectuals claim that the politicos are not concerned with intellectual excellence and are bending to political pressure. The politicos insist that there is no such thing as a universal or objective standard and the pure intellectuals are primarily concerned with maintaining their cultural dominance.[2] Such a two-sided, simplistic presentation of the debate has had the effect of distorting the character of its participants.

The word "canon" is an ecclesiastical term that originated in the Middle Ages and defined the sacred texts of the Church. Because the medieval Church was a powerful entity in Europe and controlled much of education, those select few who had access to knowledge of the canon held a particularly powerful position in society. As education became more secular, the term "canon" was increasingly applied to texts that embodied the knowledge necessary to a particular nation-state in its project to define the national character. Because the majority of those who had access to education were generally of the privileged class, a knowledge of these texts indicated one's position in a particular society. In the nineteenth century, as education became more available to the middle classes in nation-states like England, thinkers such as the middle-class poet and essayist Matthew Arnold, in his famous work *Culture and Anarchy* (1859), would attempt to

First published in Mary Ann Caws, Patricia Laurence, and Sarah Bird Wright, eds., *Issues in World Literature: The HarperCollins World Reader* (New York: HarperCollins College Publications, 1994), 17–22.

redefine "culture" according to a more democratic standard. For Arnold, the cultured person is the one who transcends the limitations of his class and caste so as to become "human." No longer belonging to any of society's actual segments, [he] can stand above the spectrum of warring factions, dispassionately appraising, balancing, stabilizing and renewing."[3] An acquisition of culture, those texts that exemplified the good and the beautiful of the national character and to which educated citizens, whatever their class, should be exposed so as to transcend the differences that might throw a nation into anarchy.

If one knows the history of Western education, it becomes clear that the particular texts chosen for inclusion in the canon, as it is now called, are not etched in stone, but are in fact tied to a particular nation-state's sense of what is philosophically and aesthetically important. Canons change according to changes in perception of the national character. The content of the canons, then, is decidedly affected by the nation-state's self-definition and thus partially determined by "political" as well as intellectual concerns. In fact the political realm and the intellectual realm are hardly discrete realms. When one looks at the debate in the latter half of the twentieth century about the "American Literary Canon" in this way, one can see why there is such furious rhetoric. What is at stake is the meaning of terms like "culture," "American" and "Western." The debate may also determine who is considered an American and who is not, who determines standards of the good and the beautiful and who does not.

American educational institutions have continually changed the content of the canon in different academic disciplines. There was a time when American literature, or more precisely Anglo-American literature, was not considered a worthy subject of study, since the only literature worth studying was from England. Now, however, few American English departments do not include a course on, say, the American Renaissance or on writers such as Nathaniel Hawthorne, Herman Melville, or William Faulkner. That shift in curriculum had much to do, interestingly, with the increasing power of the United States internationally, as well as with Anglo-Americans' growing awareness of their distinctiveness, of the ways in which their national character is quite different from that of the British. I think that most contemporary American scholars and teachers of literature would say that the restructuring of the curriculum to include American literature, that is, literature written almost exclusively by white American men, intellectually enriched our educational institutions rather than diluting our standards.

One important result of this refiguring of the canon has been the increase in revered and respected scholars who study specifically periods of American literature. For the field was found to be so rich and complex that one could even focus on a particular epoch as one's main interest, just as someone else might specialize in, say, seventeenth-century British literature. Such an intensity of focus has generated an enormous amount of scholarship, some of which has greatly illuminated our understanding of "American" culture. While there were practical dilemmas, such as how to organize a course given the inherent limitations of time—an objection often posed by teachers who are, after all, on the front lines—because there was an awareness of the intellectual necessity for Americans to know their own literature, resourceful people took on the challenge of refiguring the curriculum so that today most students who go to high school must study American literature.

Since significant changes in the curriculum of American educational institutions have not only been envisioned but have occurred before and American educators have been able to adapt to them somehow—often in remarkably enriching ways—we should welcome and support a broad infusion of cultures that will let our vision range still further.

Many of us have forgotten or perhaps have never known that "multiculturalism" as a term did not originate in the educational debates of the 1980s. The term was, in fact, very much alive during the 1960s when African-Americans, Native Americans, and other ethnic Americans in many places in this country demanded that their traditions be studied and explored on high school and college campuses. What many of the students of the 1960s realized was that, unless the knowledge of a group is validated by the entire society, that knowledge is in danger of being denigrated, misunderstood, even lost. What even these students did not know—and how could they when it was not a part of their education?—is that there had been black intellectuals, such as W. E. B. DuBois at the turn of the century, who had already been worried about the ways in which the American educational system denied blacks their history and culture and denied, in fact, all Americans a knowledge of that central element of their history and culture without which, as Toni Morrison puts it, American culture is incoherent. For example, major movements of the nineteenth century such as the abolitionist movement and the women's rights movement, movements that changed the character of American life, could not really be understood without a knowledge of black writers such as Frederick Douglass and Frances Harper, or without an understanding of the slave narrative or the sentimental romance.

Because art is generally defined in the West as that which transcends temporal matters and is apart from, rather than a part of, everyday existence, and because, in contrast, African-American writers have tended to see their work as having to have a use in present and future worlds, African-

American literature has too often been labeled "political" or "propagandistic," characteristics with negative overtones in the Western philosophies of art articulated in the last hundred years or so.

Because of African-Americans' particular history, the intellectual as well as the expressive traditions of blacks in the New World may be of particular importance to today's rapidly changing world, where heterogeneity rather than homogeneity of racial populations is becoming more and more the norm. Perhaps the history, experience, and culture of New World blacks may have relevance to those, such as North Africans in France, who have experienced colonialism in their own land but are only now beginning to contend with the restrictions and fears that are the result of being a racially distinct minority population. An understanding of the social and cultural effects on an entire society caused by the exclusion of New World Blacks may even be of some use to those who, although they may be in the majority in a certain region, are beginning to realize that none of us lives in a homogenous space. Peoples from different parts of the world have always been in contact with others; now, however, as a result of Western colonization and modern technology that rate of contact has greatly accelerated.

African-American literature differs from many other literary forms in that it has for some three hundred years occupied at least two intellectually differentiated spaces at the same time; it has been both a part of, yet different from, the European-American tradition. Because of the history of African-Americans, their literature has, of necessity, had to confront the reality of different races living in a shared space, and what it means when one of those races has been and wants to continue being culturally, socially, and politically dominant, to the detriment of other groups. At the same time, their literature also celebrates, in fact has, despite "Western" imposition of ways of thinking about the world, tenaciously held on to culturally expressive elements, which are judged by standards as rigorous as any from the West, that are uniquely African-American.

The written word is exalted in Western societies as a mark of the civilized, one reason why African-Americans have written. They have written in order to explore, analyze, and articulate the ways in which the concept of race has been constructed in this society, and the debilitating, sometimes deadly effects that construct has had on people, especially but not exclusively in American society. Because issues of sexuality and gender were and still are central to the denigration of African-Americans, both female and male, and because generally speaking they have tended to be economically deprived, African-American writers have pointed to the effects of the intersections of the categories we now call race, class, and gender. But African-Americans have also written to express the forms, vitality, and philosophical tradition of their own culture, which has its roots in Africa and has been influenced by other cultures, such as the cultures of native Americans, even as it has developed in the cauldron of racism. As a result, African-American writings, whether they are fiction, poems, plays, or essays, have tended to be concerned with issues of social justice within and outside of the culture and with issues of personal growth, joy, and sorrow, with philosophical thought, morality, wisdom, and spiritual regeneration as well.

We have to resist the tendency to make peoples of color into a monolith and work to obliterate the idea that people of color make no distinctions in their own cultures as to what is excellent and what is not, what works best and what does not.[4] Yet any devotee of jazz, for example, will tell you that Miles Davis was who he was because of his artistry as well as his political resistance, intertwined as they were. In other words, all African-American texts are not the same. There are standards, not always the same as those upheld in the West, that African-Americans hold to in determining what is the good and the beautiful.

The issue of multiculturalism is complex. I am sure that there are Chicanos, native Americans, Asian-Americans, Latinos, and Southeast Asian–Americans who perceive the world quite differently from African-Americans, for we have had distinctly different histories even as we have all been gravely affected by the racism of this country. If those who support multiculturalism support it only as an opposition to the West, then our identities remain defined by the West, just as it says they are. Nor is Western culture as monolithic as it is often represented. It too has its differences and hierarchies, a paradigm we do not need to imitate.

In acknowledging, exploring, and valuing the complexity of this country, and of this world, American educational institutions could prepare their students for the world that is already here. We might be able to value difference as a creative charge rather than a threatening reality.[5]

18 A Rough Terrain: The Case of Shaping an Anthology of Caribbean Women Writers (1995)

At present I am engaged along with one of my sisters, Opal Palmer Adisa, in constructing an anthology of English-speaking Caribbean women's creative and critical writings especially for use in college classrooms. Opal and I have for many years bemoaned the fact that such a text does not exist, particularly since Caribbean women's writing in the Islands as well as in the United States, the United Kingdom, and Canada is flourishing. If "merit" were the measure, if the appearance of new forms and concerns and different approaches to language were criteria, these writers would, we thought, be at the top of reading lists in English, comparative literature, and other literature courses.

In one sense, the constructing of such an anthology might seem to be a focused endeavor. Yet I have found in my attempt to frame it as accurately and as fully as possible that conceptualizing this collection is fraught with both possibilities and contradictions, and brings up issues not only about the politics of articulating a Caribbean identity but also about the politics of a literature defined by racial or gendered identity in general. Especially when confronted, on the one hand, with this postmodernist critical moment and, on the other, the movement toward diversity, shaping a field (which is what anthologies tend to do) is at bottom a sociopolitical as well as an educational act.

This exploratory essay is more a meditation of thoughts generated by this project than a presentation on Caribbean women writers. I found that much of my thinking about anthologizing this particular body of writing has been affected by my own personal assessment of present "multicultural"

First published in David Palumbo-Liu, ed., *The Ethnic Canon: Histories, Institutions, and Interventions* (Minneapolis: University of Minnesota Press, 1995), 241–59. The proposed anthology of Caribbean women's writing was not completed.

educational movements in this country, as well as my own belief that very few of us know or recall the *history* of these movements.

As a result of many decades of activism on the part of U.S. intellectuals of color, and the political factor of changing demographics, some U.S. institutions of higher learning have begun to accept the premise that their curricula have been largely Eurocentric and that possibly there may be non-European intellectual traditions that students need to know. From my experience as a speaker and workshop leader, teachers all over the country are trying to diversify their courses, particularly in the areas of history and literature. But most of these teachers have themselves not been educated in the literatures of racial minorities in the United States, much less of other peoples, such as those of the Caribbean. Even scholars of one of these groups, let us say, African Americans, are not necessarily knowledgeable about Chicano or Asian American literatures. That realization has been most forcefully felt at the University of California, Berkeley, with the passage of an American Cultures requirement, which is predicated on the idea that there are many intersecting American cultures. How does one begin to teach about those groups with whose *intellectual* tradition one has had little contact?

Even when there is a clearly defined Ethnic Studies department that focuses on American ethnic racial minorities, as there is at my university, there are major concerns as to what and whom we should study; for the "Four Food Groups," as my students sometimes call our simplistic categorization of American minorities, are not as discrete as they seem to be. For example, there are distinct groups of people with distinct histories, cultures, and concerns whom we label "Latinos." Puerto Ricans come from a Caribbean island colonized by Spain and most recently by the United States. They are racially Black, Indian, or white, but most likely a combination of these three racial groups, and have had a long history of migration to the East Coast, where racial differentiation is a critical issue. Some Chicanos have resided in the Southwest even before it was wrested from Mexico by the United States, whereas others have just recently migrated from Mexico. Moreover, the identities of many groups labeled Latinos, Hispanics, African Americans, or Asians are not fixed. The migrations of the sixties and seventies have resulted in the mingling and mixing of many groups—those who have migrated from Central and Latin American, African Americans and recently arrived Jamaicans and Africans, Vietnamese and Southeast Asian Americans. What we often forget is that even though these groups are all peoples of color and have experienced racism in the United States, race and another social construct, gender, have not meant the same thing for each of them, either in the "old country" or here in the United States.

Issues of fluctuating identities, then, must be understood as central to the achievement of multicultural education in the United States, lest we misrepresent peoples of color as static and unchanging. In this complex construct of cultures, anthologies become extremely important, for it is often to an anthology that one turns, at least as a guide, when one knows little about an intellectual area.

If American teachers are not generally knowledgeable about the "Four Food Groups" of the United States, consider how scanty might be their knowledge of a region as complex as that of the Caribbean, which consists of many islands, first populated by Indians, colonized by various European powers who imported large numbers of African slaves, and in some cases indentured East Indians, and to which other peoples such as the Chinese and various Arab peoples have migrated. For at least a century, this region has been a fulcrum of different races and cultures, anticipatory of the present condition of the United States. The Caribbean is also a region that, because of its proximity to the United States (even before it was part of the United States), has both had much impact on and been gravely affected by its large, sometimes superpower neighbor.

I suppose some people would consider me a Caribbean woman writer, although I have studied and written primarily on African American women. My formative years were spent in the Caribbean, which affected my sense of the oral and written language of cultural forms and referents. Still, I have spent most of my adult life in the United States as an African American of Caribbean descent. It is interesting that many notable African American critics—for example, Arnold Rampersad, the distinguished biographer of Langston Hughes—are also originally from the Caribbean and have, like me, lived much of their adult life in the United States. As such, we bridge two cultures—or is it three or four? Rampersad, for instance, is partially East Indian in origin, as are many Afro-Caribbean peoples. If we extend the articulation of a Caribbean identity to the many linguistic domains of the region—English, Spanish, French, Dutch, not to mention Creole—the quest of identity is even more complex, although those residing in the region would insist that there are certain similarities that transcend language.

Recent collections that include the works of Caribbean women are indications of the myriad ways in which the writing of a Caribbean American woman writer like myself might be framed. Responding to the fact that collections on Caribbean writers are rare, and that generally speaking, because of the marginalization of the region, even those rare collections are primarily male-oriented,[1] Caribbean women writers have included themselves in United States–based anthologies such as

Diasporic Black Women's Writing
African American Women's Writing
Third World Women's Writing
Women of Color Writing
Women Writers of the Americas

These categories are not arbitrary and are in fact engendered within political strategies that are engaged in the question of how a body of thought might be studied within the academy. Anthologies are often the mode by which categories such as racial, ethnic, regional, linguistic, gendered, and political affiliations taken on visibility. It is important, particularly now, to think about what these differentiated constructs signify in this age of official multiculturalism.

Of course I find it exhilarating and important that Caribbean women can be so variously characterized. Such a multiplicity of selves, at least in relation to linguistic labeling, speaks to the complexity of my experience historically and presently, and is certainly an advance over the long centuries of repression and of coerced silence or narrowly constricted language within which those like myself have had to maneuver. Still, I am concerned about what each of these categories really signifies in terms of who I was, am, have meant, and, even more important, might be or mean. To what extent does each of these categories liberate the voices of Caribbean women and authentically communicate their experiences and history? To state my concern in a broader way: Is there a false unity camouflaging dominance and subordination for various groups of women writers depending on the category within which they are studied? To what extent do anthologies reproduce modes of exclusion or dominance? How does the use of one category or another affect curriculum, institution building, configurations of study within academic institutions as to what is significant enough to be studied about these various groups? Who are the users and the used, the communicators, the consumers, the audience?

In forging out the meanings—or, to be more accurate, the *changing* meanings—of these categories, I have found myself turning to the history of the terms themselves, at least as I have experienced them within the American university system. For me and for many women literary activists in the United States, the point at which we could be studied in the academy was first sharply articulated within the cultural nationalist movements of the 1960s. It is to that period that I will go for some clarification as to political strategies embodied in different academic configurations of study. I will then focus on some recent anthologies and the way in which they have tried to resolve some of these issues.

Not often mentioned about the cultural nationalist movements of the 1960s is the degree to which they were influenced by liberation movements in the Third World. This fact is *crucial* for the evolution of the academic nomenclature of the time. The Mau Maus in Kenya, the Cuban Revolution, the Independence Movement in India and Ghana, the Vietnam War, to name a few such liberation struggles, influenced major thinkers such as LeRoi Jones (later Imamu Baraka), as well as ordinary people like myself, in terms of how we saw the world. Jones would document the effects of the Cuban Revolution on his art and politics in his essay, "Cuba Libre," explaining how his visit to that country made him see the relationship between art and politics.[2] And in 1962, Harold Cruse, one of the major intellectual critics of that period, was already seeing "Negroes as a potential revolutionary force aligned to that of the Third World."[3] The term "the Third World," which had been used at the 1955 Bandung Conference of African and Asian nations to characterize those countries colonized by the West and/or held under control by the struggle between the West and the Communist East, began to replace, in many progressive groups, the pejorative term "underdeveloped countries."

What was significant about the many and various societies of the Third World was that most of these countries had experienced colonialism (the unacknowledged cause of their supposed underdevelopment), and that these peoples were darker peoples while the colonizers were usually whites. Racism and colonialism were intertwined, a phenomenon that Richard Wright astutely analyzed in his collection of essays, *White Man, Listen!* (1951). Given that analysis, one could posit that African Americans, although they lived within the United States, were, because of their historical experience of slavery and contemporary experience of racism, an internally colonized group just as the colored folk in the majority of the world were oppressed under the yoke of colonialism.[4] The making of that link between colored folk in the United States and those in the Third World would be crucial to the cultural nationalist movements in African Americans and to Puerto Ricans, Native Americans, Chicanos, and Asian Americans who followed the lead of African Americans.

Frantz Fanon's *The Wretched of the Earth* (1961/1966) did much to underline not only the material exploitation of colored folk by the West that even Marx had not pinpointed, but also the ways that material exploitation was made possible by strategies of psychological oppression, that is, by the colonizers' attempt to eliminate every culture as useless unless it emanated from the white West. Cultural exploitation was integral to political and economic exploitation, a point that many politicos of color in the West have yet to understand. That Fanon was from Martinique in the Caribbean was certainly a factor in his growing awareness of the use of hegemonic, neocolonial strategies as well as his studies of the overtly, psychically abusive oppression of the Algerians.

When I took part in the City College of New York (CCNY) student strike of 1968–69, some of us were really concerned as to whether our focal demand for Black Studies was enough—should it not be for Third World Studies? We had been influenced by Third World struggles and by the folk in our movement—Caribbeans, Puerto Ricans, Africans, East Indians, and Chinese—who embodied these struggles. The Vietnam War was also raging, a galvanizing force in our thinking about ourselves. Still, there were those of us who warned that an international focus was so much more glamorous than a local one and might deflect from the difficult job of dismantling racism in the United States, of giving worth to our cultural contributions and dilemmas in the United States. So often progressive peoples like to focus on broad abstract issues of economic exploitation and racism but are not interested in the lives of people of color who are living but a few miles from them. That tension was dramatically acted out at Six PAC, the Sixth Pan African Congress (1974), over the debate as to whether Cubans should be allowed to participate, since it was not clear that these Caribbean people were Black. For some, the tension resolved itself in Malcolm X's visit to Mecca, where he declared the revolutionary possibility of the equality of races under Islam.

On the academic and literary front, the cultural nationalist impetus of the sixties resulted in anthologies like *Black Fire* (1968), and generic ones on Chicano literature, Third World writers, and so on, and in the demand for not only Black but also Chicano and Ethnic Studies programs and departments within the university as other groups of color in the United States began to articulate their own exclusion. If there was anything we activists in the sixties learned, it was that we did not know our official history and that to know it and to keep it alive for generations, we had to institutionalize it. At the same time, outside the United States in my natal world, the Caribbean, where there had also been liberation and independence movements, the realization that cultural Western hegemony was rampant resulted in Afro-Caribbean movements that brought to the fore the African influences on cultures within which we all lived, cultures that had been declared by our Western Masters (and too often by ourselves) to be nonexistent. Many of these movements underscored the dominance of European culture over African cultures, which were usually depicted by Western culture as pathological.

As Black Studies and Ethnic Studies departments were being precariously institutionalized in but a few places, another nomenclature began to surface in the United States. Ethnic peoples of color were increasingly being lumped together by officials and policymakers under the label "minority," a term that implicitly dissociated these groups from the majority of the world who were people of color. The term "minority" undercut the connotation of that multiuniverse and of the possibility of the strength in numbers that the phrase "Third World people" had suggested.

As the Vietnam War and the War on Poverty ended, it seems to me that there was a new attempt on the part of the dominant culture to undercut the possibilities of the sixties. Perhaps the most devastating blow to the discourse on racism that developed at that point were the many Euro-American appropriations of the term "ethnic." That word had, in the sixties, meant those peoples in America who were not considered by the general populace to be "real" Americans because of their race and non-European cultural base. European Americans began challenging that concept by declaring that they too belonged to specific ethnic groups. Why, then, should Ethnic Studies not include the study of Italian or German Americans? In refusing to accept how the experience of racism against a group was the kernel of the definition of the word "ethnic" as it had been used in the sixties, whites could camouflage the primary thrust of the just-emerging Ethnic Studies movement as well as the new scholarship just beginning to be produced on the histories, literatures, and cultures of the United States peoples of color.

Coalitions of peoples of color were experiencing conflict within their own ranks, for we found that we often did not know each other and that there were critical historical and cultural differences among the groups. Those differences were also exacerbated by the official favoring of some groups over others, for instance, the labeling of Asians and West Indians as "model minorities." Coalitions based on the idea of racism as a common group experience were confronting difficulties because of the claim to a unity that was often a false one, especially in the context of the power dynamics of American society.

One effect of that uncoalitioning, I believe, is the fact that few men of color writers and scholars seemed to be collaborating with each other across ethnic-color lines to produce new concepts or anthologies of writing. Much of the discourse on race in anthologies was, in fact, just that—academic discourse (one exception was Ishmael Reed's *Yard Bird Lives!* [1975] and his organization, Before Columbus). Thus, collections of creative writing began to give way to collections of critical writing or of major writers of the past. For example, I recall the publication of only one major anthology of contemporary Afro-American literature in the 1980s: *Breaking Ice* (1990), edited by Terry MacMillan, who is of course labeled a writer rather than a scholar.

The major exception to this trend of fragmentation in the Black and Ethnic Studies literary movement of the 1970s and 1980s was the coalescing of women in the African American, Chicano, Native American, and Asian groups. As the term "Third World" gave way to the more limited term "Minority" (in the official discourse), women, colored and white, were beginning to articulate themselves as women. Contrary to what some of our major scholars are saying today, the second wave of American feminism and the call for Women's Studies followed Black and ethnic movements and, in pivotal ways, resulted from women's objections to being largely excluded from their nationalist groups' definitions and concerns. White women learned from their experiences in the civil rights movement how restricted they were as women, as Sara Evans documents in her book *Personal Politics* (1979). And women of color in their respective cultural nationalist groups discovered that not only were they not perceived as central, they were in fact subordinated to men. One can see the beginnings of that realization, for example, in Toni Cade Bambara's anthology, *The Black Woman,* which was published in 1970. But because of the access white women had to the American media, the United States women's movement was often characterized as an exclusively white women's movement.

As a result of the sexism women were experiencing in their own political nationalist groups and their exclusion from the white women's movement, Chicanas, African, Asian, and Native American women formed their own organizations and, particularly on the West Coast, came together in women of color organizations. One result of this coalescing was the explosion in publishing in the 1970s by African American women writers, who published more than they ever had before, and beyond that an explosion of Chicana, Native American, and Asian American writing in the 1980s.

Pivotal anthologies in the late seventies and eighties pointed to new frames for the study of women's writing. The anthology *All the Women Are White, All the Blacks Are Men, But Some of Us Are Brave: Black Women's Studies* (1982) articulated the unique space within which African American women writers, scholars, and activists moved since Black women were not perceived as central to their own ethnic, racial, and sociopolitical organizations or to the white Women's Studies movement. The anthology *The Black Woman Cross-Culturally* (1981), edited by Philomena Steady, and *Sturdy Black Bridges* (1979) took, respectively, diasporic social-scientific and humanistic approaches to the study of Black women. The anthology *This Bridge Called My Back* (1981), which focused on similarities and differences among United States women of color, signaled growing alliances among writers in the different colored ethnic groups. On an international level, women from the previously colonized countries of the world challenged, at international conferences, American women's right to define feminism. Many United States women of color activists agreed with the concerns of Third World women outside the United States. One result was anthologies on the writings of postcolonial women such as the special edition of *Inscriptions,* "Travelling Theories, Travelling Theorists," brought out by the group for the Critical Study of Colonial Discourse at the University of California at Santa Cruz. Another development was the production of anthologies by "local" women such as *Jamaica Woman* (1980) and *Savacou* (1977). Such anthologies, however, were hampered by their lack of access to the publishing and distributing muscle of the metropolis and are therefore not very well known or accessible to many people or to the academic institutions that are often the lifeline for anthologies.

One reason anthologies on Caribbean women published in the United States are so important is precisely because of the issue of access, even as that access signals the dominant role that American publishing companies play in the literary world. Scholars and writers who publish in the United States and include Caribbean women writers in their anthologies have considerable effect on the ways these writers are perceived in the academy. In the last decade, these scholars and writers have used different strategies to shape the ways in which Caribbean women's texts might be read. By calling attention to the following anthologies, I do not intend to privilege them over other anthologies on this subject or to insist that any one of them is superior to another. Rather, I am concerned with what each of them tells us about its ideological literary position. I am also interested in the purposes to which they might be put to use in different kinds of classroom settings.

I have selected two different groups of anthologies featuring Caribbean women writers in order to discuss the complexities of anthologizing in this movement of institutionalized "multiculturalism." The first group I am calling the "Metropolis Frame"—that is, those editions by non-Caribbean scholars who include these writers in a frame that is wider than that of a specific Caribbean "identity." The second group I am calling "Placed and Displaced Caribbean Frames"—anthologies generated by varying concepts of what it means to be a Caribbean woman.

Reading Black, Reading Feminist is comprised primarily of essays on African American women's writing by critics noted for their work in African American literature. As is true of Gates's orientation, critics featured here are Africans, African Americans, and Euro-Americans. There is a focus in this volume on what might be considered "major writers" in the tradition. It is interesting that the recent tendency to canonize *Black* female writers results in a plurality of essays on *African American* writers, and that the only Caribbean writer featured in *Reading Black, Reading Feminist* is Jamaica Kincaid. Her singular presence seems somewhat tokenistic, for her inclusion in the volume seems to signal that she belongs to the African American canon ("Black" in this anthology). Kincaid has lived in the United States for many years and could, I suppose, be considered an African American writer. I wonder whether her being chosen for this volume has as much to do with her cultural origins as a Caribbean women as it does with her popularity among critics. Although Kincaid's work is certainly about the Caribbean, and about Caribbean peoples who have migrated to the United States, hers is but one view of the region and of the process of migration. Readers who know little about the history and politics of the region may accept her perspective as if it were the only view—the danger, of course, in including only one writer from the region. In a real sense, Kincaid's writing is culturally displaced in this volume by a frame that privileges the metropole and marginalizes those outside it. Gates's collection is useful, however, particularly for those classrooms in which knowledge of the latest critical writing on African American literature is the goal—classes on African American literature and literary theory, even Black feminist theory.

While *Reading Black, Reading Feminist* consists almost entirely of critical writing by or about well-known authors, Gloria Anzaldúa's *Making Face, Making Soul* is a compilation of personal narratives, poetry, and critical essays by U.S. women of color writers, many of them not well known, a kind of sequel to *This Bridge Called My Back,* the first anthology that framed women writers as women of color and one that Anzaldúa also helped to edit. *Making Face* includes more Caribbean writers: two creative writers from Jamaica and Puerto Rico, and even a few critics, as well as the writings of two well-known women of Caribbean descent, June Jordan and Audre Lorde. However, none of the works selected for the volume by these writers has to do with a Caribbean context. Rather, the writings by Caribbean women are primarily related to positions they share as women of color with other women of color in the United States.

Anzaldúa's collection is fresh, filled with creative writing and innovative critical works, and would be a fine text for inspiring especially women students of color, informing and challenging them about issues of the interrelatedness of race and gender and sexual preferences. But in order to do that, this anthology tends to flatten out the contextual differences of the various women of color groups in the United States as an argument for coalitions for struggle. Given the history of the last decade, the naive reader might assume more homogeneity among these groups than there really is. Finally, because the writings of women of color who share Spanish as part of their linguistic heritage has been neglected in the past, the volume tends to foreground that literature. Perhaps because of that focus, two of the four women writers featured in *Making Face* are Puerto Ricans, a reminder that the Caribbean is also a part of that linguistic construct.

An important difference between Gates's anthology and Anzaldúa's that might have much to do with their respective approaches is that while *Reading Black, Reading Feminist* is published by a New York mainstream publishing company, Meridian, Anzaldúa's is published by a small press on the West Coast, Aunt Lute Foundation. Gates's selections tend to privilege an East Coast mainstream view, while Anzaldúa's choices indicate a literary landscape beyond that of the mainstream publishing East, as far south as Texas, as far west as Seattle. Her volume suggests the variety of places in the United States to which Caribbean women have migrated and begins to refute the much-believed idea that Caribbean peoples reside only on the East Coast.

While Anzaldúa focuses on color and gender in the United States, Joanne Braxton and Andrée McLaughlin's *Wild Women in the Whirlwind* uses a different frame—that of women writers writing in the African Diaspora (Africa, the United States, the Caribbean, Great Britain). In her introduction, Braxton proclaims the existence of a literary and activist Black Women's Renaissance. This volume is unique in that it relates Black women's activism to Black women's folklore and literature, to the oral as well as to the literary traditions, a frame that might do much to illuminate Caribbean women's writings. Yet even as the introduction expresses a belief in the African Diaspora, most of the essays are on African American women writers and activists and are written by African American women critics. What Braxton and McLaughlin's collection indicates is the difficulty, at least at present, of compiling an African diasporic collection when Black women writers from Africa and the Caribbean, Great Britain, and Canada as well as from the United States are in themselves quite varied in their historical and cultural contexts. The volume is significant *because* it announces the possibility that there are common themes, issues, and forms in the African *female* diaspora, but the volume does not fulfill its promise perhaps because those who attempt to discover women writers in the diaspora and outside of the United States find that the task is difficult for many Black women writers outside the United States to be heard. This volume at least lets us know they are there. *Wild Women* suggests the possibility of multiple Black women's writings beyond the United States and may well pave the way for more focused anthologies that more fully explore their histories, cultures, and literary forms.

Anthologies of Black feminist, diasporic, and women of color writings have not included many Caribbean women authors, whose racial, cultural, and ethnic identities are varied, sometimes fluid, and for whom the issue of the relationship between orality and literacy is a complex one. However, collections specifically focused on these women are now beginning to be published. In this second group, what I call "Placed and Displaced Caribbeans," I am going to discuss three anthologies: *Out of the Kumbla* (1990), edited by Carole Boyce Davies and Elaine Savory Fido, scholars of Caribbean and African literature; *Caribbean Women Writers* (1990), edited by Selwyn Cudjoe, a scholar of Caribbean literature and politics; and *Green Cane and Juicy Flotsam* (1991), edited by Carmen C. Esteves and Lizabeth Paravisini-Gebert, scholars of Caribbean literature.

As if responding to the absence of historical context so often a characteristic of anthologies, Carole Boyce Davies introduces *Out of the Kumbla* with a searching essay on the history of the Caribbean and how women occupy specific roles in this history. Davies articulates as well differences among Caribbean women according to which island they came from, their class, nationality, and language. She asks a pivotal question—whether writers who were born in the Caribbean but migrated to Great Britain, Canada, or the United States should be called Caribbean writers. The economic necessity to migrate is a characteristic of Caribbean societies themselves, but when does one stop being a Caribbean and become African American or British Black?

Davies also questions the tendency of scholars to avoid the obvious multiplicity of ethnicities in the Caribbean—not only African and European Caribbeans exist and write, but also East Indians, Chinese, and Arabs. However, even as her introduction signals these issues as significant to our understanding of the Caribbean context, the critical essays in *Out of the Kumbla* focus on well-known writers, most of whom have left the Caribbean and come from relatively privileged backgrounds. As Davies notes, one reason for this might be that many Caribbean women who are writing in the Caribbean operate in the oral tradition, in poetry and theater, arts that are communal and are not necessarily written down for the reading public of the metropolis. Sistren, a theater group in Jamaica, is an example of the tremendous creativity of women; yet much of Sistren's work is not available to a reading public.

One other important characteristic of *Out of the Kumbla* is that it is comprised entirely of critical essays. Many of the creative writings on which the essays are based are not readily accessible to the audience to which they are addressed. Perhaps Davies thought that the existence of criticism would lead to an increased awareness that these writers are there, and to the publication of more anthologies that might feature the writers themselves. That she chose to emphasize critical works might also indicate the great influence the academy has on what is considered "literature" (and what is not). As such, *Out of the Kumbla* is an excellent anthology for classes in critical theory as well as in literature and Women's Studies classes. Yet in this volume the voices of the writers themselves are not heard.

Davies's anthology is an example of the cultural force that anthologies can have, for it helped to galvanize the first Conference of Caribbean Women Writers in the United States (1989), the conference upon which Selwyn Cudjoe's anthology *Caribbean Women Writers* is based. Like Davies's anthology, Cudjoe's collection is primarily a collection of criticism. What distinguishes his collection, however, is that it includes a significant number of essays by the writers themselves concerning what they think they are doing and why. A Caribbeanist, Cudjoe has written on the politics of resistance in the Afro-Caribbean region. Heretofore, when he wrote on literature, he focused primarily on male writers who seemed to be emblematic of that resistance. This new anthology also charts overtly political territory, now including feminist or at least women's writing as part of that terrain, an important advance. Perhaps because his view of literature is that of opposition to injustice, and because historically it is clear that opposition has occurred throughout the Caribbean, Cudjoe does present an overview of the Spanish and French Caribbean. Still, most of the essays in this collection are from the English Caribbean.

A recently published anthology on Caribbean women's writing called *Green Cane and Juicy Flotsam,* edited by Carmen C. Esteves and Lizabeth Paravisini-Gebert, is a sign that some scholars are attempting to correct the American academic view of the region as only that of the English-speaking islands. Importantly, this volume is published by a well-known academic press (Rutgers University Press), an indication that the academy is beginning to pay more attention to the writings of Caribbean women. The editors, two scholars of Caribbean literature, assume that the "Caribbean" means an integral geographical region regardless of the differences in history, language, and, to some extent, culture. A collection of short stories by women writers, this anthology shapes the field in a particular way—Caribbean women, regardless of whether they come from Cuba, Guadeloupe, or Jamaica, or are of African, Indian, or Chinese descent, share a history of slavery, servitude, colonialism, literary voicelessness, and patriarchal oppression. The collection privileges similarities that the editors perceive among different groups residing in these islands. One gets a sense of the integrity of the region in terms of women writers' concerns, themes, forms, so that the narratives create in themselves a larger story—one of community, coalition, and possibility. The editors demonstrate, through their juxtapositions, what the themes, forms, customs, concerns of Maryse Condé from Guadeloupe have in common with those of Opal Palmer Adisa from Jamaica or Rosario Ferre from Puerto Rico.

Yet, in order to forge such a unity, the editors had to sacrifice certain important elements in their construction of Caribbean women's writings. Most obvious is the fact that there are differences in the colonial histories of these many islands. Differences between the histories and representations of Spanish, French, Dutch, and British slavery and colonialism tend to be minimized in this volume. Of course, the islands have not remained static since they became "independent." Cuba has pursued a socialist path. Guadeloupe has remained very close to its mother country, France. Jamaica has had movements toward and away from socialism and has been greatly influenced by its giant neighbor, the United States. To what extent and in what ways have the islands' "modern" histories effected different views of race and gender, sexuality and ethnicity? For example, do Dominican women writers of African descent use the same forms, have the same concerns, as their white Dominican sisters?

Unlike many anthologies on the Caribbean, *Green Cane* presents writings by Caribbean women from all over the region rather than critical essays or historical analyses. The anthology foregrounds Caribbean women's voices. It is an excellent introduction to those voices—except that the exclusive genre represented in the anthology is narrative fiction. This is an important point since in the Caribbean the prevalent literary/oral arts of women tend to be those of poetry and theater. The question that the construction of this anthology poses for me is whose voices are being heard, who writes fiction as opposed to other forms—class concerns that one cannot ignore if one is to accurately represent Caribbean women's voices. Because the authors do not provide us with historical distinctiveness about class as well as regional and ethnic differences, the unknowing reader or teacher might assume that the emphasis on sexual repression is the same in an English-speaking island like Jamaica and a Spanish-speaking island like the Dominican Republic and that women who till the soil or work in factories or go to school or become housewives are concerned with the same issues. In effect, this anthology might suggest that one is voiceless if one does not publish fiction. *Green Cane* leaves me with the difficult issue that many women in the Caribbean do not operate in the sphere of literacy even as that sphere is the primary one that is privileged in the West. Still, because this anthology does present the voices of Caribbean women as represented by writers, rather than criticism or history, it does open up spaces for more varied, experimental manifestations of Caribbean women's linguistic activities.

As I reflect upon this case study, my attempt to shape an anthology on Caribbean women's writings, I want to return to the questions I posed at the beginning of this essay. The first was, To what extent do the different types of anthologies liberate the voices of the women in the categories within which I, as an African American Caribbean woman, might be included?

I am impressed, first of all, by what anthologies can do. Anthologies do chart a field, as the cultural nationalist anthologies of the sixties and the women's anthologies of the seventies demonstrate. They can be a significant cultural force in creating interest in a field, as in the case of Carole Boyce Davies's *Out of the Kumbla*. They are not fixed in stone, as revisionist women of color anthologies exemplify. Anthologies as an intersection of many identities do develop, change, revise themselves. Obviously, the process of anthologizing is worth it for those of us in "new fields." And yet I am also struck by the limitations of anthologies, limitations that recall another of my initial questions: Is there a false unity camouflaging dominance and subordination? Do anthologies reproduce exclusion or dominance? Anthologies can appear to be comprehensive when they are not, since specific historical moments affect their shaping. Thus it is important for the anthologist to indicate her/his frame, limits, purposes, so as not to mislead the teacher or the reader. For example, an anthology that emphasizes the subject of immigration, a particularly hot topic today in the multicultural marketplace, might give the impression that this topic is the only one about which Chicano or Asian Americans write.

Creating overarching paradigms is a tendency among academic scholars. If paradigms such as Diaspora, Women of Color, Oppositional or Postcolonial Literature become the frame, the gain for a literature such as that of Caribbean Women's Writings is that links between racism, sexism, and class exploitation can be perceived and studied so that one can see commonalities in the workings of these phenomena. Yet such linkages, unless carefully analyzed, camouflage the ways in which some categories, depending upon the particular historical moment, are more privileged than others. As important, the difference of historical process among various configurations of groups, as well as their specific cultural mores, are hidden under abstract declarations of unity. For example, often African American women become the spokeswomen for women of color, as if we were all the same, or Caribbean women become subordinated to women of color categories without an acknowledgement of their quite different definitions of race and gender. Such a process is itself the epitome of racism, for we become homogenized, dehumanized under terms that are primarily oppositional to whites. As such, "white definitions" remain the norm.

I am also intrigued by anthologies' effects on the publishing trends of the literatures they present, effects that recall my question about configurations of study within academic institutions, the purposes in fact of literatures becoming part of the academy. For one, I find that as a group's literature becomes more institutionalized in the academy, its contemporary literature, that is, the literature coming into being in the present, is less and less discussed and analyzed in academic publications. In the beginnings of each of the socio/political/literary movements I have mentioned, the writers emphasized these connections with their own communities, a recommendation for doing anthologies on specific groups. As these literatures begin to be legitimized by the academy, more and more critics contribute historical and literary stances. Thus a critical language and a tradition of critical studies develops, an important aspect of any community's literary and scholarly tradition. What is sometimes lost, however, is that as the literature, let us say of African Americans, becomes more acceptable to the academic world of the metropolis, the past literature of that group becomes the norm for study, and few examples of that group's contemporary literature, its contemporary utterances, appear in anthologies. Fewer and fewer anthologies featuring specifically contemporary literature are published. At the present time, for example, few anthologies of contemporary African American poetry are being published, in contrast to the many anthologies that were published in the late sixties and early seventies. At times, one result of this tendency is the split between critical approaches and contemporary stances of the writers themselves, or even more important, the decline of a dialogue between contemporary critics and writers. Anthologists might do well to consider the ease with which they can chart the past without engaging the pressing debates, expressions of the present.

Anthologies also confront us with the issue as to whether a community of women writers (or any writers, for that matter) actually represent their community, a critical issue about which I am constantly thinking—since so often cultures are represented in the classroom by writings, either by critical studies of a particular group or of writings by that group. In contrast, many cultures invest much in oral traditions and increasingly in visual media. This issue also reminds us that we often think of the users, the consumers of literature, as limited to those in the classroom, or to the "intellectual marketplace." Caribbean women writers, after all, do not write primarily for the purpose of being taught in the classrooms of the metropolis. They write for many reasons, not the least of which is speaking to those who do not necessarily now have the means of reading their books. In other words, they write to those who may not yet read and cannot now buy their books. They write to the future as well as to the present. To create an anthology of their writings brings to mind Gayatri Spivak's statement that "to confront them [those who do not write] is not to represent them but to learn to represent ourselves."[5]

As teachers, many of us tend to equate writing with the reality of a folk, and in fact writers do express *their* view of being in a particular construct, history. Yet, as I reflect on this process, I think it is important for scholars, anthologists, and teachers to realize the limits, as well as the possibilities, of "literature" and of "writings" and to discuss these issues with students. If not, the multicultural curriculum we are trying to create may generate new, though different, stereotypes, the continuation of that academic stereotype called "others." Even as I know that creating an anthology of Caribbean women's writings of the English-speaking Caribbean is a worthwhile intellectual and political endeavor, I am increasingly aware of that endeavor's limitations and of the importance of signaling to the reader those limitations.

It is remarkable to me how fields grow, and change. Ethnic Studies, African American Studies, the intellectual terrain that I have been treading for some twenty-five years, has grown to such an extent that it is now questioning its own premises as to the meaning of racial identity. Because of the depth and extent of our scholarship, our identity from the perspective of ethnicity, race, gender, class affiliations can no longer be asserted as singular; rather, it is—or rather, they are—a multiplicity of selves. What that new configuration will mean for our present institutional labels, coalitions, and concerns is one challenge for the future. Anthologies can help us to assess our institutional stances, so that our sites in the academy keep pace with our intellectual questionings, our political developments.

Ethnic and African American Studies in the United States are, in a sense, just beginning to catch up with the complexities of the very concept of identity, complexities acknowledged by Caribbean peoples, for in that region identity is seldom characterized by a simple or single label. So, although the constructing of an anthology on Caribbean women's writings presents the anthologist with a rough, not yet leveled terrain (in other words, one that refuses to be simply and easily traveled), for that very reason, it challenges our assumptions that other terrains are as even as they seem. In testing the assumptions of a terrain as varied as that of the Caribbean, we also confront the shape of those fields that figure racial/gendered/ethnic intellectual institutions in the United States.

19 Diminishing Returns: Can Black Feminism(s) Survive the Academy? (1994)

When I was asked to speak at this conference on "Feminisms in the Twenty-First Century," at first I chose a topic that asked the question whether feminism in America is still largely conceived of as a white movement by most American institutions. Despite the impact the Anita Hill/Clarence Thomas hearings had on feminism in this country, I was amazed that when the media focused its attention on the women's movement as it did in 1992, it still featured primarily white women as its major spokespersons. For example, *Time Magazine* in 1992 featured on its oh-too-predictable March cover Gloria Steinem and Susan Faludi, representing two generations of the second wave of feminism.[1] Even *The Atlantic,* by featuring Wendy Kaminer's "Feminism's Identity Crisis," got into the fray, perhaps because of First Lady (a title I hate) Hillary Clinton's media profile. But while Wendy Kaminer's clearly conservative (backlash) piece did mention the white feminist theorist Carol Gilligan's work, it did not indicate that African-American women scholars had contributed anything of worth to American feminism(s).[2] Apparently Wendy Kaminer still thinks that feminism is a strictly white upper-class phenomena emanating from prestigious universities such as Harvard.

So much for media writers. As I thought about the concerns of this conference, however, who my likely audience would be—that of the smarter and purer folk in the academy where I am situated—I decided it would be more appropriate, more honest for me to assess my own site, hence the title of this exploration, "Diminishing Returns: Can Black Feminism(s) Survive the Academy?"

This paper was originally written for a conference entitled "Figuring Feminism at the Fin-de-Siècle," sponsored by Scripps College Humanities Institute and the Claremont Graduate Humanities Center. It was first published in David Theo Goldberg, ed., *Multiculturalism: A Critical Reader* (Oxford, U.K.: Basil Blackwell, 1994), 168–74.

I hope it is clear to everyone here that black feminisms have existed for a long time—that since the nineteenth century, black women such as activist Sojourner Truth, poet Frances Harper, and educator Anna Julia Cooper had articulated a position that stressed the interrelatedness of racism, sexism, and classism as central to this society's structure. I name these women's primary commitments because I want us all to be clear that African-American feminists have operated in many arenas, a fact that gets left out in cultural histories, even on the Left.[3] Radical black women such as turn-of-the-century feminist Ida B. Wells's hard-hitting journalistic pieces about lynchings demonstrate how racism and sexism are not separate entities, but are interdependent modes of domination which affect us all, for contrary to much contemporary white feminist theorizing, racism often expresses itself in sexist terms and sexism in racist terms. Works on African-American women are not just examples of some cultural nationalist problem, but rather a mirror image of this country's inability to deal with its hierarchical inequities. Too often race issues are seen as the "problems" of blacks and people of color, gender issues as the "problems" of women.

Contemporary black feminists have continued and developed their foremothers' tradition—especially in the literature they have produced—in which they have claimed themselves as subjects. Scholar Deborah King put it this way in her essay, "Multiple Jeopardy, Multiple Consciousness": "A black feminist ideology fundamentally challenges the interstructure of the oppressions of racism, sexism, and classism both in the dominant society and within movements for liberation."[4]

I hope it is clear also that the second wave of black feminist thought and practice did not originate or does not now reside primarily in the academy despite all the hoopla about political correctness. Rather, its roots were in popular movements, in the civil rights, black power, and women's movements of the 1960s and early 1970s as exemplified by the many voices of black women collected in Toni Cade's edition of *The Black Woman* (1970). Black feminist thought and practice is very much alive outside the academy, whether its proponents use that label or not, although I could not prove that since most studies conducted by American white women demonstrate the incidence of feminism among American women without taking into account in any real way the ways in which African-American women call themselves womanists, the word coined by writer Alice Walker to distinguish themselves and their specific perspective from white feminists. Other African-American women, like many of their women of color and white counterparts, may not call themselves feminists or even womanists, yet practice the tenets that that point of view signifies.[5]

As was true of the black women's rights movement of the nineteenth century, contemporary black feminisms have been articulated in many arenas, an important one being the literature of African-American women such as Alice Walker, Audre Lorde, Toni Morrison, and June Jordan. As I have already noted in my essay, "But What Do We Think We're Doing Anyway? The State of Black Feminist Criticism(s) or My Version of a Little Bit of History,"[6] in the seventies, the academy scarcely acknowledged the existence of black women in major knowledge areas such as literature or history, nor had a black feminist inquiry been initially central to the establishment of African-American and women's studies in the academy. For much of that decade, the subject of race was usually associated with men and the subject of gender with white women for even the most astute intellectuals. The few black women scholars who existed in the university often fell between the cracks or just managed to straddle the apparently divided terrains of race and gender.

By the early eighties, however, scholars had established a small but influential place in the academy for black women's studies, mostly as a result of the intensity and quality of African-American women's literature and scholarship. A few of us were able to excavate the neglected histories and literatures of African-American women, to articulate the interrelatedness of race, class, and gender as the core of a black feminist inquiry, and to critique the male bias of race analysis and the white bias of gender studies. The number and quality of these studies are too vast for me to cite in this essay. Suffice it to say that black feminist inquiry in all of the major disciplines of the university as well as in interdisciplinary areas, such as women's studies, African-American studies, and diaspora studies, has been substantive. As well, in collaboration with other women of color, in anthologies such as *This Bridge Called My Back* and *Making Face, Making Soul,* African-American women writers and scholars have challenged the concept of a universalized woman. As a result, the editors of the book *Feminist Theory in Practice and Process,* a collection of essays published in the women's studies journal *Signs* during the decade of the 1980s, could note "the shift away from an undifferentiated concept of woman" in recent feminist theorizing: "Just as one of the first acts in the development of a feminist theory was to reject the standpoint and experiences of white men as normative, so too, one of the first acts in developing black feminist theory has been to reject the perspectives of white women as normative, focusing instead on the concrete everyday experiences of black women as the basis for theory making."[7]

Black feminist inquiry also has had a major effect on the study of race, so that male African-American studies specialists increasingly include African-American women in their studies — to the extent that some of the major scholars in the area of African-American women's literature are African-

American men. Some African-American women critics have noticed that contemporary societal institutions still tend to choose African-American men over African-American women to be the "real" experts and spokes-men when it comes to critiquing the relationship between race and gender, again reflecting the hierarchical structure of our society in which men are always better than women.[8]

Fortunately, some male scholars are beginning to explore the other side of African-American women's studies, that constructions of masculinity in relation to race are often camouflaged in our society. Major contemporary African-American male writers such as John Wideman and Clarence Major credit African-American women's intellectual questionings in the 1970s with opening spaces for them to investigate themselves as men in relationships with family and female and male lovers, as opposed to the white/black border wars, relegated to black male writers of the past. Such an anthology is Joseph Beane's *Brother to Brother.* Some of my graduate students are engaged in this endeavor. An important anthology called *The African-American Black Male, His Person, Status, and Family,* edited by Richard Myers and Jacob Gorden, which places the intersection of race and gender in relation to men, is about to be published. As well, major intellectuals such as Cornel West and Manning Marable have used black feminist ideological positions in their analyses of black community contexts, and possibilities for liberation.[9]

African diasporic and postcolonial feminist studies have developed in the last decade. Because of its marginality in U.S. studies and its long tradition of subjugation to colonial/racial points of view that extend even beyond the celebration of left male critics' idealization of male Caribbean writer Frantz Fanon's writings, this field has understood the importance of one of the first tenets of black feminist scholarship—that of intervention and change. Postcolonial scholar Chandra Mohanty has pointed out that feminist scholarship "is not the mere production of knowledge about a certain subject. It is a political praxis which counters and resists the totalizing imperative of age-old 'legitimate' and 'scientific' bodies of knowledge."[10]

Critiques originating in black feminist thought, then, have had a sure effect on the restructuring of traditional disciplines. Positioned at the vortex of so many discourses that seem to be vying with one another for centrality, black feminist critics have had to rethink traditional constructs in the academy and the world. Many of my sister/colleagues, as well as graduate students with whom I work, have often asked ourselves the question, "To whom do I belong? Black studies? Women's studies? A specific discipline such as English or sociology?" Black feminist scholar Patricia Hill Collins recalls that she "found [her] training as a social scientist inadequate to the task of studying the subjugated knowledge of a black woman's standpoint. This is because subordinate groups have long had to use alternate ways to create independent self-definitions and self-valuations and to rearticulate them through our own specialists."[11] In creating alternative systems, black feminist critics have helped to validate the necessity for interdisciplinary approaches, such as those of cultural studies as well as the possibility of redefining the very concept of what it means to be an intellectual, since so many of our thinkers have resided outside the academy or even outside traditional black institutions.

But not only has black feminist inquiry critiqued the race bias of white feminisms, the gender bias of race matters, the usually neglected subject of class, the too-rigid boundaries of academic systems, it exists also for itself. In other words, black feminist thought is not only a critique of other systems that is at the service of the "real" points of view, it is also a distinctive, one is tempted to say, a coherent perspective, which places black women, including those from the rest of this hemisphere and Africa, at the center of its inquiry. That distinctiveness is obvious especially in the literature that African-American women have produced during the last two decades in which I would insist they have been major theorizers about gender, race, class, and sexual preference. Toni Morrison's receipt of the 1993 Nobel Prize for Literature—the first time a black woman, and an African-American has been so honored—is a sign that African-American women finally are being perceived as intellectuals within their own right, nationally and internationally. Increasingly, black feminist thought is also being articulated in critical works such as bell hooks's *Talking Back: Thinking Feminist, Thinking Black;* Patricia Hill Collins's *Black Feminist Thought;* and anthologies such as *Home Girls,* edited by Barbara Smith, *Wild Women in the Whirlwind,* edited by Braxton and McLaughlin, and *Changing Our Own Words,* edited by Cheryl Wall.

Without question, as the applications to the Ph.D. program in ethnic studies at my university indicate, more and more students are studying African-American women's thought, especially in the area of literature. I, for example, now find myself, as I am sure most of my sister/colleagues do, "an academic mother to more children than I could have possibly imagined, and to types of children beyond my conjuring . . . at a time when my white counterparts are already academic grandmothers."[12]

Clearly, black feminisms no longer are completely absent in the academy and have had some effect on the ways in which we think about the intersections of race, gender, and class, as well as the accomplishments and thought of black women. And yet—I have entitled this essay "Diminishing Returns: Can Black Feminism(s) Survive the Academy?" for, though there have been some advances, they have been achieved at much cost and have not really changed the landscape or the population of the academy. What central problems do black women and therefore, black feminisms face in the academy in the last decade of this century?

One especially important dilemma we face is who black feminist academics of the future will be. My experience during the last few years is that although African-American women's thought and literature, and intersections of race, class, gender, and even sexual preference are being focused on by some graduate students, few of them are black women or men. Of course, not all black women in the academy do feminist scholarship, nor is all black feminist scholarship done by black women. Yet, although black women are not all the same, they do bring a certain urgency to this area of study precisely because it affects them directly and emanates from their personal and historical contexts since black feminist thought, for them, is not only and primarily an artifact to be studied. It would be a tremendous loss, a distinct irony, if some version of black feminist inquiry exists in the academy to which black women are not major contributors.

My experience that there are few African-Americans entering graduate school is verified by statistics. In 1991, according to the *Journal of Blacks in Higher Education,* only 2.3 percent of the Ph.D.'s in all academic disciplines awarded in this country went to blacks, a percentage far below that of Ph.D.'s awarded in the 1970s to blacks, such as myself. There was a slight gain in overall black graduate enrollments in the late 1980s, but progress occurred mostly at professional schools such as business, law, and medicine. The *Journal* also included a survey of the status of African-Americans on the faculties of American colleges and universities. Although there were gains in the 1970s, there was a slowdown, then an abrupt drop during the Reagan/Bush years of the percentage of blacks at predominantly white institutions. The *Journal* points out that roughly half of the 19,000 black professors in the United States teach at the predominantly black colleges and universities — that is, one hundred colleges as opposed to the 3,000 "historically white" colleges and universities.[13] Even then, only 2.5 percent of all professors in the country, 4.2 percent of associate professors, 6.0 percent of assistant professors, and 6.7 percent of instructors were black.[14] How are African-American women faring? In 1987, African-American women received 54 percent of the doctoral degrees awarded blacks; that is 2 percent of the doctorates awarded that year. In 1985, 0.6 percent of all full professors were black women, 1.4 percent were associate professors, 2.5 percent were assistant professors, and 3.2 percent were instructors.[15]

Even I, suspicious of numbers and statistical studies, could see that the situation for African-American women graduate students and faculty is dismal. While I could have some measure of pride in the fact that such a small percentage of black feminist academics had had such a significant impact on intellectual inquiry in the 1970s and 1980s, any optimism I have about our situation was greatly outweighed by the reality of the minuscule number of black women entering the academy. Why are African-Americans, and especially women, not going into academic areas at a time when issues of race and gender have become increasingly acknowledged as central to intellectual inquiry?

I recall the many students I've worked with, very bright, intellectually oriented, and interested in graduate study, who decided to go into business, law, or medicine. I think about the many African-American students who didn't have the opportunity to make such a choice since they had not finished high school or did not have *access* even to the knowledge about these choices. For them, making it big in music or sports continues to be their only options out of poverty or the violence of an early death.

Some of us African-American academics have focused much of our attention on those students who manage to graduate from high school. I've learned in my twenty years at the University of California, Berkeley, that students of color who supposedly could not succeed in college often did very well when they learned about, were inspired by, the possibilities that other students had taken for granted from the time they were born. Still, many of those students, though interested in pursuing graduate study, moved into more "practical" areas such as the professional schools, community activism, and journalism. They felt, for some reason, that life in the academy would be unrewarding. While life in the professions might be difficult, at least they could make some money and pay back the debts their education incurred, even as they might be able possibly to affect our contemporary society.

As I was working on this essay, a new volume was published, exploring specifically the issue of black women faculties' survival in white universities. Called *Spirit, Space and Survival: African-American Women in (White) Academe,* this anthology, a collection of black women's voices from inside the academy, voices concerns that we black women faculty talk about when we see each other at conferences, usually the only time we do see each other since so many of us are the only black woman, or one of a few, at our respective universities. In fact, this volume grew out of such a meeting at a conference. The editors, Joy James and Ruth Farmer, say that the objective of the volume is to examine the voices of African-American women "struggling with Eurocentric disciplines, students, faculty and administrators in predominantly white institutions." Most African-American women faculty, they inform us, are at the bottom of the academic hierarchy and, even in comparison to the fewer black male academics, are paid less, have higher workloads, and get fewer returns. For most African-American academics, research and writing does not come easy, beleaguered as they are by demands within their institutions as well as in their families and communities, demands that they feel they must meet if they are to fulfill their many roles in their diverse communities.

I am aware of how better off African-American women are in the academy than they are in many sectors of our community. After all, we have the possibility of doing work we like to do, an opportunity that probably only 2 percent of the planet has got. Still it is important that we raise our voices about the inequities we face in our terrain and how it affects our daily lives, for our "complaints" nuance a site of possible resistance.

In their introduction to their courageous volume, Joy James and Ruth Farmer remind us that African-American women academics work in environments which often are not only nonsupportive but, at times, outright hostile. They (we) are expected to perform mightily—with little reward—and to be grateful that we are allowed in the halls of learning. Overworked and underrecognized, we are forced to cope with office and university politics as well as the racism, sexism, and homophobia inherent in these environments and the larger society.[16]

Perhaps my students are smarter then I think. Salaries paid to business, law, and medical graduates are considerably more than those paid to non-tenured, even tenured, professors. For African-Americans, most of whom come from families who are struggling to survive, the issue of monetary returns is not a mercenary concern but a communal one. In addition, as Martin Anderson, a senior fellow at the Hoover Institution at Stanford University, has pointed out, "the time necessary to earn a Ph.D. has gradually lengthened in recent years . . . that after receiving a bachelor's degree, the median time it takes to earn a Ph.D. is now 10.5 years. For women the median time to earn a Ph.D. has reached 12.5 years . . . the time it takes for black Americans to earn the Ph.D. stretches out to 14.9 years."[17]

Pursuing one's intellectual interests might seem frivolous to many African-American students, especially women, who are generally perceived as necessary contributors to their family and community's financial well-being.

In the essay "Balancing the Personal and the Professional," Adrianne Andrews extends the knowledge we have about African-American women academics by interviewing a number of black women faculty at different universities around the country about their lives. Inevitably she found they faced issues of concern to Euro-American women, but also issues specifically related to being black and female in the academic environment:

[t]he issues they felt were the most pressing ones facing them as black women, were not only the impact of gender and salary discrimination based on male dominance in the profession, and struggling to get tenure, but racial discrimination and a type of role conflict and professional burnout that was compounded by the fact of race, as well.[18]

One respondent noted:

Most women have family responsibilities, and when black women have family responsibilities, they're even more difficult for us than for the white woman because for us many of us are the first, second generation at best [in university life].[19]

Other respondents described how the black woman professor is often called upon to serve as mentor, mother, and counselor in addition to educator to African-American students who experience the academy as a hostile and alien place and that she often is expected to serve on committees to make certain the minority and woman perspective are represented. Some of my sister/colleagues refuse to be what they call "academic mules"; yet they are also aware that it is usually our communities who lose if we do not attempt to fulfill the demands of our respective institutions.

Many of the women in this study also are struggling with the issue of finding a suitable mate who could contend with a woman who has a doctorate, and whose professional life would involve much of her time. The question as to whether the feminist movement has negatively affected women's marital status or whether that idea is a media hype is one that Susan Faludi explores in her book *Backlash*. The situation in African-American communities perhaps might be different, an example of how an important mainstream "theory" might take on different ramifications if it is viewed from the point of view of African-Americans, and possibly other people of color. African-American men have been under severe attack from the judicial system and levels of poverty that affect their ability to be breadwinners. I note that in the last month, my local paper, the *Oakland Tribune*, ran a Sunday feature article about the fact that one-third of African-American women in the ages from eighteen to fifty who express heterosexual desires are not able to find a mate. Whether that fact is true or not (I always doubt newspaper articles), the experiences of many of my colleagues, as well as my own personal experience, indicate that African-American women academics very often are single, or single mothers, with little prospect of intragroup heterosexual relationships, if that is what they desire. As well, African-American women academics, whether they are heterosexual or homosexual, often are living in areas where there is no vibrant African-American presence, so that they suffer from cultural isolation.

But the problems of monetary returns, time concerns, probably work overload, and distorted personal relationships are not the only issues confronting an African-American woman who might want to go into the academy. When the *Journal of Blacks in Higher Education* asked black feminist scholar Professor Johnnetta Cole why there is a shortage of black professors, she not only cited these restraints but also that "many African-Americans entering the academy today do so because they have been lured by the promise of alternative models of research and action-oriented scholarship. . . . [But] anything not fitting the traditional model is considered less than scholarly."[20] While some African-American women are willing to endure financial and personal lifestyle sacrifices because they love intellectual inquiry and understand its importance, some are deterred by the realization that they will likely have to do the *kind* of work they want to do in a hostile environment, or they might have to change their sense of themselves and the position from which they explore ideas if they are to succeed in the academy.

In her essay "Teaching Theory, Talking Community," Joy James, who teaches courses on African-American women in political movements in Women's Studies at the University of Massachusetts at Amherst, passionately delineates this theoretical dilemma: "If it is assumed that we only speak as 'black' women — not as *women* — or 'black' people — not as *human beings* — our stories and theorizing are considered irrelevant or not applicable to women or people in general; they are reduced to descriptions of a part rather than analyses of a whole (humanity)."[21]

The way in which the writings of bell hooks is viewed by some white scholars, female and male, is one example of this reduction. While my graduate students use her work extensively and cite her quite extensively in their dissertations, while her books are widely used in sociology and literature classes as well as in women's studies and African-American studies classes, I have heard many a white scholar, female and male, insist that hooks does not articulate theories. Rather she reacts to others' theories, uses inappropriate language, and has no scholarly methodology. I believe, although it is never really said, that her work is suspect because it is so popular. While I certainly do not agree with everything hooks has ever written, I consider her work to be an example of theorizing, of making connections between many different forms of intellectual disciplines, as well as between the so-called popular cultural terrain and intellectual marketplaces. She has emphasized how she has consciously chosen to locate her work "in the margin." Not one "imposed by oppressive structures" but one she has chosen as a "site of resistance — as location of radical openness and possibility."[22]

Perhaps some academics' assessment of bell hooks and other black intellectuals has to do with another bias. Professor Andrew Hacker, the author of the much celebrated study *Two Nations: Separate, Hostile and Unequal,* believes that many black intellectuals "rely on more discursive modes of analysis as opposed to the more schematic linear method embodied in the multiple-choice matrix and—later on—the formats expected for academic research." Thus, "they are seen as failing to internalize and adapt to white mental ways," that is, of not assimilating intellectually.[23] Whether all African-American intellectuals can be so characterized is a question for debate. The point, however, that Hacker is making has more to do with the monolithic standard as to what "real" scholarship is and how it should be expressed.

Can one be a *successful* academic, artist, or writer and still be seen as an African-American woman? I recall the many times television and radio commentators stated, on the occasion of Toni Morrison's receipt of the Nobel Prize for Literature, that she was not *just* an African-American woman writer, she was a universal writer. I wrote a piece on Morrison's receipt of the Nobel Prize which emphasized that she wrote as an African-American woman writer. I got letters in response from white women readers who were upset that I had "limited" her by locating her in that tradition. In other words, if you're really good, you somehow are no longer an African-American woman. African-American writers have had to contend with such responses, ones that have "limited" their access to the literary establishments of the West and, thus, to other "Third World" countries whose educational systems take their cue from the West. Clearly, the literary tradition is surviving that assault, and I suspect that black feminism(s) in the academy will, too.

Besides, the point is, and it is an important point, that there is joy in struggle, a fact that a few genuinely wonderful students of mine, female and male, African-American, colored, and white, have understood and have demonstrated in their teaching, writing, and campus and community activism, thus regenerating these old bones of mine. We will survive in the academy.

Still, it is important that those of us who understand the importance of black feminist thought's role in the academy be clear about the dire situation that African-American women academics face; in other words, praxis is central to our survival. We need not only fancy treatises on *Beloved* or smart feminist theses that include black feminisms. We need nuts and bolts action. We need to ask questions that at first glance may seem to have nothing to do with scholarship but are central to our survival. For example, how many African-American women and men graduate students are there at my institution? Can we conceive of that idea that oftentimes their projects and the ways in which they pursue them might be incomprehensible to our sense of what scholarly enterprises should be about? Can we think about how narrowly defined our own definition of scholarship might be? Do we really subscribe to the idea the feminist scholarship should be interventionist, should change our view of society, and therefore of our site, the university?

I fear that if we do not engage these issues, potential black feminist scholars, faced with diminishing returns, may have to reconsider whether the academy is a suitable site for them or whether more gains in scholarship and intellectual inquiry may lie elsewhere. If that occurs, the academy will be the loser.

20 Camouflaging Race *and* Gender (1996)

University of California Regents voted last night to *kill* affirmative action in admissions, hiring, and contracting after a marathon meeting that *erupted* into an *angry, raucous protest* causing regents to find another room in which to cast their historic vote.

—*San Francisco Chronicle,* 21 July 1995 (emphasis added)

For as long as I can remember, my daughter has been interested in the law, possibly because my father, uncle, brother, and cousin are impressive lawyers with an intense appreciation for the law. In high school she took courses in law in which she earned As, and in her junior year she auditioned for and got on the mock trial team. She did really well on the team; partly because of her efforts, her team made it to the finals in the state's competition. It was for her the most educational and social event of her high school experience.

Juniors on the mock trial team who audition in their senior year usually make the team again. My daughter had done very well in her junior year, so she auditioned again for the senior year and expected to get on the team. Surprisingly, of all the seniors, including a few black men, she did not make the team. She was devastated. A usually composed young woman who did extremely well in school, she collapsed in tears and was barely able to function.

Since her rejection from the team had been so unexpected, I went to her high school to find out how to explain this to her. Had she been terrible in her second audition? I'd been to most parent/teacher meetings. Yet it took me four days to find the teacher/mentor of the mock trial team despite the tens of messages I left him and the fact that I went to her high school on three successive days. I shudder to think of parents who would not have the time to pursue the matter or the confidence to question their child's teacher about the reasons for her "failure." When I did find my daughter's teacher, he told me that she had been very good on the team, but as a black girl, she spoke "too well" for the roles they needed on the

First published in *Representations* 55 (Summer 1996), 120–28.

present team. They needed blacks to play witnesses, blacks who sounded like "inner-city girls."

This was not the first time my daughter had been expected in school to "be" the stereotypical black girl, in other words, a gum-cracking, slurred-speaking, sassy girl—the image, unfortunately, even teachers often have of who black girls are supposed to be. My daughter had found herself during her years in high school to be the *only* black girl in calculus, and so on. But this was the ultimate blow for her. She'd loved the mock trial team, had devoted hours and hours to it, fitting it into her homework, giving up social time to succeed at it. She was devastated. And here it was again—as she said to me, "If you're black, you can't win for losing."

I begin this reflection on affirmative action debates within the University of California system with this incident because so often the opponents of such policies insist that the issue of race is dead—that poverty rather than race is the real issue—that we should give special "preference" *only* to the poor. Remarkably, within this construct, no one says the issue of gender equity is dead; its significance to affirmative action debates is typically sidelined, though, despite the fact that there are people of color who are also female. While I'd like a thorough restructuring of this country's characterizations and treatment of the poor *it* produces, I find this shift in rhetoric disingenuous in that so many of the people who use the argument that the issue of race is dead also insist that there is no such thing as "class" in America.

Nonetheless, as an intellectual, as a black woman, and as a feminist, I have tried to answer the question, Why should race and gender or precisely race/gender be taken into account? Doesn't the foregrounding of race privilege middle-class people who just happen to be black? Why is gender a hidden, though powerful, construct in the anti–affirmative action arsenal?

Although in this essay I do not wish to focus on the long-standing debates among blacks about whether race or class is the primary root of our oppression, some history may be useful. I was born in the Caribbean, in a society like the United States that is saturated with racism, but unlike it in that blacks are in the majority. Certainly that majority status is one of the reasons the Caribbean has produced so many scholars who have focused on class oppression as primary. As descendants of European colonialism, and as inhabitants of societies where people of the same race were often managers of their own people for the colonists, Caribbean scholars tend to foreground *class* as the basis for our analysis of racism. Scholars such as C. L. R. James and Walter Rodney have emphasized how class oppression is at the root of poor people's condition around the world as well as in the

Caribbean. Still, when you come to *this man's country* (*this man's country* is a phrase that Caribbeans have used for the United States since the 1920s), Caribbeans discover that class analysis of their oppression is undermined by *this man's country*'s discourse on race. Especially after studies of difference emerged in the 1980s, scholars all know that there are different forms of racism and that there is a form of racism that is specifically American in its contours.[1]

Debates among blacks as to the relationship between class and race have not until recently included the centrality of gender to knowledge production. During the 1970s and 1980s, a much-fought-for realization among many scholars became increasingly important in public discourse, that there was more than *the woman question* that the traditional Left had proposed; rather, gender was central to the critical choices human beings could make.

The affirmative action debates have tended to foreground race as the central issue of controversy. Yet I tend to agree with Gloria Steinem that the anxieties caused by affirmative action policies may be more about gender than about race, since people of color have made but small increases in their numbers, whether one counts students, faculty, or contracting agencies. Rather, it is white women who appear to have forged ahead, who present more of a threat. That appearance of success may in fact be short-lived. In the 1990s, there has been a steady attack not only on welfare mothers but also on professional women. For example, on 8 January 1996, the *New York Times* reports: "Equal Opportunity Recedes for Most Female Lawyers." It is a report that relates to my daughter—I clipped it out for her—though most people would think of this report as having to do only with white women. While nearly half of the students in the nation's law schools are women, "women have been disproportionately hurt by the recent shrinking of law firms after a rapid expansion in the 1980s."[2] As Steinem mentioned in a 1995 talk in the City Arts and Lectures series in San Francisco, the issue of race (including the perception that immigrants of color are taking over America) might well be a camouflage for the issue of gender, since race in this country is such a trigger point. Rather than being rewarded for their accomplishments, black women are sometimes punished precisely because they are *successful* black women.

My theoretical and literary writings on the intersections of race, class, and gender did not prepare me for this country's assault on black girls. I submit to you the case of my daughter, the daughter of a UC professor, an excellent student who went on to major in sociology at UC Santa Cruz, graduated with highest honors in her major, and is presently at Georgetown

Law School—clearly a middle-class black. She was dealt the major blow of her high school career not because she was poor but precisely because she was a successful black middle-class student who spoke "too well," in other words, who did not exhibit the signs of blackness that are equated with black poverty and the inner city. That experience was so pivotal for my daughter that her personal statement in applications to law school began with her remembrance of the mock trial incident and the strategies she'd used to turn it into a strong determination to pursue her dreams of becoming a lawyer.

And yet I wonder how many other young middle-class black women have experienced some variation of this experience and how many have decided like my daughter that "if you're black you can't win for losing." And if you're a woman, you've somehow got to overachieve. Why, in any case, should they have to overcome this emotional trauma? "Merit, merit," I had preached to my daughter. And here it was. Merit was turned into disadvantage because she did not fit the stereotype of what so many conceive of as being a black woman in this society. Lord knows what such a characterization might mean for those inner-city black women who do "speak well."

I think of the scholar Thomas Sowell's insistence that Caribbean Americans constitute a model minority: immigrants who work hard, go to school, and ignore the racial nibblings at our soul that are alive in American society.[3] In that context, my Afro-Caribbean American daughter's *mock* trial experience could be interpreted as the peak of model minorityness. Ironically, she was born in the United States. My brother was not. A partner in a major law firm, one of few such blacks, my brother has remarkable achievements, though his are not as remarkable as those of my father, who clawed his way up through a plantation system to become a lawyer at a time when class background in the Caribbean was central to mobility. Yet even though my brother's way was easier, the psychological battering of racism in the United States has turned him into an angry black man. My father, who remained in the Caribbean, cannot fathom the depths of his son's anger at the "glass ceiling" he's repeatedly bumped his head against. The primacy of racism in the United States has been for my brother, as well as for so many other model minority Caribbean Americans, the initiation into the "American Way." My brother's point of view is a tribute to the tremendous impact of the psychological battering of racism—by racism I mean not just lynchings or beatings but also the assault on the spirit.

In that regard, I think of myself here at UC Berkeley as a person who feels, despite her accomplishments, alienated from the culture of this university. What do my black and colored students feel if I still feel strange and often unappreciated, despite my accomplishments at *this* university? One of my Caribbean American colleagues, Opal Palmer Adisa, writes in one of her pieces that "racism drains [her] energy leaving [her] feeling psychically weak and wasted so that it takes a concerted effort to will [her]self to continue to move, to smile at [her] children, to not detonate from anger."[4] The UC Regents meeting might have been *angry* and *rancorous;* my life, for more than a night, has been too often fired by the emotion of anger. It is this effect of racism that whites who talk about poverty as the only disease we face refuse to acknowledge. It is not only poverty that explains the inner cities. It is this nibbling at the spirit, this wasting of the soul. Those of us who sustain these war injuries, what Alice Walker calls "warrior marks," understand only too well that the interpretation of any issue in this society is based on one's position and stance.[5]

I hold a relatively unique position at this university. I am one of a handful of black women who are full professors in the University of California system (we could comfortably sit around a lunch table), a position I reached partly because of the "liberal" atmosphere of the 1970s. Although I received a Ph.D. with high honors from Columbia University, I am well aware that the few black women academics that preceded me were restricted to appointments in the historically sexist black universities and that they had very limited access to historically racist and sexist white universities until the 1970s, when a few, and I mean a very few, of us gained entrance into what was considered to be *the* American academy. And unlike most actors in the affirmative action debate, I have been a part of the process of affirmative action at UC Berkeley, for I have been a faculty participant on the Special Admissions Committee, possibly the most time-consuming committee service I have ever done for the university (and one that minorities are typically expected to perform—in a sense, part of our affirmative action benefits). My participation in the Special Admissions Committee, as well as my position as one of the few full professors in the system who is a black woman, has informed the theoretical bases of my work. That is, at the center of my work is the notion that it is the intersections of differences rather than one single difference that is always at work.

I was appalled at how misinformed the discussants at the Regents meeting were about *how* the UC system actually admits students. So many claimed that standards had declined as a result of affirmative action. Yet in the last twelve years, eligibility standards have been raised five times; in fact, standards are higher than ever before in UC's history. There are three tiers of admission to the university. The first 50 percent of students are admitted based on grade point averages and SAT scores, as well as on special talents. The next 45 percent are the top students (defined by grade point averages; test scores; and assessments of essays, activities, and awards) from categories of students defined by UC diversity criteria. Such criteria include socioeconomic disadvantage, ethnic underrepresentation, geographic origin, athletic recruitment, age, special talent, and disability. Also considered are applicants whose academic index scores narrowly missed the requirements for the first tier. The remaining 5 percent are admitted based on a particularly intensive, qualitative, case-by-case evaluation by a Special Admissions Committee. Students considered in this tier are from the diversity categories defined above who have not been admitted in the first two tiers but who demonstrate a high probability of achieving success at Berkeley. For example, there are exceptional music students who do not do well in math but who will, without question, succeed at Berkeley.

The affirmative action debate has focused especially on race, sometimes on gender. Legislators, even some UC faculty, seem to believe that race and gender are the only factors taken into consideration in special admissions. In fact, there are many factors the committee considers: gender; race; region; and special situations such as disabilities, special talents, special hardship situations, and the challenges faced by returning students.

The Special Admissions Committee consists of faculty members, students, and administrators, each of whom reads and critiques each student's application. In other words, there is a discussion of each individual student's possibilities, the problems the student has faced, and how that student has dealt with those problems. We look at students' personal statements, their records, their SATs and grade points, comments from their teachers, as well as notes taken by administrators of the students' interviews. We carefully consider the case of, for example, a Chicana whose family is opposed to her going to college, even to the extent of restricting the hours she can go to the library, who yet manages to achieve a 3.4 grade point average; or a white working-class man from a rural area in northern California, whose family wants him to work rather than go to college, but who has, against tremendous odds, achieved a 3.5. We do not simply admit students when there are special situations that affect their performance. We may consider whether the student would benefit more by going first to community college or to special bridge programs. But the committee is aware that maturity, persistence, and intellectual focus are factors as important for educational growth as grade point averages and SAT scores, as many studies of successful college students have shown.

The idea of difference as an energizing force was proposed by the poet and theorist Audre Lorde, whose thoughts filtered into universities as well as society at large through the work of scholar-activists like myself, who stormed the intellectual barricades during the 1970s.[6] It was a result of policies like affirmative action that the monolithic intellectual community of that time was allowed access to our thoughts. White middle-class students (the public's image of *the* college student) have benefited, perhaps even more than students of color or disabled students, from the diversity of *bodies* and *minds* in the classroom. Through it they have come to know the America they are living in, the world they are living in. Contrary to my colleague Todd Gitlin's most recent study on multiculturalism, which tends to be very critical of cultural balkanization, I think that the separativeness of groups of students at Berkeley is in fact the seed of their ultimately understanding one another. Students are more honest, I often think, than faculty are. They know you've got to really get to know yourself, your "group," and then struggle to know others, not just their bodies, but their histories, points of view—what I call cosmologies—if you are to really know yourself and others. They know that change has to be honest if it is to be lasting. Often, "adult" faculty want a ready-made solution based on their desires for a better world, without being willing to work out power relations, racial and ethnic relations, gender relations. Often adults want a pretty picture of integration.

The classes at Berkeley, at least my classes, are like a United Nations, filled with students from a multitude of backgrounds—Bangladeshi, West African, Canadian, East Asian, Latin American, European—who are Americans. Scholars and students of color have generated entire new areas of inquiry on, for example, diasporas, sexualities, borders, and languages. The young people I teach (including young white men) are engaging each other in a conversation that is inclusive of ethnicities and cultures worldwide, the kind of conversation we need if we are to save this planet. Not only are these young people concerned with issues of race, ethnicity, gender, sexual preference; they also confront other major issues of our time, such as the environmental devastation of the planet and the intense injustices brought about by political waste.

I am not an affirmative action beneficiary per se. Yet I am, in the sense that the work I did on such African American women as Audre Lorde, Alice Walker, and Toni Morrison would not have been heard if it had not been for affirmative action policies. I do not apologize for the atmosphere created by affirmative action. American universities and society at large have gained much from what African American women writers and scholars have written during the last thirty years. In fact, we have produced a golden age of writing—one that this country has yet to acknowledge despite Toni Morrison's winning of the Nobel Prize. The University of California system has produced the very best scholars of American literature, and by that

I mean *American* literature, precisely because a few like me were allowed into its halls. But what a price we have paid. More than it was worth, I sometimes think, since, in this anti–affirmative action atmosphere, we continue to be called upon to defend our right to inclusion. And yet all I hear from the media is that white men are upset.

I too am upset. The July Regents' decision marks people like myself, faculty hired in good faith by the university, as people who somehow do not make the grade. I really resent this effect of the Regents' decision, perhaps even more than its effects on students. Faculty members like myself have introduced into this university vital intellectual issues of our society to which white students, as much as any other group, are responding. Faculty of color have, against great odds, constructed an alternative canon that has made it possible for such writers as Frances Harper, the most famous African American women writer and thinker of the nineteenth century, as well as such twentieth-century writers as Toni Morrison, Ishmael Reed, and Alice Walker, to be taken seriously.

I take the Regents' insult against faculty personally because I risked my entire academic career to do the work that I have done. We (and by *we*, I mean the few African American scholars admitted into the historically white universities in the early 1970s) have launched an industry that has invigorated academic departments and disciplines throughout the entire university. We get very little in return for our labors. In a published essay, "Diminishing Returns: Can Black Feminism(s) Survive the Academy," I explore the apparent contradiction that, while there has been a tremendous surge of interest in African American literatures and studies, the number of black Ph.D.'s has declined.[7] I am concerned that the message of the Regents' decision, especially to African American graduate students, who now comprise only 4.4 percent of our total graduate student population, is that they are not wanted at UC, an embarrassing situation that I have had to contend with when I have spoken, since the decision, at universities in Europe as well as in this country.

Academics of color have not just performed a civil service. We have extended the landscapes of American and British literature (to include, for example, Irish and South Asian traditions within the United States and Britain). We are forging ahead to transform the concept of American literatures as including the literature of South America, possibly the richest in the world today. And we are transcending the borders of disciplines to produce interdisciplinary studies.

Academics of color are being used as scapegoats for California's problems because the state is unwilling to face the real issue underlying the affirmative action debate. The real issue is that the state is not using its vast resources to create what some of my colleagues, in an open letter to the UC Regents printed in the *New York Times,* call "the need for a robust, healthy educational environment."[8] This state's governing bodies have been criminal in their refusal to provide resources for our educational system and in their propagandizing against the very educational systems they are weakening through budgetary legislation and "symbolic actions" such as the Regents' decision on 20 July.

In its political process, this state is destroying one of the world's greatest public universities, even as private institutions such as Stanford are broadcasting their support for affirmative action. The Regents have made UC a laughingstock among universities even as they, like many of the state's governing bodies, are overtly using fears about race, and covertly those about gender, as a camouflage for their actions. The university may never again be able to recuperate what already has been lost and what will surely be lost as a result of the 20 July decision—unless it is rescinded as soon as possible.

Finally, the question—the *real* question—is not about that decision, but about whether the system will abandon its responsibility to the educational process and allow its role in the affirmative action debate to camouflage the political machinations of the supporters of the California Civil Rights Initiative.[9]

Afterword

NAJUMA HENDERSON

After my mother, Barbara Christian, died in 2000, I began thinking about how to keep her work, as well as her memory, alive. I wanted the important work she did to remain available to others, and not be forgotten. I agreed to donate her papers to the Bancroft Library at the University of California, Berkeley, and wondered what else to do. After thinking it over and discussing it with many people, it became clear that an updated book of her essays would accomplish these desires. I was pleased to learn that one of my mother's literary colleagues, Gloria Bowles, and two of her former students, M. Giulia Fabi and Arlene Keizer, all were interested in seeing such a book come to fruition. I met these three women through my mother at different stages in my life, spanning from infancy to adolescence. They knew my mother and her work intimately, critically, and I knew that my mother's work would be well taken care of in their capable hands.

I wanted this book, *New Black Feminist Criticism,* published because, without a doubt, my mother's work is important. *Black Women Novelists* was the first book of its kind. My mother recognized the brilliance of writers like Alice Walker, Toni Morrison, and Paule Marshall long before they became the deservedly well-recognized public figures that they are today. It is important that this work not only remains available to those already familiar with my mother's writings, but that it remains available to a new generation of readers. My mother spent her life educating people. Her ability to reach out to people is clear in her writing, and through her writings, and now this book, she continues to reach out and educate.

As a child, and even as a young adult, I was always too embarrassed to read my mother's work. I had periodically attended her classes from

Najuma Henderson, the daughter of Barbara Christian, is an attorney, and lives in California with her husband.

infancy to adulthood, so I knew what a wonderful teacher she was and how she motivated and encouraged her students. But for whatever silly teenage reason I did not pick up her written work: perhaps because I was present at so many conversations she had with friends and colleagues on the subject of her work, perhaps because I had seen her television appearances and watched her discuss her work and had also watched her teach her classes. Maybe it was simply because it felt strange for my "mother" to be this well-known, published scholar when to me she was just simply "Mom." Her life-work was always around me, a part of my life without my ever needing to pick up her books. I was there when she was writing. I was there during telephone radio interviews, or when she had students over to the house and they would talk about books and authors and ideas. I was there when even the authors themselves visited her both as friends and colleagues, and sat in our living room talking and laughing. But when she died, that all stopped. The ideas, and my mother's passion for her work, ceased to surround me.

After a while (in truth, a couple of years), I picked up *Black Women Novelists* and started reading. And I realized that though I had gained so much through my passive involvement in the educational and intellectual activities of my mother, there was still more that I could take away from her writing. I had read books by African American women writers through the years that my mother had recommended, but reading her essays expanded my curiosity to other works I had not yet read. The ideas she discussed surrounding these books related to issues both new and old, that still relate to my life today. Speaking almost from the grave, her work is making me think, making me want to read more, and learn about more ideas. I am glad that another generation will be able to glean such a fresh curiosity as mine through *New Black Feminist Criticism,* and that in the process my mother will be able to continue teaching, to continue toward her goal of bringing African American women's voices in our society to the forefront, and to continue speaking to us . . .

Notes

Introduction

1. "Being the Subject and the Object: Reading African-American Women's Novels," in *Changing Subjects: The Making of Feminist Literary Criticism,* eds. Gayle Greene and Coppelia Kahn (London: Routledge, 1993), 195.

PART I: DEFINING BLACK FEMINIST CRITICISM

1. The major essays in this debate are reprinted in Winston Napier, ed., *African American Literary Theory: A Reader* (New York: NYU Press, 2000).

Chapter 1: But What Do We Think We're Doing Anyway

1. *Black World* 23, no. 10 (August 1974).
2. Toni Cade, *The Black Woman* (New York: New American Library, 1970).
3. Alice Walker, "In Search of Our Mothers' Gardens," *Ms.* 2, no. 11 (May 1974): 64–70, 105.
4. Mary Helen Washington, "Black Women Image Makers," *Black World* 23, no. 10 (August 1974): 10–19; quote, 11.
5. Originally published as Barbara Smith, "Toward a Black Feminist Criticism," *Conditions II* 11 (October 1977): 25–44. Cited from Judith Newton and Deborah Rosenfelt, eds., *Feminist Criticism and Social Change* (New York: Methuen, 1985).
6. Ibid., 3–4.
7. Ibid., 5.
8. Ibid., 16.
9. Ibid., 8–9.
10. "The Black Sexism Debate," *Black Scholar* 10, nos. 8–9 (May–June 1979): 17.
11. Audre Lorde, "The Great American Disease," *Black Scholar* 10, nos. 8–9 (May–June 1979): 17.

12. Deborah E. McDowell, "New Directions for Black Feminist Criticism," *Black American Literature Forum* 14, no. 4 (Winter 1980): 153–59.

13. Michele Wallace, "Who Dat Say Who Dat When I Say Who Dat?" *Village Voice Literary Supplement,* April 12, 1988, 18–21.

14. Barbara Christian, *Black Feminist Criticism: Perspectives on Black Women Writers* (New York: Pergamon Press, 1985).

15. Marjorie Pryse and Hortense J. Spillers, eds., *Conjuring: Black Women, Fiction, and Literary Tradition* (Bloomington: Indiana University Press, 1985).

16. Hortense J. Spillers, "Afterword: Cross-Currents, Discontinuities: Black Women's Fiction," in Pryse and Spillers, *Conjuring,* 249–61.

17. For a current overview of canonical issues in American literature see Frederick Crews, "Whose American Renaissance?" *New York Review of Books,* October 27, 1988, 68–81. For an alternative view on the dangers of canonical formation in Afro-American literature, see Theodore D. Mason, Jr., "Between the Populist and the Scientist: Ideology and Power in Recent Afro-American Literary Criticism, or The Dozens as Scholarship," *Callaloo* 11, no. 3 (Summer 1988): 606–15.

18. Spillers, "Afterword," in Pryse and Spillers, *Conjuring,* 259.

19. Hazel Carby, "Woman's Era: Rethinking Black Feminist Theory," in *Reconstructing Womanhood: The Emergence of the Afro-American Woman Novelist* (New York: Oxford University Press, 1987), 16.

20. Ibid., 17.

21. Valerie Smith, "A Self-Critical Tradition," *Women's Review of Books* 5, no. 5 (February 1988): 15.

Chapter 2: What Celie Knows That You Should Know

1. Harriet E. Wilson, *Our Nig; or Sketches from the Life of a Free Black* (New York: Vintage Books–Random House, 1983), 6.

2. Ibid., 13.

Chapter 3: Fixing Methodologies

1. Barbara Christian, "'Somebody Forgot to Tell Somebody Something': African American Women's Historical Novels," in *Wild Women in the Whirlwind: Afra-American Culture and the Contemporary Literary Renaissance,* eds. Joanne M. Braxton and Andrée Nicola McLaughlin (New Brunswick, N.J.: Rutgers University Press, 1990), 326–41.

2. Toni Morrison, interview, *All Things Considered,* National Public Radio, WNYC (New York), February 16, 1986.

3. I owe this insight to Alberto Perez, a graduate student in the Ethnic Studies Department at the University of California, Berkeley.

4. Sweet Honey in the Rock, *The Ancestors,* Flying Fish, 1978.

5. John Mbiti, *African Religions and Philosophy* (New York: Anchor-Doubleday, 1970), 32.

6. Ibid., 35.

7. Ibid., 208.

8. Morrison, *Beloved* (New York: Knopf, 1987), 274.

9. Mbiti, *African Religions and Philosophy*, 21–22.

10. Ibid., 144.

Chapter 4: The Race for Theory

1. Audre Lorde, *Sister Outsider: Essays and Speeches* (Trumansburg, N.Y.: Crossing Press, 1984), 37.

Chapter 5: Does Theory Play Well in the Classroom?

1. *Original editor's note:* Barbara Christian's essay is taken from her longer presentation at the Summer Institute in 1991. It deals in part with an earlier essay she wrote, "The Race for Theory" (*Cultural Critique* 6 [Spring 1987]: 51–63), and with passages from Toni Morrison's *Beloved*, particularly pages 86–88. Though shortened for inclusion in this volume, the essay highlights the salient points and retains much of the personal tone of her remarkable presentation.

2. Alice Walker, "In Search of Our Mothers' Gardens," in *In Search of Our Mothers' Gardens: Womanist Prose* (New York: Harcourt Brace Jovanovich, 1983).

3. Harriet A. Jacobs, *Incidents in the Life of a Slave Girl, Written by Herself* (1861; repr. Cambridge, Mass.: Harvard University Press, 1987).

4. William Wells Brown, *Clotel; or The President's Daughter: A Narrative of Slave Life in the United States* (London: Partridge & Oakley, 1853).

5. Middleton A. Harris et al., comp., *The Black Book* (New York: Random House, 1974).

6. Toni Morrison, *Beloved* (New York: Knopf, 1987), 86.

7. Ibid., 87–88.

8. Ibid., 88.

PART II: READING BLACK WOMEN WRITERS

1. Barbara Christian, "'Somebody Forgot to Tell Somebody Something': African-American Women's Historical Novels," in *Wild Women in the Whirlwind: Afra-American Culture and the Contemporary Literary Renaissance,* eds. Joanne M. Braxton and Andrée Nicola McLaughlin (New Brunswick, N.J.: Rutgers University Press, 1990), 333.

2. Barbara Christian, "Being the Subject and the Object: Reading African-American Women's Novels," in *Changing Subjects: The Making of Feminist Literary Criticism,* eds. Gayle Greene and Coppelia Kahn (London: Routledge, 1993), 195.

3. Barbara Christian, "Paule Marshall," in *African American Writers,* ed. Valerie Smith (New York: Charles Scribner's Sons, 1991), 292.

4. Christian, "'Somebody Forgot,'" 334.

5. Barbara Christian, "Layered Rhythms: Virginia Woolf and Toni Morrison," in *Virginia Woolf: Emerging Perspectives,* eds. Mark Hussey and Vara Neverow (New York: Pace University Press, 1994), 166.

6. Christian, "Being the Subject and the Object," 198.

7. Christian, "'Somebody Forgot,'" 331.

8. Christian, "Layered Rhythms," 171–72.

9. Ibid., 165.

10. Barbara Christian, "Gloria Naylor's Geography: Community, Class, and Patriarchy in *The Women of Brewster Place* and *Linden Hills*," in *Reading Black, Reading Feminist: A Critical Anthology,* ed. Henry Louis Gates, Jr. (New York: Meridian, 1990), 369.

11. Christian, "Layered Rhythms," 173.

12. Christian, "'Somebody Forgot,'" 341.

13. Christian, "Layered Rhythms," 166.

14. Christian, "Paule Marshall," 299–300.

15. Christian, "Gloria Naylor's Geography," 372.

16. Barbara Christian, *Black Women Novelists: The Development of a Tradition, 1892–1976* (Westport, Conn.: Greenwood Press, 1980), x.

17. Christian, "Being the Subject and the Object," 200.

18. Christian, "Layered Rhythms," 175.

19. Christian, "Being the Subject and the Object," 176.

20. Ibid., 200.

21. Christian, "Gloria Naylor's Geography," 350.

22. Barbara Christian, introduction to *The Hazeley Family,* by Mrs. A. E. Johnson (New York: Oxford University Press, 1988), xxvii.

23. Ibid., xxvii.

24. Christian, "'Somebody Forgot,'" 338.

25. Christian, "Being the Subject and the Object," 200.

26. Christian, "Layered Rhythms," 165.

27. Christian, "Being the Subject and the Object," 197.

28. Ibid., 195.

29. Ibid., 198.

30. Barbara Christian, *Black Feminist Criticism: Perspectives on Black Women Writers* (New York: Pergamon Press, 1985), 65.

31. Ibid., 65.

32. Barbara Christian, "Conversations with the Universe," *The Women's Review of Books* 6, no. 5 (February 1989): 9.

33. Barbara Christian, "Epic Achievement," *The Women's Review of Books* 9, no. 1 (October 1991): 6.

34. Barbara Christian, "Remembering Audre Lorde," *The Women's Review of Books* 10, no. 6 (March 1993): 6.

35. Christian, "Conversations with the Universe," 9.

36. Christian, "Remembering Audre Lorde," 5.

37. Ibid., 5.

38. Barbara Christian, "There It Is: The Poetry of Jayne Cortez," *Callaloo* 26 (Winter 1986): 236.

39. Christian, "Remembering Audre Lorde," 5.

40. Christian, "There It Is," 235.

41. Christian, "Conversations with the Universe," 9.

42. Christian, "Epic Achievement," 6.

230   *Notes to Pages 70–77*

43. Barbara Christian, "A New Dawn. Review of *A Brighter Coming Day: A Frances Ellen Watkins Harper Reader* (1991)," *Belles Lettres* 6, no. 3 (1991): 5.

44. Christian, "There It Is," 235.

45. Christian, *Black Feminist Criticism*, 65.

46. Barbara Christian, "A Checkered Career," *The Women's Review of Books* 9, nos. 10–11 (July 1992): 18.

47. Ibid., 19.

48. Ibid., 19.

49. Christian, "There It Is," 239.

50. Christian, *Black Women Novelists*, 239.

Chapter 7: "Somebody Forgot to Tell Somebody Something"

1. Toni Morrison, interview with Ntozake Shange, Steven Cannon's *It's Magic*, WBAI (New York), 1978.

2. Margaret Walker, *How I Wrote Jubilee* (Chicago: Third World Press, 1972).

3. "Alice Walker and *The Color Purple*" (TV Documentary), BBC, 1986.

4. Alice Walker, interviewed by John O'Brien, in *Interviews with Black Writers*, ed. John O'Brien (New York: Liveright, 1973), 186–221.

5. Toni Morrison, "Distinguished University of California Regent's Lecture," (lecture, University of California, Berkeley, October 13, 1987).

6. Toni Morrison, *Beloved* (New York: Alfred A. Knopf, 1987), 275.

7. Sherley Anne Williams, "Author's Note," in *Dessa Rose* (New York: William Morrow, 1986).

8. See Gerda Lerner, ed., *Black Women in White America: A Documentary History* (New York: Vintage, 1973), 60–63, for the Margaret Garner story.

9. See June Jordan, "The Difficult Miracle of Black Poetry in America or Something Like a Sonnet for Phillis Wheatley," in *On Call: Essays* (Boston: South End Press, 1985).

10. See Barbara Christian's "Shadows Uplifted," in *Black Women Novelists: The Development of a Tradition, 1892–1976* (Westport, Conn.: Greenwood Press, 1980), for a discussion of this question.

11. Walker, *How I Wrote Jubilee*.

12. Barbara Chase-Riboud, *Sally Hemings* (New York: Avon Books, 1979).

13. Morrison, "Regent's Lecture."

14. Morrison, *Beloved*, 95.

15. Williams, *Dessa Rose*, 5.

16. Ibid., 5.

17. Valerie Babb, "*The Color Purple*: Writing to Undo What Writing Has Done," *Phylon: The Atlanta University Review of Race and Culture* 47, no. 2 (Summer 1986): 107–16.

18. Morrison, *Beloved*, 200.

19. Ibid., 216.

20. Williams, *Dessa Rose*, 119.

21. Ibid., 236.

Chapter 8: Gloria Naylor's Geography

1. Gloria Naylor, *The Women of Brewster Place* (New York: Penguin, 1982), 60.
2. Ibid., 141.
3. Gloria Naylor, *Linden Hills* (New York: Tucknor and Fields, 1985), 141.
4. Marilyn French's *Beyond Power* and bell hooks's *Feminist Theory: From Margin to Center* both summarize this orientation and suggest theoretical dilemmas that result from it.
5. William Wilson's *The Declining Significance of Race* and Thomas Sowell's *Ethnic America* discuss this phenomenon from different points of view.

Chapter 10: Layered Rhythms

1. Toni Morrison, *Playing in the Dark: Whiteness and the Literary Imagination* (Cambridge, Mass.: Harvard University Press, 1992), xi.
2. Susan Blake, "Toni Morrison," in *Dictionary of Literary Biography*, vol. 33, *Afro-American Fiction Writers After 1955*, eds. Thadious Davis and Trudier Harris (Detroit: Gale Research, 1984), 189.
3. See Harold Bloom, *Toni Morrison* (New York: Chelsea House, 1990).
4. Ralph Ellison, *Shadow and Act* (New York: Random House, 1964), 59.
5. See Jane Marcus, *New Feminist Essays on Virginia Woolf* (Lincoln: University of Nebraska Press, 1981).
6. See Stephen Spender, *The Struggle of the Modern* (Berkeley: University of California Press, 1963).
7. Toni Morrison, "Rootedness: The Ancestor as Foundation," in *Black Women Writers (1950–1980): A Critical Evaluation*, ed. Mari Evans (Garden City, N.Y.: Anchor/Doubleday, 1984), 342.
8. Virginia Woolf, *A Room of One's Own* (New York: Harcourt, Brace, 1929), 89.
9. Toni Morrison, *The Bluest Eye* (New York: Holt, Rinehart & Winston, 1970), 47.
10. Toni Morrison, interview with Ntozake Shange, Steve Canon's *It's Magic*, WBAI (New York), 1978.
11. Toni Morrison, "Interview in Swiss Italian Series on African American Writers," California Newsreel, 1991.
12. A sister student of Toni Morrison who works at Sacramento State University told me this.
13. Morrison, "Interview in Swiss Italian Series."
14. For a discussion of the Dreadnought Hoax, in which Virginia Woolf and friends dressed as Abyssinian men in a protest against British policy in North Africa, see J. J. Wilson, "Virginia Woolf," in *Dictionary of Literary Biography*, vol. 36, *British Novelists, 1890–1929: Modernists* (Detroit: Gale Research, 1985), 292–313.
15. See Gerda Lerner, *Black Women in White America* (New York: Pantheon Books, 1972), for a discussion of the reasons why African American families, in contrast to much of American society in the early part of the twentieth century, felt it necessary that their daughters, even more than their sons, needed higher education.
16. Epigraph in Paula Giddings, *When and Where I Enter* (New York: William Morrow, 1984).
17. Toni Morrison, "Interview with Bill Moyers," PBS, 1987.

18. See Quentin Bell, *Virginia Woolf: A Biography* (New York: Harcourt Brace Jovanovich, 1972).

19. See Sandra M. Gilbert and Susan Gubar, *The Madwoman in the Attic: The Woman Writer and the Nineteenth Century Literary Imagination* (New Haven, Conn.: Yale University Press, 1979).

20. Woolf, *A Room of One's Own,* 80.

21. See Claudia Tate, "Allegories of Black Female Desire; or Rereading Nineteenth-Century Sentimental Narratives of Black Female Authority," in *Changing Our Own Words,* ed. Cheryl Wall (New Brunswick, N.J.: Rutgers University Press, 1991), 98–126.

22. See Barbara T. Christian, *Black Women Novelists: The Development of a Tradition, 1892–1976* (Westport, Conn.: Greenwood Press, 1980).

23. See Rachel Blau DuPlessis, *Writing Beyond the Ending: Narrative Strategies of Twentieth Century Women Writers* (Bloomington: Indiana University Press, 1985), for extensive discussion of this concept.

24. Claudia Tate, "Interview with Toni Morrison," in *Black Women Writers at Work,* ed. Claudia Tate (New York: Continuum, 1983), 122.

25. Wilson, "Virginia Woolf," 294.

26. Toni Morrison, *Sula* (New York: Knopf, 1973), 7, 14.

27. Ibid., 15.

28. Virginia Woolf, *To the Lighthouse* (New York: Harcourt, Brace, 1927), 201.

29. Toni Morrison, *Jazz* (New York: Plume, 1992), 7.

30. Bell, *Virginia Woolf,* 3–4.

31. Morrison, "Rootedness," 340.

32. Ibid., 342.

33. Virginia Woolf, *The Common Reader, First Series* (New York: Harcourt, Brace, 1925), 300–301.

34. Ralph Freedman, *The Lyrical Novel: Studies in Herman Hesse, André Gide and Virginia Woolf* (Princeton, N.J.: Princeton University Press, 1963), 187–88.

35. See Barbara T. Christian, "Somebody Forgot to Tell Somebody Something," in *Wild Women in the Whirlwind: Afra-American Culture and the Contemporary Literary Renaissance,* eds. Joanne M. Braxton and Andrée Nicola McLaughlin (New Brunswick, N.J.: Rutgers University Press, 1990), 326–41, for discussion of this point.

36. Freedman, *Lyrical Novel,* 228.

37. Woolf, *Common Reader,* 189–90.

38. Tate, "Interview with Toni Morrison," 122.

39. Morrison, "Rootedness," 341.

40. Morrison, *Jazz,* 226.

41. DuPlessis, *Writing,* 163–64.

42. Wahneema Lubiano, "Toni Morrison," in *African American Writers,* ed. Valerie Smith (New York: Scribners and Sons, 1991), 321.

43. Virginia Woolf, *A Writer's Diary* (London: Hogarth Press, 1953), 139.

44. Morrison, "Rootedness," 341.

45. Toni Morrison, *Song of Solomon* (New York: Knopf, 1977), 280.

46. Woolf, *Room,* 39.

47. I owe this insight to Stanford instructor Cheri Ross's lecture, "*A Room of One's Own* and the Reevaluation of Space," May 1993.

48. Tate, "Interview with Toni Morrison," 124.

49. Morrison, "Rootedness," 344.

Chapter 12: Conversations with the Universe

1. Alice Walker, *Living by the Word: Selected Writings, 1973–1987* (New York: Harcourt Brace Jovanovich, 1988), 51.

2. Ibid., 179–80.

3. Ibid., 7–8.

Chapter 13: Epic Achievement

1. Carolivia Herron, *Thereafter Johnnie* (New York: Random House, 1991), 7.

2. Ibid., 232.

3. Ibid., 108–9.

Chapter 15: Remembering Audre Lorde

1. Audre Lorde, "Coal," in *Chosen Poems: Old and New* (New York: W. W. Norton, 1982), 11.

2. Audre Lorde, "A Litany for Survival," in *The Black Unicorn* (New York: W. W. Norton, 1978), 31–32.

3. Audre Lorde, "The Uses of the Erotic," in *Sister Outsider* (Trumansburg, N.Y.: Crossing Press, 1984), 58.

4. Audre Lorde, "Age, Race, Class, and Sex," in *Sister Outsider,* 114–23.

5. Audre Lorde, "Among Ourselves," in *A Burst of Light* (Ithaca, N.Y.: Firebrand Books, 1988).

6. Audre Lorde, "Against Apartheid," in *A Burst of Light.*

7. Ibid., 130.

8. Ibid., 110–11.

PART III: BLACK FEMINIST CRITICISM IN THE ACADEMY

1. Barbara Christian, "But Who Do You Really Belong To — Black Studies or Women's Studies?" *Women's Studies International Forum* 17 (1989): 17–23.

2. "Fewer Blacks Admitted to UC Berkeley," *Berkeley Voice,* 23 April 2004, A2. The decline was also attributed to a lack of money for "outreach efforts into low-income K12 schools." Then-Chancellor Robert Berdahl called the figures "flat-out unacceptable."

Chapter 16: Being "The Subjected Subject of Discourse"

1. [Editor's note] Questions posed by Ann duCille, Sharon Marcus, and Sylvia Schafer:

1. In its original formulation this project was conceived as a "polylogue between generations" of feminist scholars. To cast the history of a feminist presence in the

academy as one of "generations" engages us in a complex familial metaphor. We are reminded of a variety of intergenerational dynamics including (among other possibilities) rebellion or obedience on the part of the "youthful," and tyranny or nurturance on the part of the "elders." At heart, "generation" (in this context) seems to presume an essential distinction drawn from our institutional identities as teachers and students. It also seems to point towards our differing historical experiences of the place and weight of feminism in the academy. Do you see signposts of open "generation" or even a "generation gap" within recent feminist thought? Is there a feminist "patrimony" (matrimony?) to keep "in the family"?

We are also intrigued by the way in which "generation" cuts across feminism's reigning and problematic familial metaphor of "sisterhood," and, conversely, by the way in which "sisters," as divided among themselves as they have been, have managed to reproduce new generations of feminist offspring. What explains the success of this process of intellectual reproduction? Are there obstacles to intergenerational sisterhood? Finally, are there tropes which bypass the family model altogether that might be useful alternatives in describing the relations between feminist students and their feminist teachers?

2. In her introduction to *A World of Difference,* Barbara Johnson writes: "Whether one is in the university or the army, the real world seems to be the world outside the institution. It is as though the institution existed precisely to create boundaries between the unreal and the real, to assure docility, paradoxically, through the assumption of unreality. Yet institutions are nothing if not *real* articulations of power. They are strategies of containment (to use Jameson's phrase) designed to mobilize some impulses and to deactivate others." How does identifying oneself or being identified as a feminist scholar affect one's position within the university as a system of power relations? Have the academy's strategies of containment changed in significant ways since you began your academic career? Has feminism's position in the university shifted in recent years as attention focuses more insistently on other categories of difference—race, ethnicity, the third world, sexual orientation, and so forth? What strategies have proven most effective in resisting masculinist institutional discipline and its project of normalization? What would you signal as the most positive and the most negative aspect of pursuing an active feminist course within the "unreal" world of university life?

3. "Race," "ethnicity," "class," "gender," "diversity," "sexual preference"—all are words that liberally populate the pages of current feminist discourse, reflecting the degrees to which "difference" has come of age in the academy. Yet, some scholars have accused the discourse of paying no more than "lip service to the significance of race and class, racism and classism" (Spelman 81), in particular, as it continues to treat the experiences of middle-class white women as normative. Our questions here are several: What happens to your own assessment of the achievements of the new (literary critical and/or historical) scholarship on women when it is interrogated by such variables as race, class, and region—for example when "women" are not assumed to be white, middle class, heterosexual, and East Coast American? How can we bridge this gap between rhetoric and result; that is to say, how can we guard against generating, endorsing, and insti-

tutionalizing scholarship that makes the right noises but does not fundamentally alter our sense of who "women" are?

4. Once all but ignored as historical subjects, black women in general and black women writers in particular have become popular sites of socio-historical and literary investigation. While black women scholars have indeed played a critical role in bringing this about, a significant portion of the new scholarship on black women has been written by white feminists and by men whose work has frequently achieved greater critical and commercial success than the work of black female scholars. This observation suggests a number of questions: How do you account for this explosion of interest in the lives and art of black women? Is the current popularity of black women and subjected subjects of discourse a silver lining that is not without its cloud? What does it mean, that the *New York Times* repeatedly calls on male authors—white and black—to review the work of black women? Approaching this subject more broadly, please comment on such issues as men in feminism, the benefits of cross-cultural, gender-specific investigation, and the problems and possibilities of race and gender essentialism.

5. Extrapolating from a friend's extrapolation: "'all the women are white, all the blacks are men' . . . and everybody is heterosexual." As black lesbian feminist Cheryl Clarke has asked (Monique Wittig notwithstanding), "Ain't lesbians women, too?" (205). Do you see the heterosexual presumption as still dominant in academic feminism? What suggestions do you have for future feminist work on questions of sexuality? Is redefining, revisioning, and retheorizing the category "lesbian," as well as "woman," and "man," an essential part of the process?

6. Feminist scholarship has been one of the most active realms of interdisciplinary labor in recent years. How have these interdisciplinary dialogues affected your work? What have you learned from other fields of study, and what disciplines besides your own have had the most powerful impact on you? What are the most productive tools, concepts, or projects that your field has to offer to feminist collaborations? Have you encountered any unbridgeable gaps or moments of extreme dissonance in your efforts to transcend or transgress? Do you see a need for more highly articulated common ground(s) for future interdisciplinary feminist work?

7. What has surprised you most about the development of women's studies and feminist theory? What tendencies within early women's studies and feminist theory did you find the most productive? the most problematic? Who have been feminist studies' worst enemies? most unlikely friends?

8. What are some of the words, concepts, practices, and methods which you have been happy to see feminist critiques add to and eliminate from our institutional lexicon? What concepts do you consider to be sorely in search of names and methods? What new work do you find useful and promising?

9. Is feminism alive and well in the academy? Is the problem that it is alive and well *only* in the academy? In light of recent events on the macro world scene, what do you see as the future of U.S. feminism both within and without the academy in the 90s? How do you envision the future of U.S.-centered feminism in light of the diminishment of U.S. hegemony, projections of a unified Europe, reconfigurements in the second world, and continuing struggles in the third world?

2. Norma Alarcon, "The Theoretical Subject(s) of *This Bridge Called My Back* and Anglo-American Feminism," in *Making Face, Making Soul = Haciendo Caras,* ed. Gloria Anzaldúa (San Francisco: Aunt Lute Foundation Books, 1990), 356–69.

Chapter 17: Whose Canon Is It Anyway?

1. For this formulation of the multicultural debates, see Troy Duster, *The Diversity of California at Berkeley: An Emerging Reformulation of "Competence" in an Increasingly Multicultural World.* Publication forthcoming. [Editor's note: Duster's book was not published].

2. There are many books and essays that follow this line of thought—too many for me to cite. Perhaps the most famous of these studies are: Dinesh D'Souza, *Illiberal Educations: The Politics of Race and Sex on Campus* (New York: Free Press, 1991), and Arthur Schlesinger, Jr., *The Disuniting of America: Reflections on a Multicultural Society* (New York: Norton, 1992). Even as I write this essay, a new book on the topic, this time from England, has just been published: David Bromwich, *Politics by Other Means: Higher Education and Group Thinking* (New Haven, Conn.: Yale University Press, 1992).

3. Mitchell Breitwieser, "Multi-Culturalism: Oxymoron or Redundancy?" Presented to the Humanities Program, University of San Francisco, April 9, 1992.

4. Troy Duster's discussion of the multiplicities of perspectives among Berkeley students from different cultural backgrounds, e.g., Asians, Latinos, and African-Americans, is particularly instructive. See Duster, *The Diversity of California at Berkeley.*

5. Audre Lorde, *Sister Outsider* (Trumansburg, N.Y.: Crossing Press, 1984). Lorde's essays are primarily concerned with the creativity that can result from our valuing difference rather than shedding or abhorring it. This is an insight—one might even call it a theory—that African-American writers like Audre Lorde have for many years articulated and explored.

Chapter 18: A Rough Terrain

I want to acknowledge my gratitude to Dr. Giulia Fabi, now of the University of Bologna, Italy, and also a Ph.D. graduate of the Ethnic Studies program at Berkeley, for her illuminating comments on this essay. I also want to thank Alberto Perez, a Ph.D. student in ethnic studies at Berkeley, for critiquing this essay.

1. Major collections of Caribbean literatures include Andrew Salkey, ed., *West Indian Stories* (London: Faber and Faber, 1971); O. R. Dathorne, ed., *Caribbean Narrative* (London: Heinemann Educational Books, 1973); Stewart Brown and Mervyn Morris, eds., *Caribbean Poetry Now* (London: Hodder and Stonghton, 1984); Steward Brown, Mervyn Morris, and Gordon Rohlehr, eds., *Voice Print* (London: Longman, 1989).

2. LeRoi Jones, "Cuba Libre," in *Home: Social Essays* (New York: William Morrow, 1966), 11–62.

3. Harold Cruse, "Revolutionary Nationalism and the Afro-American," *Studies on the Left* 2, no. 3 (1962): 22–28.

4. African American writers such as LeRoi Jones, and political activists such as Stokely Carmichael, were, as early as 1964, articulating the concept of internal colonialism long before it became an operative theory in the academy.

5. Gayatri Spivak, "Can the Subaltern Speak?" in *Marxism and the Interpretation of Culture,* eds. Cary Nelson and Lawrence Grossberg (Urbana: University of Illinois Press, 1988), 271–313.

Chapter 19: Diminishing Returns

1. See "The Backlash Debate," *Time,* 139, no. 10 (March 9, 1992): 50–57. Also see "'I'm Not a Feminist, But . . .'," *San Francisco Chronicle, This World* section (February 23, 1992): 7, 9–11.

2. Wendy Kaminer, "Feminism's Identity Crisis," *The Atlantic,* 272, no. 4 (October 1993): 51–68. Even Susan Faludi's more respectable study, *Backlash* (New York: Crown, 1991), does not pay much attention to African-American women's contributions to the development of feminist concepts.

3. See Paula Giddings's *When and Where I Enter* (New York: William Morrow, 1984), a marvelous historical study of African-American women except that it gives short shrift to the women involved in cultural transformation, such as Frances Harper.

4. Deborah King, "Multiple Jeopardy, Multiple Consciousness: The Context of a Black Feminist Ideology," in *Feminist Theory in Practice and Process,* eds. Micheline R. Malson, Jean F. O'Barr, Sarah Westphal-Wihl, and Mary Wyer (Chicago: University of Chicago Press, 1989), 105.

5. For a popular view of the way in which most white women in this country do not call themselves feminist, while a good proportion of them believe in and/or practice its basic tenets, take a look at Wendy Kaminer's quite conservative article in *The Atlantic,* October 1993. See also Susan Faludi's *Backlash.*

6. Barbara T. Christian, "But What Do We Think We're Doing Anyway?" in *Changing Our Own Words: Essays on Criticism, Theory and Writing by Black Women,* ed. Cheryl Wall (New Brunswick, N.J.: Rutgers University Press, 1991): 58–74.

7. "Introduction," *Feminist Theory in Practice and Process,* eds. Micheline R. Malson, Jean F. O'Barr, Sarah Westphal-Wihl, and Mary Wyer (Chicago: University of Chicago Press, 1989), 1–13.

8. See Barbara T. Christian et al., "Conference Call," *Differences* 2 (Fall 1990): 52–108. For a comprehensive and brilliant analysis on this issue published after I completed this essay, see Ann duCille, "The Occult of True Black Womanhood: Critical Demeanor and Black Feminist Studies," *Signs: Journal of Women in Culture and Society* 19, no. 3 (Spring 1994): 591–629.

9. See Patricia Hill Collins, *Black Feminist Thought: Knowledge, Consciousness and the Politics of Empowerment* (Boston: Unwin Hyman, 1990).

10. Chandra Talpade Mohanty, "Under Western Eyes: Feminist Scholarship and Colonial Discourses," *Boundary 2,* 12, no. 3 (1984): 333–58.

11. Collins, *Black Feminist Thought,* 202.

12. Christian et al., "Conference Call," 57.

13. Andrew Hacker, in Martin Anderson et al., "Why the Shortage of Black Professors?" *Journal of Blacks in Higher Education* 1, no. 1 (Autumn 1993): 32.

14. "Vital Signs," *Journal of Blacks in Higher Education* 1, no. 1 (Autumn 1993): 15–24.

15. "Introduction," in *Spirit, Space and Survival: African-American Women in (White) Academe,* eds. Joy James and Ruth Farmer (New York: Routledge, 1993), 2.

16. Ibid., 3.

17. Hacker, in Anderson et al., "Why the Shortage of Black Professors?" 34.

18. Adrianne Andrews, "Balancing the Personal and the Professional," in *Spirit, Space and Survival,* eds. Joy James and Ruth Farmer (New York: Routledge, 1993), 183. See also Yolanda Moses's study, *Black Women in Academia: Issues and Status* (Baltimore: Project on the Status of Education of Women, August 1989).

19. Andrews, "Balancing the Personal," in James and Farmer, *Spirit, Space and Survival,* 190.

20. Johnnetta B. Cole, in Anderson et al., "Why the Shortage of Black Professors?" 30.

21. Joy James, "Teaching Theory, Talking Community," in James and Farmer, *Spirit, Space and Survival,* 121.

22. bell hooks, *Yearning: Race, Gender and Cultural Politics* (Boston: South End Press, 1990), 153.

23. Hacker, in Anderson et al., "Why the Shortage of Black Professors?" 33.

Chapter 20: Camouflaging Race *and* Gender

1. For example, see Henry Louis Gates, Jr., ed., *"Race," Writing, and Difference* (Chicago: University of Chicago Press, 1986).

2. "Equal Opportunity Recedes for Most Female Lawyers," *New York Times,* January 8 1996, A10.

3. Thomas Sowell, *Civil Rights, Rhetoric or Reality?* (New York: Morrow, 1984).

4. Opal Palmer Adisa, "For the Love of My Children," *Oakland Voices Quarterly Community* 1 (Fall 1995): 13.

5. Alice Walker and Pratibha Parmar, *Warrior Marks: Female Genital Mutilation and the Sexual Blinding of Women* (New York: Harcourt Brace, 1993).

6. Audre Lorde, *Sister Outsider* (Trumansburg, N.Y.: Crossing Press, 1984).

7. Barbara T. Christian, "Diminishing Returns: Can Black Feminism(s) Survive the Academy?" in *Multiculturalism: A Cultural Reader,* ed. David Theo Goldberg (London: Basil Blackwell, 1995), 168–79.

8. Hispanic Coalition on Higher Education, "An Open Letter to the Regents of the University of California," *New York Times,* July 20 1995, A11.

9. Proposition 209, an initiative constitutional amendment, "Prohibition against Discrimination or Preferential Treatment by State and Other Public Entities," was passed by 54 percent of the popular vote in November 1996. [Editor's note.]

Selected Bibliography of Works by Barbara Christian

Books

Black Feminist Criticism: Perspectives on Black Women Writers. New York: Pergamon Press, 1985.

Black Women Novelists: The Development of a Tradition, 1892–1976. Westport, Conn.: Greenwood Press, 1980.

Ed. *"Everyday Use"/Alice Walker.* Women Writers: Texts and Contexts Series. New Brunswick, N.J.: Rutgers University Press, 1994.

Ed., with Elizabeth Abel and Helen Moglen. *Female Subjects in Black and White: Race, Psychoanalysis, Feminism.* Berkeley: University of California Press, 1997.

Ed. "Literature Since 1970" section of *The Norton Anthology of African American Literature.* New York: W. W. Norton, 1997.

Essays

"Alice Walker: The Black Woman Artist as Wayward." In *Black Women Writers: 1950–1980: A Critical Evaluation,* edited by Mari Evans, 457–77. Garden City, N.Y.: Anchor Press/Doubleday, 1984.

"Alternate Versions of the Gendered Past: African American Writers vs. Ivan Illich." *Feminist Issues* (Spring 1983): 23–28.

"Being the Subject and the Object: Reading African-American Women's Novels." In *Changing Subjects: The Making of Feminist Literary Criticism,* edited by Gayle Greene and Coppelia Kahn, 195–200. London: Routledge, 1993.

"Being 'The Subjected Subject of Discourse.'" *Differences* 2, no. 3 (1990): 57–65.

"But What Do We Think We're Doing Anyway: The State of Black Feminist Criticism(s) or My Version of a Little Bit of History." In *Changing Our Own Words: Essays on Criticism, Theory, and Writing by Black Women,* edited by Cheryl A. Wall, 58–74. New Brunswick, N.J.: Rutgers University Press, 1989.

"But Who Do You Really Belong To—Black Studies or Women's Studies?" In *Across Cultures: The Spectrum of Women's Lives,* edited by Emily K. Abel and Marjorie L. Pearson, 17–23. New York: Gordon and Breach, 1989.

"Camouflaging Race *and* Gender." *Representations* 55 (Summer 1996): 120–28.

"The Contrary Women of Alice Walker: A Study in Female Protagonists in *In Love and Trouble.*" *The Black Scholar* (March–April 1981): 21–30, 70–72.

With Deborah McDowell and Nellie McKay. "A Conversation on Toni Morrison's *Beloved.*" In *Toni Morrison's* Beloved: *A Casebook,* edited by William Andrews and Nellie McKay, 203–22. New York: Oxford University Press, 1999.

"Diminishing Returns: Can Black Feminism(s) Survive the Academy?" In *Multiculturalism: A Critical Reader,* edited by David Theo Goldberg, 168–74. Oxford, U.K.: Basil Blackwell, 1994.

"Does Theory Play Well in the Classroom?" In *Critical Theory and the Teaching of Literature: Politics, Curriculum, Pedagogy,* edited by James F. Slevin and Art Young, 241–57. Urbana, Ill.: National Council of Teachers of English, 1996.

"Fixing Methodologies: *Beloved.*" *Cultural Critique* 24 (Spring 1993): 5–15.

"Gloria Naylor's Geography: Community, Class and Patriarchy in *The Women of Brewster Place* and *Linden Hills.*" In *Reading Black, Reading Feminist: A Critical Anthology,* edited by Henry Louis Gates, Jr., 348–73. New York: Meridian, 1990.

"The Highs and the Lows of Black Feminist Criticism." In *Reading Black, Reading Feminist: A Critical Anthology,* edited by Henry Louis Gates, Jr., 44–51. New York: Meridian, 1990.

Introduction to *Bake Face and Other Guava Stories,* by Opal Palmer Adisa, ix–xii. Berkeley, Calif.: Kelsey Street Press, 1986.

Introduction to *The Hazeley Family,* by Mrs. A. E. Johnson and edited by Henry Louis Gates, Jr., xxvii–xxxvii. Schomburg Series of 19th-Century Afro-American Women Writers. New York: Oxford University Press, 1988.

"Layered Rhythms: Toni Morrison and Virginia Woolf." In *Virginia Woolf: Emerging Perspectives. Selected Papers from the Third Annual Conference on Virginia Woolf,* edited by Mark Hussey and Vara Neverow, 164–77. New York: Pace University Press, 1994.

"No More Buried Lives: The Theme of Lesbianism in Audre Lorde's *Zami,* Gloria Naylor's *The Women of Brewster Place,* Ntozake Shange's *Sassafras, Cypress and Indigo* and Alice Walker's *The Color Purple.*" *Feminist Issues* 5, no. 1 (Spring 1985): 3–20.

"Nobel Laureate Is Our Saving Grace." *San Francisco Chronicle,* October 10, 1993, 5.

"Nuance and the Novella: A Study of Gwendolyn Brooks' *Maud Martha.*" In *A Life Distilled: Gwendolyn Brooks, Her Poetry and Fiction,* edited by Maria K. Mootry and Gary Smith, 239–53. Urbana: University of Illinois Press, 1987.

"On Reading Afro-American Women's Novels: Being the Subject and the Object." *Social Studies Review* 29, no. 1 (Fall 1989): 50–54.

"Politically Incorrect: Struggles/Syndromes." In *Defining Ourselves: Black Writers in the 90s,* edited by Elizabeth Nunez and Brenda M. Green, 137–46. Boston: Peter Lang, 1999.

"The Race for Theory." *The Nature and Context of Minority Discourse,* edited by Abdul R. JanMohammed and David Lloyd. Special issue of *Cultural Critique* 6 (Spring 1987): 51–63.

"Ritualistic Process and the Structure of Paule Marshall's *Praisesong for the Widow.*" *Callaloo* 18 (Spring–Summer 1983): 75–84.

"A Rough Terrain: The Case of Shaping an Anthology of Caribbean Women Writers." In *The Ethnic Canon: Histories, Institutions, and Interventions,* edited by David Palumbo-Liu, 241–59. Minneapolis: University of Minnesota Press, 1995.

"Somebody Forgot to Tell Somebody Something: African American Women's Historical Novels." In *Wild Women in the Whirlwind: Afra-American Culture and the Contemporary Literary Renaissance,* edited by Joanne M. Braxton and Andrée Nicola
McLaughlin, 326–41. New Brunswick, N.J.: Rutgers University Press, 1990.

"Trajectories of Self-Definition: Placing Contemporary Afro-American Fiction." In
Conjuring: Black Women, Fiction, and Literary Tradition, edited by Marjorie Pryse and
Hortense J. Spillers, 233–48. Bloomington: Indiana University Press, 1985.

"The Use of Nature and Community in the Novels of Toni Morrison." *Journal of Ethnic
Studies* (February 1980): 66–78.

"What Celie Knows That You Should Know." In *Anatomy of Racism,* edited by David
Theo Goldberg, 135–45. Minneapolis: University of Minnesota Press, 1990.

"Whose Canon Is It Anyway?" In *Issues in World Literature: The HarperCollins World
Reader,* edited by Mary Ann Caws, Patricia Laurence, and Sarah Bird Wright, 17–22.
New York: HarperCollins College Publications, 1994.

"Your Silence Will Not Protect You: Tribute to Audre Lorde." *Crossroads* (February
1993): 14–16.

Reviews

"A Checkered Career." Review of *The Street,* by Ann Petry. *The Women's Review of Books*
9, nos. 10–11 (July 1992): 18–19.

"A New Dawn." Review of *A Brighter Coming Day: A Reader of Frances Watkins Harper,* by
Frances Ellen Watkins Harper. *Belles Lettres* 6, no. 3 (Spring 1991): 5.

"Conversations with the Universe." Review of *Living by the Word: Selected Writings, 1973–
1987,* by Alice Walker. *The Women's Review of Books* 6, no. 5 (February 1989): 9–10.

"The Dynamics of Differences." Review of *Sister Outsider,* by Audre Lorde. *The Women's
Review of Books* 1, no. 11 (August 1984): 6–7.

"Epic Achievement." Review of *Thereafter Johnnie,* by Carolivia Herron. *The Women's
Review of Books* 9, no. 1 (October 1991): 6–7.

"The Heart of Maya Angelou." Review of *The Heart of a Woman,* by Maya Angelou. *In
These Times* (January 1982): 20–26.

"Home Girls and Black Feminists." Review of *Home Girls: A Black Feminist Anthology,* by
Barbara Smith. *New Women's Times Feminist Review* 34 (July–August 1984): 1–2, 16.

"Rediscovering Voodoo Culture." Review of *Tell My Horse,* by Zora Neale Hurston. *In
These Times* (16 September 1981): 15–17.

"Remembering Audre Lorde." *The Women's Review of Books* 10, no. 6 (March 1993):
5–6.

Review of *An Ordinary Woman,* by Lucille Clifton. *The Black Scholar* 7, no. 1 (September
1975): 52–54.

"The Short Story in Process." Review of *You Can't Keep A Good Woman Down,* by Alice
Walker. *Callaloo* (Winter 1981): 195–99.

"Testing the Strength of the Black Cultural Bond." Review of *Tar Baby,* by Toni Morrison. *In These Times* (14 July 1981): 19.

"There It Is: The Poetry of Jayne Cortez." Review of *Coagulations: New and Selected
Poems,* by Jayne Cortez. *Callaloo* 26 (Winter 1986): 235–39.

Index

Print (with Mervyn Morris and Gordon Rohlehr), 237n1

Brown, William Wells, 22, 59; *Clotel,* 89–92, 94

Burst of Light, A (Lorde), 166

Bush, [George H. W.], 209

Cade, Toni. *See* Bambara, Toni Cade

Cancer Journals, The (Lorde), 166–67

Cane (Toomer), 7

Carby, Hazel V., 16–17, 162

Carmichael, Stokely, 237n4

Chase-Riboud, Barbara: *Sally Hemings,* 94–95

Chaucer, Geoffrey, 129

Chesnutt, Charles W., 43, 79

Chinaberry Tree, The (Fauset), 84

Chosen Place, the Timeless People, The (Marshall), 46, 71, 100

Christian, Barbara: "Being 'The Subjected Subject of Discourse,'" 171, 173–81; "Being the Subject and the Object," 74–75, 120–26; *Black Feminist Criticism,* 13–14, 75, 77; *Black Women Novelists,* 9–11, 30, 71–72, 78, 225–26; "But What Do We Think We're Doing Anyway," 2, 5–19, 177, 206; "Camouflaging Race and Gender,"171, 216–24; "Checkered Career," 77–78, 157–63; "Conversations with the Universe," 76–77, 147–51; "Diminishing Returns," 171, 204–15, 223; "Does Theory Play Well in the Classroom?" 2, 51–67; "Epic Achievement," 76–77, 152–56; "Fixing Methodologies," 2, 31–39, 58–59; "Gloria Naylor's Geography," 99–119; "Introduction to *The Hazeley Family,*" 79–85; "Layered Rhythms," 74, 127–41; *The Norton Anthology of African American Literature,* 172; "The Race for Theory," 1–2, 40–50, 51–58, 229n1; "Remembering Audre Lorde," 76, 164–67; "Rough Terrain," 172, 187–203; "'Somebody Forgot to Tell Somebody Something,'" 32, 86–98; "There It Is," 76, 142–46; "What Celie Knows That You Should Know," 2, 20–30; "Whose Canon Is It Anyway?" 182–86

Civil Wars (Jordan), 14

Clarke, Cheryl, 236n1

Cleaver, Eldridge: *Soul on Ice,* 158

Clifton, Lucille, 12

Clinton, Hillary, 204

Clotel (Brown), 89–92, 94

Coagulations (Cortez), 142–46

Cole, Johnnetta, 213

Collins, Patricia Hill, 207–8

Color Purple, The (Walker), 11, 20–31, 46, 84, 88, 96, 100, 107, 118, 148, 154, 162

Conde, Maryse, 199–200

Confessions of Nat Turner, The (Styron), 96

Cooper, Anna Julia, 205

Cortez, Jayne, 76, 78, 142; *Coagulations,* 142–46; *Firespitter,* 143–44; *Mouth on Paper,* 143–44; *Scarifications,* 143

Country Place (Petry), 158

Craft, Ellen, 81

Crews, Frederick, 228n17

Cruse, Harold, 191

Cudjoe, Selwyn, 198–99

Dathorne, O. R., 237n1

Davies, Carole Boyce: *Out of the Kumbla* (with Elaine Savory Fido), 198–99, 201

Davis, Angela, 95, 96

Davis, Miles, 186

Dessa Rose (Williams), 65, 88–92, 94–98

Douglass, Frederick, 55, 184

"Down by the Riverside," 63

Dreiser, Theodore, 15

D'Souza, Dinesh, 237n2

Du Bois, W. E. B., 131, 184

Ducille, Ann, 234n1, 238n8

Dumas, Henry, 144

Dumas, Leon, 144

Dunbar, Paul L., 79

Dunbar-Nelson, Alice, 150

Duplessis, Rachel Blau, 135, 137

Duster, Troy, 237n1, 237n4

Ellison, Ralph, 11, 24, 46, 55, 131; *Invisible Man,* 31, 120, 158; *Shadow and Act,* 43, 127–28

Esteves, Carmen C.: *Green Cane and Juicy Flotsam* (with Lizabeth Paravisini-Gebert), 198–200

Johnson, Charles: *Middle Passage,* 65;
  Oxberding Tale, 65
Jones, Jacqueline, 96
Jones, Leroi. *See* Baraka, Imamu Amiri
Jordan, June, 5–8, 12, 49, 58, 92, 143,
  161–62, 196, 206; *Civil Wars,* 14
Joyce, James, 136
Jubilee (Walker), 70, 92–94, 113

Kaminer, Wendy, 204, 238n5
Keizer, Arlene R., 1, 225
Kincaid, Jamaica, 196
King, Deborah, 205
King, Martin Luther, Jr., 151

Lacan, Jacques, 48
Larsen, Nella, 54, 150; *Quicksand,* 157
Lee, Andrea: *Sarah Phillips,* 100–101, 162
Lerner, Gerda, 10, 96, 231n8, 232n15
Linden Hills (Naylor), 87–88, 99–104, 106,
  108–12, 115–19
Living by the Word (Walker), 76–77, 147–51
Locke, Alain, 129
Lorde, Audre, 7–8, 18, 49, 58, 76, 143, 161,
  164–67, 179, 196, 206, 221–22; *A Burst of
  Light,* 166; *The Cancer Journals,* 166–67;
  Our Dead Behind Us, 166; *Sister Outsider,*
  12, 50, 166, 237n5; *Zami,* 166
Lubiano, Wahneema, 138

MacMillan, Terry: *Breaking Ice,* 193
Major, Clarence, 207
Malcolm X, 192
Malson, Micheline R.: *Feminist Theory in
  Practice and Process* (with Jean F. O'Barr,
  Sarah Westphal-Wihl, and Mary Wyer),
  206
Marable, Manning, 207
Marcus, Jane, 232n5
Marcus, Sharon, 234n1
Marshall, Paule, 7, 49, 54, 73, 125; *Brown
  Girl, Brownstones,* 7, 9, 70, 74–75,
  87, 102, 112–14, 117–18, 120–23; *The
  Chosen Place, the Timeless People,* 46, 71,
  100; *Praisesong for the Widow,* 87–88,
  100–101, 107, 117–18
Marx, Karl, 191

Mason, Theodore D., Jr., 228n17
Mbiti, John, 36–38
McDowell, Deborah E., 158; "New Direc-
  tions for Black Feminist Criticism,"
  12–13
McKay, Nellie Y.: *The Norton Anthology of
  African American Literature* (with Henry
  Louis Gates Jr.), 172
McLaughlin, Andrée: *Wild Women in the
  Whirlwind* (with Joanne Braxton), 197,
  208
Melville, Herman, 129–30, 183
Meridian (Walker), 87–88, 112, 150, 162
Middle Passage (Johnson), 65
Milton, John, 140
Mirikitani, Janice, 167
Miss Muriel and Other Stories (Petry), 158
Mitchell, Margaret: *Gone with the Wind,*
  93
"Modern Fiction" (Woolf), 138
Mohanty, Chandra, 207
Moraga, Cherríe, 167; *This Bridge Called
  My Back* (with Gloria Anzaldùa), 196,
  206
Morris, Mervyn: *Caribbean Poetry Now*
  (with Steward Brown), 237n1; *Voice
  Print* (with Steward Brown and Gordon Rohlehr), 237n1
Morrison, Toni, 7–8, 12, 30, 41, 43, 49, 54,
  56, 70, 73, 86, 99, 122, 127–41, 170, 184,
  206, 208, 222–23; *Beloved,* 2, 20, 31–39,
  52, 58–67, 78, 88–92, 94–98, 132, 136–37,
  140, 149, 214; *The Bluest Eye,* 10, 37,
  74–75, 87, 100, 112–13, 123–26, 128, 132,
  137–39, 154; *Jazz,* 132–33, 137, 140; *Playing in the Dark,* 232n1; *Song of Solomon,*
  11, 37, 86, 87–88, 100–101, 116, 118, 137,
  139–40, 162; *Sula,* 87–88, 102, 112–14,
  116–17, 132, 137, 139–40, 162; *Tar Baby,*
  87, 100–101, 118, 137–39, 162
Moses, Yolanda, 239n18
Mouth on Paper (Cortez), 143–44
Moynihan Report, 11, 112, 160
Mrs. Dalloway (Woolf), 132, 136
Mumbo Jumbo (Reed), 47
Myers, Richard: *The African-American
  Black Male* (with Jacob Gorden), 207

GLORIA BOWLES is the founding coordinator of women's studies at the University of California at Berkeley, where she received her Ph.D. in comparative literature. Her books include *Theories of Women's Studies, Strategies for Women's Studies in the Eighties,* and *Louise Bogan's Aesthetic of Limitation.* She has completed a memoir, *Living Ideas,* on the formative period of women's studies at Berkeley, when Barbara Christian served on the women's studies board. In recent years, she has added Spanish to the languages (French, German) that she speaks and studies.

M. GIULIA FABI is associate professor of American literature at the University of Ferrara, Italy. She is the author of *Passing and the Rise of the African American Novel* and a contributor to several other volumes, including *The Oxford Companion to African American Literature* and the *Cambridge Companion to the African American Novel.* She is the author of an Italian-language concise history of African American literature and the editor of the Penguin Classics edition of William Wells Brown's *Clotel* and of a series of Italian translations of African American novels.

ARLENE R. KEIZER is associate professor of English and American studies at Brown University. She is the author of *Black Subjects: Identity Formation in the Contemporary Narrative of Slavery.* She has published scholarly essays and poems in a wide range of journals, including *African American Review, American Literature,* and *Kenyon Review.* Her chapter on black feminist criticism will appear in the forthcoming *Cambridge History of Feminist Literary Criticism.*

The University of Illinois Press
is a founding member of the
Association of American University Presses.

Composed in 10.3/13 Hoefler Text
with Myriad Pro display
by Jim Proefrock
at the University of Illinois Press
Designed by Dennis Roberts
Manufactured by Thomson-Shore, Inc.

University of Illinois Press
1325 South Oak Street
Champaign, IL 61820-6903
www.press.uillinois.edu